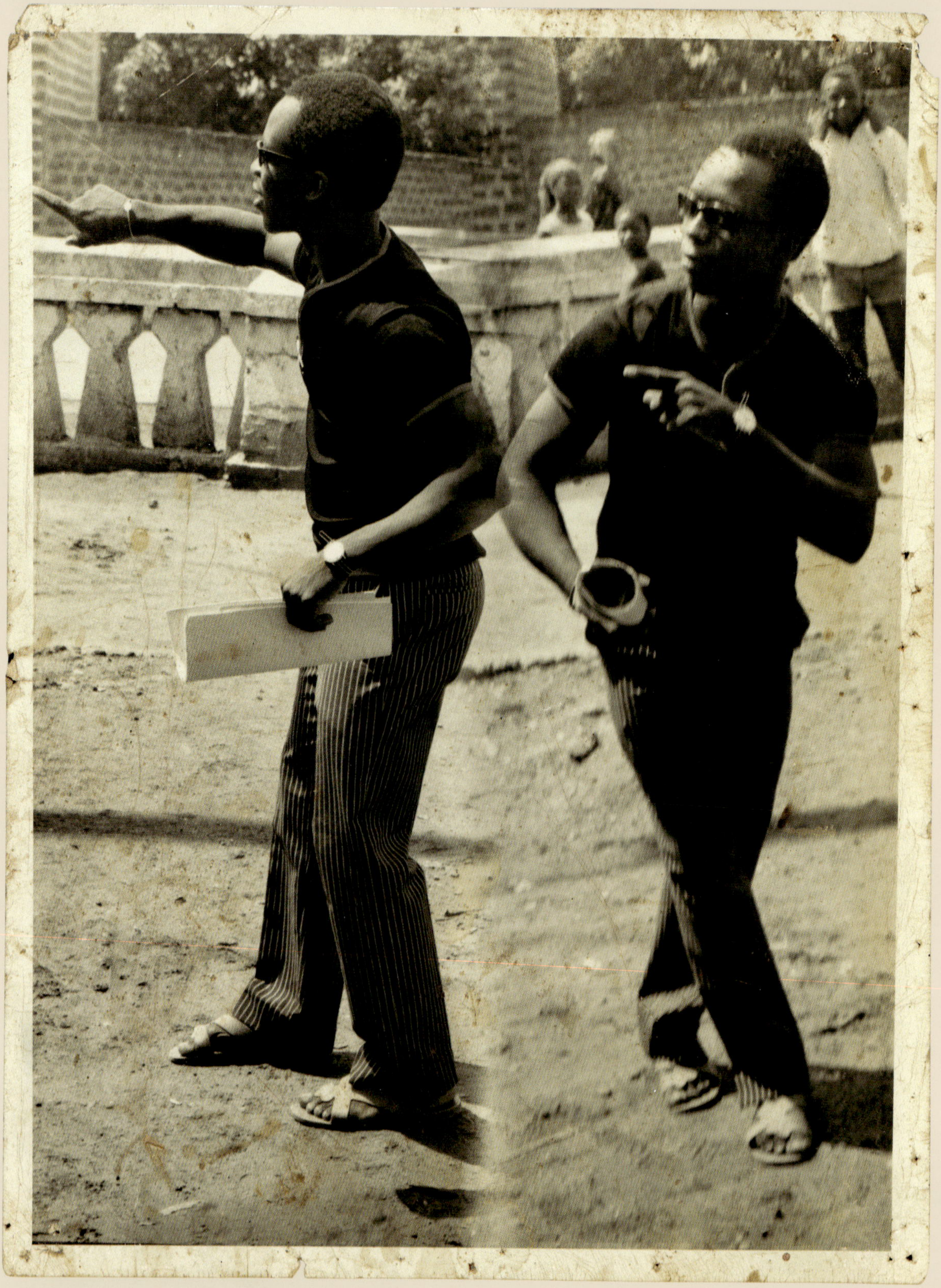

1 Double-exposure self-portrait in Place du Paysan Noir (Black Farmer Square), c. 1970

VOLTA PHOTO

starring

SANLÉ SORY

and the

PEOPLE OF BOBO-DIOULASSO

in the small but musically mighty

COUNTRY OF
BURKINA FASO

Steidl | The Art institute of Chicago

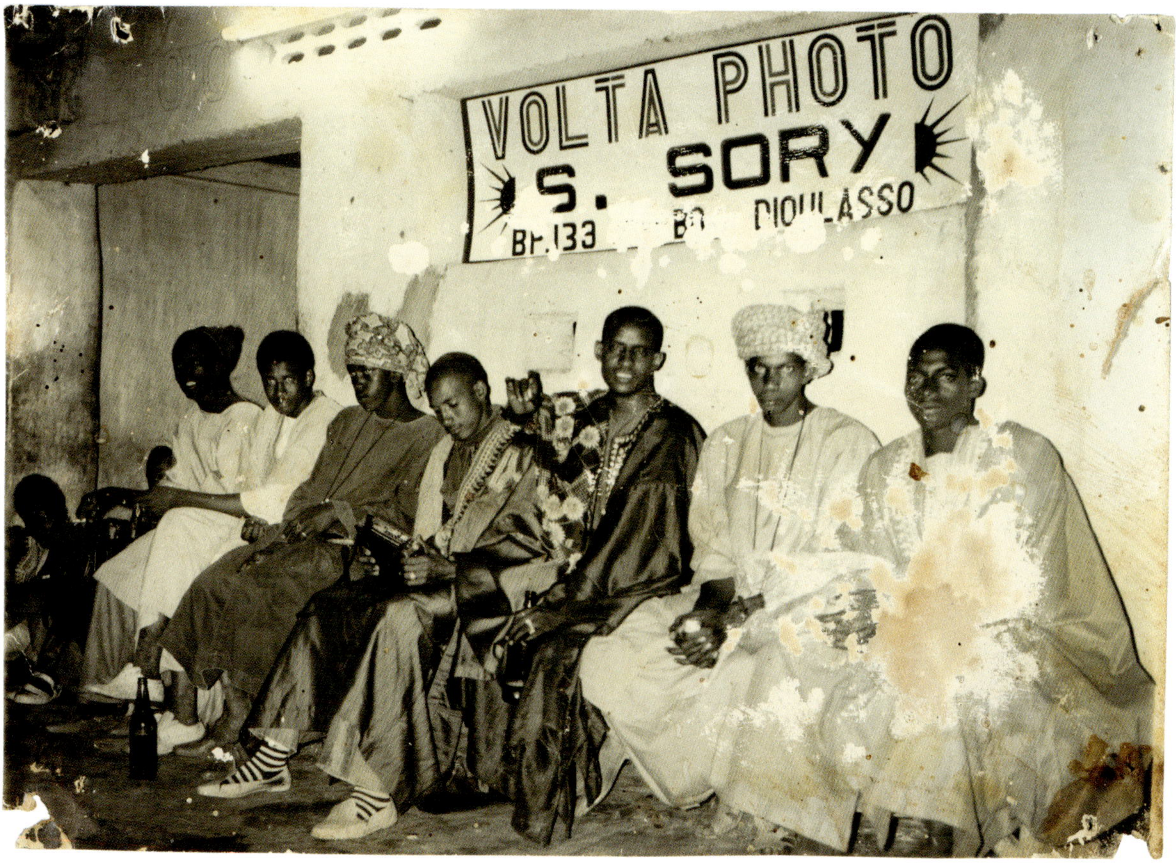

2 Fula men seated outside the Farakan studio, 1970/80

INTRODUCTIONS

Sanlé Sory:
I'm very happy to be here. I'm the old photographer Sanlé Sory (laughs), generally called Sory. I'm here to talk about my photos from long ago with Mr. Florent, *l'homme infatigable* (the tireless man).

Florent Mazzoleni:
I am the tireless man called Florent. I was lucky to find a large part of Sory's archives several years ago when I was making a book on the music of Burkina Faso. It's been a nice story ever since.

Antawan Byrd:
I'm a scholar of contemporary African art, with a focus on sound and photography, and an assistant curator at the Art Institute of Chicago; I'm here to interview Sory for an exhibition opening in Chicago next April.

Matthew Witkovsky:
I'm in charge of Photography at the Art Institute and curator of Sory's exhibition. Sory, when did you arrive in Bobo from the village of Naniagara?

SS: 1957.

MW: Did you already have a camera? Had you seen a photograph or was it something new?

SS: There were none where I came from.

Volta Photo: Starring Sanlé Sory and the People of Bobo-Dioulasso in the Small but Musically Mighty Country of Burkina Faso is published in conjunction with an exhibition organized by The Art Institute of Chicago and held there April 27–August 19, 2018.

Lead support for the exhibition is provided by Helen and Sam Zell. Major support is provided by The Artworkers Retirement Society. Additional support is provided by Kenneth and Christine Tanaka and Ralph and Nancy Segall.

Annual support for Art Institute exhibitions is provided by the Exhibitions Trust: an anonymous donor; Neil Bluhm and the Bluhm Family Charitable Foundation; Jay Franke and David Herro; Kenneth Griffin; Caryn and King Harris, The Harris Family Foundation; Liz and Eric Lefkofsky; Robert M. and Diane v.S. Levy; Ann and Samuel M. Mencoff; Usha and Lakshmi N. Mittal; Sylvia Neil and Dan Fischel; Thomas and Margot Pritzker; Anne and Chris Reyes; Betsy Bergman Rosenfield and Andrew M. Rosenfield; Cari and Michael J. Sacks; and the Earl and Brenda Shapiro Foundation.

Cover photograph by Chris Gallagher (see pp. 182–183).

Sanlé Sory stamp on half-title page is taken from the reverse of plate 65 (p. 108).

CONTENTS

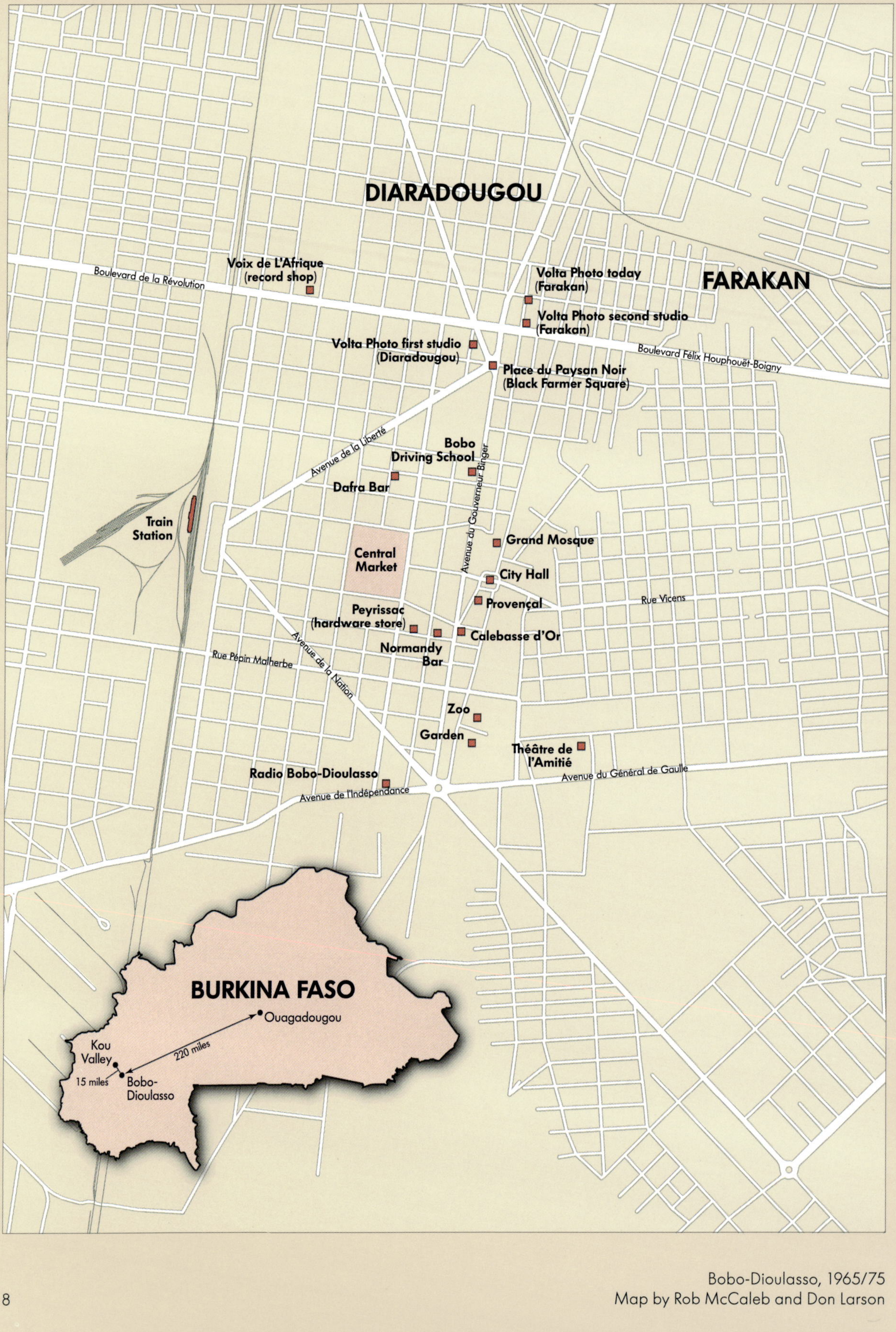

Bobo-Dioulasso, 1965/75
Map by Rob McCaleb and Don Larson

ACKNOWLEDGMENTS

This book accompanies an exhibition—the first at the Art Institute of Chicago to focus on a photographer from the African continent—that had its start in an impromptu meeting between myself and music historian Florent Mazzoleni in May 2016. For the initial introduction I am grateful to Quentin Bajac, chief curator of photography at the Museum of Modern Art, New York. I thank Florent tremendously, meanwhile, for bringing Sanlé Sory's work to my attention and guiding me these past two years in learning about the music and cultural history of Francophone West Africa. Florent had come to Chicago to make a set of records of popular music from Bobo-Dioulasso, illustrated by Sory's photographs, with the Numero Group, which first brought an intertwined attention to Voltaic photography and music that is developed here from another angle. It has been a real pleasure to visit Burkina Faso and Mali with Florent and Antawan Byrd, and to think through the project with them. Antawan in particular has been a rich source of ideas and scholarly references, and a true partner in shaping the contents of this book.

James Rondeau, President and Eloise W. Martin Director of the Art Institute, has championed this undertaking and the museum's sustained interest in modern and contemporary art in Africa. He has my great thanks, as do Greg Nosan, executive director of Publishing and editor of the manuscript; the departments of Project Management, Registration, and Imaging; Constantijn Petridis, chief curator of African and Amerindian Art; and the exceptionally committed and professional staff in the Department of Photography. Gerhard Steidl and his team have produced a handsome, engaging book in record time.

The presentation at the Art Institute has been made possible through the lead generosity of Helen and Sam Zell and a key initial contribution from the Artworkers Retirement Society. Additional support is provided by Kenneth and Christine Tanaka, and Ralph and Nancy Segall. Antawan's travel to Mali was funded through the Bamako Encounters, African Biennial of Photography and the Mellon-COSI Fellowship between the Art Institute and Northwestern University.

The greatest pleasure for the book's contributing authors has been getting to know Sory. His combination of a veteran's affectionate memories, of studio photography and popular music as he advanced them in the later twentieth century, and a youthful willingness to keep reinventing his practice in the early twenty-first century is nothing short of admirable. On behalf of all involved, I offer thanks to Ibrahima Sanlé Sory, his daughter Djénéba and son Adama, and his extended family, and ask for their blessing on this undertaking.

Matthew S. Witkovsky
Richard and Ellen Sandor Chair and Curator
Department of Photography
The Art Institute of Chicago

NOTE TO THE READER

Unless stated otherwise, the pictures in this book illustrate gelatin silver photographs taken by Ibrahima Sanlé Sory. Those accompanying the interview are reproduced from editioned modern prints or original negatives. Others show uneditioned period prints. All original materials come from Sory through the intermediary of Florent Mazzoleni. The record sleeves, for which Sory likewise took the photographs unless otherwise noted, are offset lithographs. Any titles to photographs are descriptive and are drawn from comments by the photographer, while date attributions that differ from the default (1965/75) derive from circumstantial information (for example the approximate dates of Sory's first and second studios) and the authors' study of clothing or music in the images.

Full information for plate illustrations appears at the back of the book, in a list that also correlates plates and essay figures with objects shown in the Art Institute exhibition. Thumbnails accompany photographs included in the exhibition and not otherwise reproduced in this book. Not mentioned there are illustrations made directly from negatives, or works not by Sory. All prints belonging to the Art Institute are identified with an accession number, or for gifts awaiting accession, a six-digit object identification number.

The photographer's name is given here in Western order, with family name last. Sory can also be a first name, and it is common in Burkina Faso to refer to individuals by family name first or only. This has caused confusion over name order in previous scholarship. Sory's birth date has also been given at times as 1948, beginning with the first published writing on his work, by Kerstin Pinther in the exhibition catalogue *Snap Me One! Studiofotografen aus Afrika*, ed. Tobias Wendl and Heike Behrend (Prestel, 1998). It appears that this birthdate was assigned to him for documentation purposes at age four or five and that he was born in 1943. This earlier birth date may be taken as unconfirmed, however, as should the dates given here of Sory's apprenticeship with Kojo Adomako and his founding of Volta Photo (1957 and 1960, respectively).

The conversation with Sory published here, which has been translated from the French by Matthew S. Witkovsky and edited for length and clarity, took place in the garden of the Mandé Hotel and a room at the Loft Hotel during the 11th African Biennial of Photography, Bamako (Mali), December 4–6, 2017.

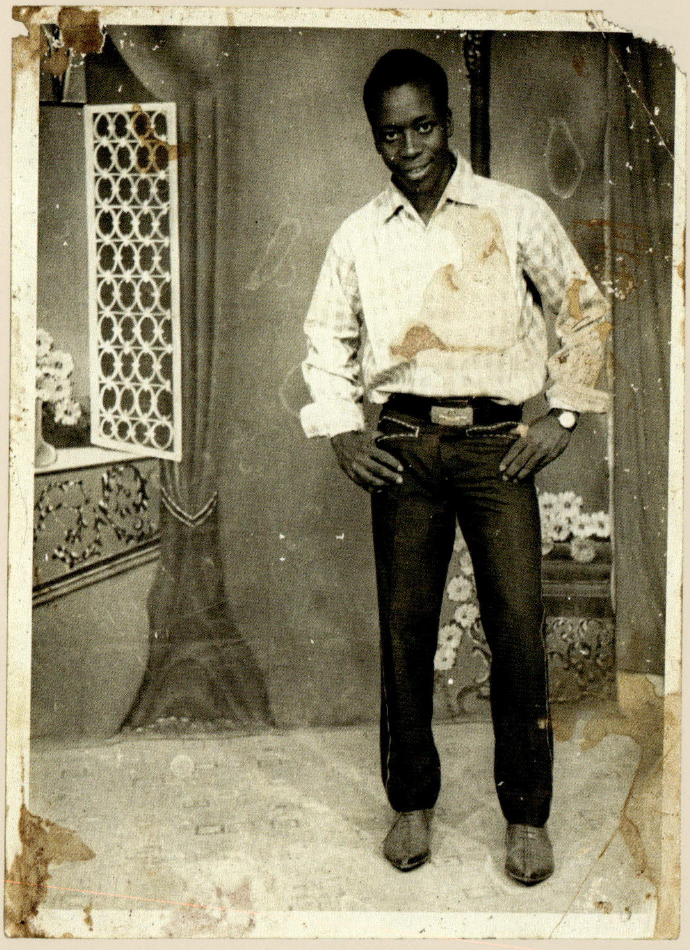

fig. 1 Self-portrait at the studio of Kojo Adomako, 1960/70
22.5 × 16.6 cm (image); 23.7 × 17.8 cm (paper). Private collection

TO RECOGNIZE ONE'S PICTURE

Matthew S. Witkovsky

Volta Photo—Starring Sanlé Sory and the People of Bobo-Dioulasso in the Small but Musically Mighty Country of Burkina Faso. This intentionally lengthy and playful title casts Burkinabé photographer Ibrahima Sanlé Sory (born 1943 in Naniagara; lives and works in Bobo-Dioulasso) as the lead in a cinema vérité film with a large cast and a soundtrack that matters as much as its cinematography. Florent Mazzoleni sets forth in these pages a detailed history of Volta Jazz, the band founded by Sory's cousin Idrissa Koné, and which Sory photographed for a series of record covers; Antawan Byrd discusses Sory's photography and popular music of the time in Bobo as interrelated forms of "amplification." The photographer himself—who came through an open window, as it were (fig. 1), and inscribed a jaunty, early self-portrait (plate 35) with the phrase "Sory, Directeur de la Photographie"—provides a major textual contribution in the form of an extended interview with the three other authors. This wide-ranging conversation, held over several days in Bamako, Mali, in December 2017, structures the book as a series of guiding themes, the last of which is titled "Afterlives of Images."

I want to expand upon this perhaps metaphysical closing subject, drawing principally from comments Sory made throughout the interview. In it, he appears as a humble artisan with inventive business practices, particularly his organization of all-night "bush parties" for which he and a trio of assistants supplied music, lights, and photos; these gatherings drew together youthful locals in the Bobo countryside from the early 1970s through the mid-1990s. Through this enterprise above all—selling tickets to the parties and souvenir pictures to the partygoers—Sory made innovations in an indigenous photographic system that, sociologist and theoretician Jean-Bernard Ouédraogo has argued, "accustomed Africans to the monetization of social relations." Studio photography in Burkina Faso, Ouédraogo has explained, developed from a colonial structure that aimed to "express the new identity of a subject emerging from communitarian constraints" and instantiated a political order that substituted personal identity for any traditional identification with family, village, or ethnic collectives.[1]

The replacement of group identification with individuated identity found its most adequate expression in the identity photograph, or ID photo, that colonial administrations required in Bobo and across Africa. To have one's identity specified and recorded, not (only) as an ethnographic type but as a juridical subject, marked a rite of initiation into modern society. As Sory notes near the start of the interview: "ID pictures were necessary only when you moved to a city; you had to register soon after with the authorities." (To the colonial powers, "'Civilization' meant citification," as Mazzoleni supposes in reply.) In Sory's case, this initiation marked a wholly new beginning, for the decision to become a photographer, in his telling, was taken at the moment he posed for his ID picture, soon after moving from his tiny birth village to the commercial hub of Bobo. He spent three years as an assistant to Kojo Adomako, the very photographer who had snapped his likeness, then set up his own business, where he—like most African studio operators, it seems—found in turn that customers generally came asking for ID photos.

"A photograph addressed to the administration," Ouédraogo writes, "seems to constrain shoulders to stiffness and faces to seriousness... Public affairs are not matters of fantasy."[2] But African customers and photographers alike swiftly found a way to assert their subjecthood by modifying the very apparatus of standardization and control. Amplifying, to use Byrd's quite helpful term, upon the ID photo to make what Sory and other practitioners call the "souvenir" photo permitted what Okwui Enwezor has described as the emergence of the postcolonial African subject.[3] A larger print size—9 × 13 cm or greater, as opposed to the 4 × 4 cm format of the ID picture—and a more generous framing brought into view the subjects' clothing and gestures, along with props they carried in or borrowed from the studio. Imaginative patterned or painted backdrops also played a great role, unlike the "neutral fabric to make ID photos. You can't put drawings in an ID photo," as Sory explains.

The souvenir photo has become celebrated as Africa's great gift to postwar world photography. In the 1990s, the two art-world "stars" of this genre, Seydou Keïta (1921–2001) and Malick Sidibé (1936–2016), saw their studio pictures from Bamako translated into gloriously large prints in which individuals, posed singly or in small groups, reinforce in myriad ways their belonging in a modern world. Keïta, who worked in the waning years of colonial rule, deployed (without knowing the precedent) a device used in the 1920s and '30s by Senegalese operator Mama Casset (1908–1992), whereby customers sat diagonally to the camera, causing them, in the words of Kobena Mercer, "to lean out of the frame to look straight out to the viewer," laying claim to "an interaction conducted on an equal footing."[4]

Building on this legacy of increased assertiveness, Sidibé, the near contemporary of Sory, gave face to a stylish post-independence generation progressing in step with the worldwide Sixties counterculture. Sidibé's customers flaunted identification as a process of choosing one's social network: youth groups, rock and roll, and *arrosages* (parties to mark a significant occasion). "Membership here," Ouédraogo writes of the contemporary studio system and its customer base, "is defined by refusal, in opposition to a social order declared invalid."[5] Such opposition, which crystallized around the time of independence, shaded quickly into escapism and became the hallmark of African studio photography through to the present. The studio is a space of magic or fantasy, a respite from everyday life and its cares; Ouédraogo notes a sign outside one 1990s studio in Ouagadougou, the capital city of Burkina Faso, that reads "La photo c'est la fête" (Photos are holidays or parties).[6] Updating that idea of studio image as wish fulfillment, Sory notes in the interview that he currently works with labs to offer customers a montage of their portraits onto background scenes of greenery—"Greenery means happiness," he says—or Mecca: "That's something you can do today [on the computer], and people like it."

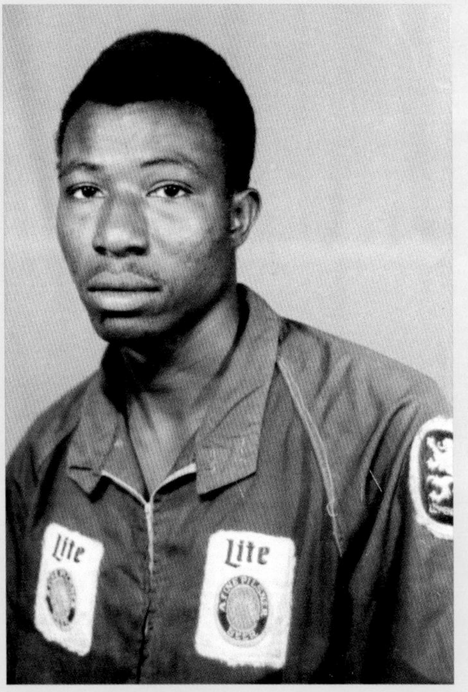

fig. 2 ID photo, 1965/75. 11.2 × 7.5 cm (image); 12.5 × 8.8 cm (paper). Private collection

*

Sory chose for his first studio in Bobo a newly built space in the neighborhood known as Diaradougou, by his account a part of town full of street life and populated with Malians, who do seem to have been particularly fashion-conscious and keen to pose for the camera (and not only in Bamako). A fan of popular music and sports, particularly bodybuilding, Sory made these personal enthusiasms into career moves. He was perpetually on the go, entrusting the studio to apprentices once it began to flourish and searching throughout Bobo for customers, especially in the city's dance clubs and music halls. Sory photographed all segments of a burgeoning pop-music culture, from fan clubs and record sellers to musicians and guests at *surpat* or "surprise parties" (a borrowed French term for private dance parties). He also became the de facto image maker for Volta Jazz, the group run by his cousin Koné, who had backed Sory's initial studio.

Around 1970 Sory was forced to move and found smaller but equally well-located quarters in the nearby Farakan neighborhood, directly on a main Bobo boulevard. At this time he developed the distinctive practice of organizing and emceeing at dance parties in the "bush," the villages surrounding Bobo that closely resembled his birthplace. Just as Sidibé, in the mid-1970s, found a second career repairing cameras, Sory's village party operation continued into the mid-1990s—some years after his studio business had begun to decline, as it did for practitioners throughout Africa.[7] He halted the parties eventually for personal reasons, limiting his travel so that he might better care for a wife afflicted with partial paralysis.

The village parties seem to Sory the most consequential of his various ventures: "In town I wasn't the only one. But it was just me in the bush. I was the only photographer doing that." The apparatuses of recorded music and recorded image became thoroughly integrated with these undertakings. First, the photographer would visit record stores throughout Bobo and commission mixed tapes of popular songs, reaching from his "house band," Volta Jazz, to regional and diasporic stars, including Bembeya Jazz, Fela Kuti, Uhuru, and James Brown.[8] Then he and three hired technicians would bring these tapes to a village in a dust-covered truck loaded with a microphone, two tape decks, an amp, megaphone-style speakers, lights, cameras, and a diesel-powered generator. The technicians and Sory would set up in gathering spaces cleared by agreement with bar owners, who paid Sory for helping to drive business their way. Also gratefully assisting were older village women who made money cooking crepes or other light fare as the night went on. Locals came when they heard the music, or Sory's voice, blasting from the speakers—Sory calls them "funnels"—that poured life into the village: "[I]t's the funnels that bring people. When the funnel's going, even 15 kilometers away, man, you heard the music and came." To gain admission cost 100 francs; to drink, eat, and buy photos of one's happy time could cost ten times as much. This is pure souvenir territory, it would seem, and a consummate example of monetizing social relations through and for the benefit of the photographic system.

*

When Sory first speaks of souvenir photos in this interview, he slips into the past tense, a rare shift from his overwhelming preference (in the original French) for describing actions from any time period in the present. The choice of verbal tense underscores Sory's nostalgia for photography as a lost art of *summoning memory*:

But 9 × 14 / 9 × 13, those were for memories. For example if people were having a dance party, or a wedding, something like that, they called you and said, I want this and that, a picture of so-and-so... If there are no pictures, there are no memories!

ID photos, he avers, are monotonous to make, and they seem in every way the opposite of a souvenir image: official, quotidian, uniform, and dull versus unofficial, personalized, and inventive. Yet the latter type of

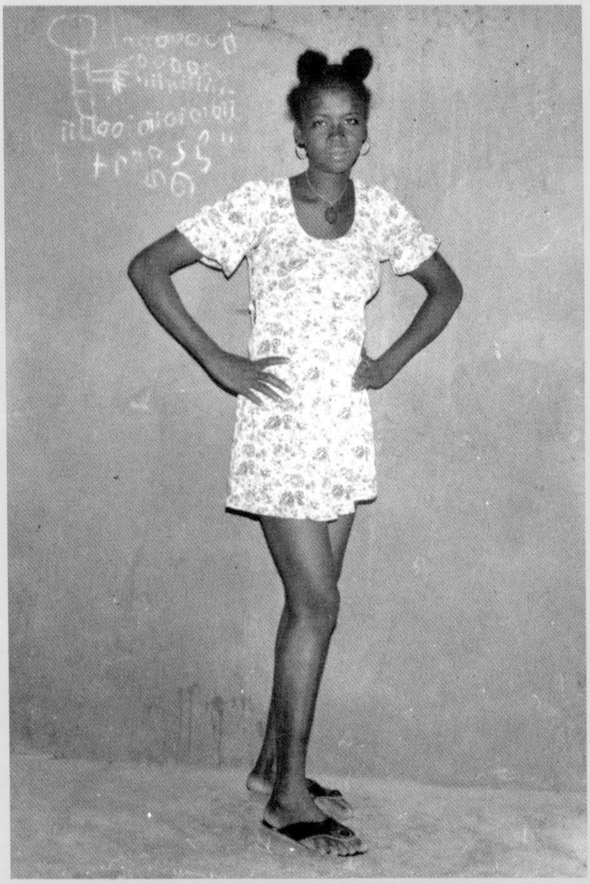

fig. 3 Teenage girl in the village of Dandé, photographed at home on market day, 1970/80. 11.5 × 7.8 cm (image); 12.8 × 8.7 cm (paper). The Art Institute of Chicago, restricted gift of Peter J. Cohen, 2017.371

photograph grows directly out of the former. Indeed, Sory makes clear that the two photographic forms were not only historically conjoined but also practically interchangeable, for they proceeded from a single source and involved the same sheets of paper. In the rudimentary setup at Volta Photo, the 6 × 6 cm film negative served in all the cameras and for all the needs imagined by Sory's customers. "I just asked them what kind of picture they wanted: ID, bust, souvenir," he recalls. "The choices were pinned up [at the entrance] so customers could choose." Rather than "souvenir" equating to pure choice, and "ID" to utter lack of choice, the two kinds of image were, to use one of Sory's favorite French words, *polyvalent,* or multipurpose.

Working in the darkroom with this single negative and a sheet of the smallest souvenir-size photographic paper (9 × 13 cm), either kind of photograph could easily be made, as Sory explains with regard to a picture of a young working man that might seem indeterminate (fig. 2): "That's an ID photo. We would crop [i.e. mask] as we were printing. We put the neg up top and projected onto the paper underneath. Then we cropped as needed. For an ID photo you fold the paper in two, light one side and then the other, and put it in the developer. You get four pictures. Then you cut them up and give them to the customer." The difference between ID and souvenir, one may say, lay not in their origin but in their afterlives.[9]

*

To understand the terms of that proposition, let us look at a photograph whose circumstances Sory recalls especially well. The picture shows a teenage girl posed against a neutrally colored wall in a modish, patterned dress that is cut well above her knees (fig. 3). From the neck up, this young lady emanates a wary poise, her face turned resolutely toward the camera. Projections of self-assurance in the eyes, but also her hairdo and accessories, are nevertheless belied to different degrees by her stance. She holds her arms bent outward, with hands on hips, in a show of resolve—yet the fingers of one hand are splayed, and those on the other are compressed in a gesture that seems equally awkward. Her hips and legs, meanwhile, are turned to the side as if the front knee and foot should hide the rear, so as not to let too much of her uncovered lower half be seen.

The young lady's pose is arresting, as is the homemade chalk inscription on the wall behind her. Sory explained that the picture was not taken in his studio but in the countryside:

This one is in the bush. A little village called Dandé… I was going to emcee a party, and since night had not yet fallen I was driving around looking for customers… I'd park, the kids would come and tell everyone the photographer had arrived. That's how I managed to enter this young lady's home. She didn't want to be seen in public. It embarrassed her to be exposed like that. She said she'd rather pose indoors.

Asked whether other members of the woman's family had also requested poses, Sory answered, "She was the only one. But as I walked around, other villagers asked for ID pictures." The longevity of that line of work becomes clear with the next remark: "We carried the one-color cloth in a bag. That worked well, and it still does today." "So this is an ID photo?" "No, it's a souvenir photo," replies Sory, although the background directly around the girl's head is monochromatic. One could imagine providing the adolescent customer a full-frame souvenir of her uneasy negotiation between shyness and bravado, then masking the negative to turn the confident head alone into an ID photo in four copies.

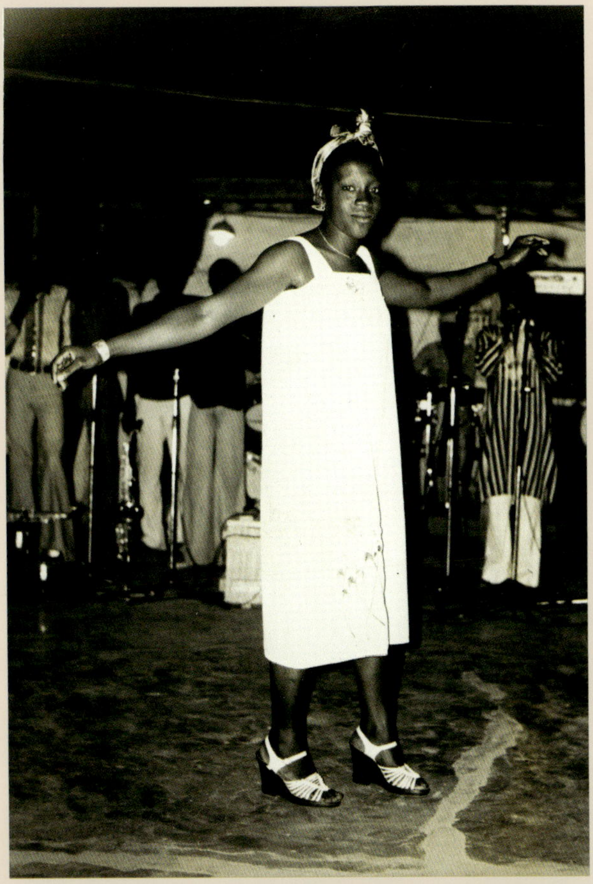

fig. 4. A customer at Calebasse d'Or (Golden Calabash, later named Volta Dancing), 1965/75. 11.4 × 7.9 cm (image); 12.5 × 8.7 cm (paper). The Art Institute of Chicago, promised gift of Ralph and Nancy Segall, 240598

Having "identity" as a widespread cultural grounding demonstrably made "identification" easier to imagine as a photographic pastime. The popularity of studio photography as a social ritual in the late colonial and postcolonial decades took shape, in other words, as a reply to administrative exigency. The more personal form of projection entailed in the souvenir photo is, however, necessarily less determined in its function or audience. Studio photography may perpetuate or record some preindustrial customs, but to judge by its first users, it was experienced as excitingly new, and as such entailed new forms of belonging.

To whom, then, does one express one's photographic identification and to what ends? For whom did the girl in Dandé—acting in relative secrecy, out of view of the village public—make her picture? One could guess that, in her hoop earrings and pendant necklace, with her well-styled hair and suggestively short dress, this teenager wished to project an identification with the liberated youth culture that independence had helped bring into vogue. That culture, it seems, came to life through music and dancing. Compare this picture to one Sory took of a customer at Volta Dancing, the house venue for Volta Jazz (fig. 4). The two photographs appear similar and (to continue the cinematic metaphor contained in our book title) could even form a narrative sequence, with this guest fulfilling the role that the younger girl aspires to play. More self-possessed and in costlier footwear, she spreads her arms in a gesture of "here-I-am" cool while an array of musicians heats up the night behind her. That image of thriving city nightlife seems the destination environment for the assisted selfie made by the teenager in the village of Dandé.

*

There is nevertheless a capital difference between the two photographs, for the one at Volta Dancing would never do as an ID photo. The background is not uniform; the face is not frontal. Here we are in a different world, governed, it would seem, by pure identification: all id, no ID. And this world is not made for memories, although it may well channel extensive historical awareness. I want to speculate that photos taken at parties are not in fact souvenir photos, but rather the third term (in the sense of early Barthes) that reveals the true relation to memory of all studio production. Dance party pictures help us to see that, while ID and souvenir photos may share a common physical basis, it is ID photos, if often lifeless, that fix a lasting memory. "Souvenirs" as such were not meant to last.

Photography set the rhythm of the music parties, particularly those made by Sory in "the bush." On the packed, flash-lit earth of a *bal poussière* (dust ball, the nickname for backstreet dance parties of any kind), Sanlé Sory became an impresario. He would take the mike, effectively merging photography and music through his patter: "Anyway do your best to show up, lots of you, I came from Bobo to emcee, so you have to do your best to keep me happy. It's a beautiful night. I'm here to keep you dancing 'til dawn. I take pictures too, hey ladies, that's what you need." The role of deejay, so important to nightlife today, was relegated to one of the three technicians. Producer, emcee, deejay, and—like the drummer in a 1930s-era jazz orchestra—bandleader, Sory deployed assistants, business partners, and guests alike in the creation of a thoroughly mediated live performance.

A battery-operated Multiblitz flash[10] performed double duty as the threshold of photographic visibility and the means for a percussive organization of leisure time.[11] "When people were at the door I went 'peep' with the flash; that lit them up, and they said, 'Hooray, the photographer is there, it's gonna be good.' It's the flash that tells you the party's started. I had that idea. [Instead of] speaking into the microphone, I went 'peep peep peep' at the door." Like crashes on a hihat cymbal, the rapid-fire flash served as a sound-and-light welcome to a music party staged with the goal of making and selling photographs.

Tellingly, no picture needed to be made for the photographic experience to be valid. "The room is full, but everyone's sitting down, so you enter and go 'peep peep peep'—not even taking pictures—and people say, 'The photographer's here.' Free of charge! It's a kind of advertising." Certainly so for Sory, who needed ultimately to sell actual prints, but for partygoing customers the ritual of being snapped might have mattered above all. The photographs, despite their salability, were less keepsakes of that experience than its necessary byproducts. "No one ever came back to ask me to reprint a picture," Sory recalls. "They don't need it, and they don't care." This remarkable observation suggests "souvenir" photography—whether undertaken in or out of the studio—as an ephemeral event, perhaps no more lasting than a dance party.[12]

The functions and audiences that one might associate with commercially made portrait photographs hold no interest for Sory, who remains resolutely a man of the people. His comment on advertising notwithstanding, he only once undertook such a commission, on a single day, to make record cover photographs for Volta Jazz. He regards official portraiture as a bureaucratic waste of time, rather than an enticement for customers: "If I took a picture of a politician, I wouldn't put it up in my studio room. People don't care, and the politicians don't need it." And publicity, surprisingly, was (with the sole exception of that single day's work) not a factor in his music photographs: "Musicians don't need any kind of photographer." Despite his thrill at photography as a mass image form, Sory seems not to have engaged much with the mass-communications potential of photographs or even their iconicity.

Some exceptionally well-off customers might frame a print for the wall, but in Sory's view, the meanings contained in such an image would be ignored by all but the immediate owners: "When people come to your house… [t]hey could care less about the photo. It's meaningless. You made the photo so you know its significance." Making is what matters—not looking. This could be true for photographers and customers alike, although the latter do, in certain cases, have photographs by Sory in albums to this day. Devastatingly, Sory concludes the interview with a sharp comment on the fallibility of memory itself. Asked what he anticipates his former customers might say upon seeing an image of themselves reproduced in this book, Sory observes with resignation: "Many have gone up to paradise. Those who have stayed behind, if they see a photograph, in their current state, they won't even recognize themselves." In mourning his departed or irreversibly aged customers, Sory is, I think, mourning the demise of the photographic métier as he advanced it: a galvanic catalyst for lived experience.

The identity photo, by contrast, is by common definition an icon: a person's true and durable likeness. (When the resemblance begins to falter, one makes a new photo.) In this respect the little pictures, which might seem less interesting as images, connect unexpectedly with the gloriously printed art-world enlargements of souvenir photos that have done so much to valorize Keïta and Sidibé. Sanlé Sory's work is now also being enlarged and editioned, and a selection of these modern prints features in the exhibition that this book accompanies; the illustrations that punctuate his interview here are printed from the original negatives in a similar manner. Such an undertaking adds a new format, audience, and mode of distribution for those same 6 × 6 cm negatives. The art-world default is to assign the subjects of these pictures a group identity, understood as telling or typical of their period, and to fasten an authorial one to their maker. By comparing photography and music here in the very structure of their production and reception, Sanlé Sory and the other contributors to this book have hopefully shown the value of treating photographs and songs alike as *polyvalent*, two forms of popular technology that shape individual identity only temporarily and on the basis of transient collective identifications. This suggests in turn that we should resist or at least relativize an iconic, memory-laden reading of either of these art forms in favor of one that keeps them alive and moving.

My great thanks to Florent Mazzoleni for introducing me to Sanlé Sory and providing details on a wide variety of African popular music; and to Antawan Byrd, who brought many of the writings cited here to my attention and engaged my thinking at every turn in this essay.

1 Jean-Bernard Ouédraogo, *Arts Photographiques en Afrique: Technique et esthétique dans la photographie de studio au Burkina Faso* (Paris: L'Harmattan, 2002), 94; also Ouédraogo, "La figuration photographique des identités sociales: valeurs et apparences au Burkina Faso," *Cahiers d'Etudes Africaines* 36:141/142 (1996), 30.

2 Ouédraogo, "La figuration photographique," 30.

3 See Okwui Enwezor and Octavio Zaya, "Colonial Imaginary, Tropes of Disruption: History, Culture, and Representation in the Works of African Photographers," in Enwezor, ed., *In/Sight: African Photographers, 1940 to the Present* (New York: Solomon R. Guggenheim, 1996), 28; Enwezor, "Gesture, Pose, Mimesis: Seydou Keïta's Portraits," in Enwezor, ed., *Contemporary African Photography from the Walter Collection: Events of the Self: Portraiture and Social Identity* (Göttingen: Steidl, 2010), 32-33.

4 Kobena Mercer, "Home from Home: Portraits from Places in Between," in *Self Evident: Ikon Gallery* (Birmingham: Ikon Gallery, 1995), cited in Enwezor and Zaya, 30.

5 Ouédraogo, *Arts Photographiques en Afrique*, 165. See also Manthia Diawara, *The 1960s in Bamako: Malick Sidibé and James Brown* (New York: Andy Warhol Foundation for the Visual Arts, 2001). "Malick Sidibé's photographs," Diawara writes, "show exactly how the young people in Bamako had embraced "rock-and-roll" as a liberation movement ... and developed a rebellious attitude toward all forms of established authority." Diawara provocatively connects this rebellion to a revival of precolonial, indeed preslavery African teachings enacted through dance and the convergence of music and language, for example in Dogon rituals from Mali, which he finds James Brown reanimating in ways to which a youthful Bamako audience responded.

6 Ouédraogo, *Arts Photographiques en Afrique*, 167.

7 One commonly cited reason for this decline—the rise of color photography and the processing labs to handle it—is treated by Érika Nimis in her essay, "Yoruba Studio Photographers in Francophone West Africa," in John Peffer and Elisabeth L. Cameron, eds., *Portraiture and Photography in Africa* (Bloomington, Indiana: Indiana University Press, 2013), 112–13.

8 In this selection alone one can see a potential difference with the dance parties captured by Sidibé, where French or white Anglo music—which Sory claims "didn't heat up" the Burkinabé villagers—enters the mix, and where stars of a transcontinental counterculture, such as Jimi Hendrix, can be as widely admired as a regionally popular band such as the Guinean group Orchestre de la Paillotte. It could be that Bamako, with its greater economic and cultural standing and larger population, held more avenues for contact with world music; it may also be the case that Sory's village audiences, or Sory himself, held a more conservative preference for music styles that were considered closer to home. At any rate, *Mali Twist* (Paris: Fondation Cartier, 2017), the recent exhibition catalogue focused on Sidibé and the Bamako music scene, places a decided emphasis on international music. This may simply reflect the preferences of its authors, who address music only in a general way. Little mention is made of African singers, for example, and Orchestre de la Paillotte figures only in a record reproduced as a small detail in one of Sidibé's photos (169).

9 To this point, see also the prints saved by Italian photojournalist Martina Bacigalupo from Gulu Real Art Studio in Gulu, Uganda. Studio owner Obal Denis makes a practice of cutting passport photos neatly out of customers' portraits, which are printed on somewhat larger paper stock. See Bacigalupo, *Gulu Real Art Studio* (Göttingen: Steidl with The Walther Collection, 2013).

10 According to the company website, Multiblitz was founded in 1948 in Cologne, Germany, to manufacture flash lighting for studio photographers.
See: http://www.multiblitz.com/about-us/.

11 Sidibé recounts his party photography in similar terms: "I would let people know I had arrived [at a party] by letting off my flash, people made way to let me in, and everyone was happy. You could feel the temperature rise right away, and the atmosphere would heat up." See *Mali Twist*, 115–16.

12 Seydou Keïta claimed with displeasure in his final published interview, "Here, no one knows what a photograph really is. A few months after you make some photographs, you see them tossing around in the street, people throw them out.... Here, in my own home, I have seen people tear up photographs.... In Europe, you'll never see that." Lydia Diakhaté, "The Last Interview: Seydou Keïta 1921–2001," *Nka: Journal of African Art* 16/17 (Fall/Winter 2002), 23, trans. Emoretta Yang. Although the experience of such indifference was understandably painful for the photographers—and may have played a part, for example, in Sory's decision to burn a part of his archive—I want to suggest it could be consistent with the customers' original expectations and even, at least unconsciously, with the logic underlying Sory's fusion of photography and music into ephemeral media events.

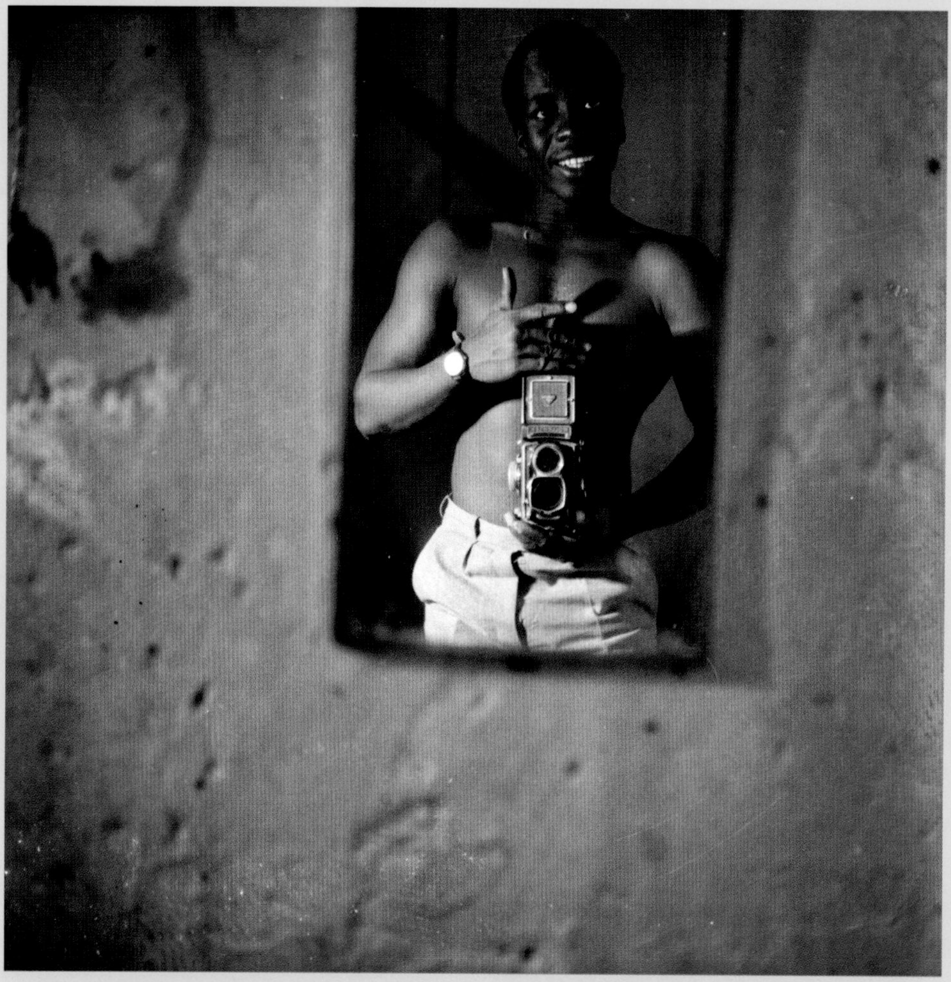

fig. 1 Untitled, 1965/75, printed 2017. 36 × 36 cm (image); 50 × 40 cm (sheet). The Art Institute of Chicago, gift of the artist and Florent Mazzoleni, 242556

BECOMING A STUDIO PHOTOGRAPHER

SS: What first pushed me to become a photographer was getting an ID photo. I went to a Ghanaian, Kojo Adomako, soon after I arrived in Bobo, and he charged 200 francs. I said, that's incredible. If I can learn it, this job could pay pretty well. In my village no one needed ID photos. Older relatives lived and died without them. It was another time. ID pictures were necessary only when you moved to a city; you had to register soon after with the authorities.

FM: I think identification started to be required from the 1940s. Upper Volta under the French comprised what are now the countries of Ivory Coast, Mali, and Burkina Faso. The territory was carved up more than once, and the current borders for Burkina were set in 1947. It inherited the name Upper Volta (which changed to Burkina Faso, "land of upright people," in 1984, under the presidency of Thomas Sankara). Living in cities made one a citizen—literally. In Senegal, for example, people in the countryside simply didn't exist for the colonial authorities. "Civilization" meant citification.

AB: How did you meet Kojo Adomako?

SS: My big brother [an influential cousin named Idrissa Koné] led me to him. He was also the one who advised me how to ask Kojo for an apprenticeship. He said I would have to pay a certain amount—25,000 francs—and a bottle of whisky (laughs).[1] So that's what I brought him. He called his photographer friends, they sat around the bottle, drank it all, and talked about me, saying that they had gained an apprentice brought to them by Idrissa.

MW: Have we skipped a step? You were having your picture taken and had the idea that this could make a good profession. You asked the photographer straightaway to hire you?

SS: You're right—first I spoke to my big brother. He asked me what I wanted to do, and I said, I like this profession here. I've just had my picture taken for 200 francs, and that's what I want to learn how to do.

MW: How long did the apprenticeship last?

SS: Three years.

AB: Can you remember the names of the other photographers?

SS: They were also Ghanaian. There was Adama Donko and—they are all dead. Everyone I'm telling you about has died, even my boss. There were two others that day, I didn't know their names, and as an apprentice I couldn't ask. They talked a lot and had us eat yams (*ignames*). They were pleased, so that's how it started. I slept in the studio together with another young guy, also an apprentice. Since I knew how to read a little, I looked right away at the instructions, and I was able to figure things out. After three years I thought, why not make something, change the décor, try this and that. I thought about it all. So after three years I opened my studio. And I commissioned my backdrops, working still with Ghanaians, other Ghanaians who made decorative paintings.

MW: What sort of work did apprentices learn to do?

SS: They teach you the chemical products for photography in black-and-white: fixative and the rest. You learn how to develop as well, because there were no labs in those days, so you handled the photos yourself.

MW: Did you learn retouching?

SS: Not so much. Back then we retouched only defects on select photos. If the film was scratched, you started over. So there was not much retouching because we weren't specialized for that. If you look bad, you look bad; there was no such thing as embellishment!

MW: Did part of the job involve getting clients?

SS: To attract clients you made a layout. You pinned photos to the wall. The best way was to organize the pictures step by step: full views, then busts, then ID photos. By size and by series, from 30 × 40 cm to 9 × 13 cm.

MW: Do you recall prices?

SS: It was less expensive. I told you that photos aren't expensive! An ID photo, for example, cost 150 to 200 francs. At 9 × 13 size we sold three prints for 300 francs. At 13 × 18, 4 prints cost 500 francs. 18 × 24, it was two prints for 600 francs. And 30 × 40 cost the most: 2000 francs.

FM: That was expensive at the time.

MW: Which were the most popular sizes?

SS: 9 × 13 and 9 × 14. When people needed an ID photo [at 4 × 4 cm], they had to come see us; they brought money, had the photo taken, and left.

MW: Not as interesting then.

SS: True! *Voilà.* But 9 × 14 and 9 × 13, those were for memories. For example, if people were having a dance party or a wedding, something like that, they called you and said, I want this and that, a picture of so-and-so, my friend is getting married tomorrow and you need to be at City Hall for the signing. You came over to act as witness. Photographers are witnesses.

MW: At last something useful!

SS: Very useful. If there are no pictures, there are no memories! If someone asks to see a picture and there's no picture to show, it is as if nothing had happened. But if the picture is there, we see what really took place.

AB: Your first studio was in the neighborhood of Diaradougou?

SS: Yes, and the second in Farakan.

MW: Can you recall how many studios were in Bobo in the late 1950s?

SS: Not many, three or four. There was a man from Benin called Quénum. And the others I've mentioned already.

MW: Were any run by Burkinabé?[2]

SS: No.

MW: Or Yoruba?[3]

SS: There was a Yoruba who trained with the Ghanaian at the same time as I did. He died young from an accident. I've forgotten his name. He was young, he married a woman from Bobo, and they had children. Then the accident happened.

MW: How big was your family?

SS: In the village? Oh, a lot of us because my father had many wives. For example my elder brother went into the army.[4]

FM: Whose idea was it to open the studio, and how did that work?

SS: It was my idea. I said, I know the business and want to set up shop. Since I didn't have enough money, [my cousin] Idrissa Koné gave me some.

MW: Not the Ghanaian?

SS: Not at all. He said that's enough. And I had paid for my apprenticeship! You could say I bought my knowledge.

FM: Well put.

MW: How did one go about opening a studio?

SS: Back then it wasn't hard. You needed authorization, that's all. You paid the government a monthly sum—can't do anything without the government taking its share. It's the same today: if you want to open a cafeteria or any business, you have to declare it. This was what Idrissa helped me with.

MW: Did he go with you to take care of paperwork?

SS: No, I did that all myself. Idrissa gave me enough to buy a camera as well. I had a Yashica-Mat—no, my first was a Shanghai.[5]

AB: The same brand that Kojo used?

SS: That's right. Then came the Yashica-Mat and, after that, Rolleiflex.

MW: And a tripod.

SS: Correct. So you open, you focus, you check lighting, then you shoot and advance the film, which has twelve or twenty-four frames.

FM: How often did you buy a new camera?

SS: It could be yearly or even more frequently if business was good. We might have had two or three at the time.

MW: What did the first studio look like?

FM: Diaradougou is a neighborhood in Bobo that used to have a lot of Malians who liked to dress up and have their photo taken. You've said you moved there for that reason.

SS: I chose a place where there were lots of people: crowds. And my studio building was the second building in the whole neighborhood to have a modern roof and a backyard.

MW: How did you arrange your studio?

SS: First I had to give it a name: Volta Photo. And then there was a large wall covered in photos. I made it look the same as the Ghanaian's. Then we started to get backdrops.

MW: How did you do that?

SS: I mentioned that there were Ghanaians who made drawings and stencils. You paid for the fabric and then the drawing—well, you described the picture you wanted, and they drew it for you on the spot.

MW: How did you choose the backdrop with the column as a design?

SS: I didn't choose this one: the Ghanaians came around with readymade designs. Later I came up with my own ideas, for example the city [scene]. That's development for you. You have to keep modifying.

MW: How many backdrops did you have in all? The column, the Volta Photo city scene, the monochrome gray cloth for ID photos…

SS: There is also the beach and the plane [see pages 46 and 60]. It's two backdrops in one, double-sided. A white man came to see me and bought it. I said no, but I needed money, and he gave me 60,000 francs.[6]

FM: A man from the Ivory Coast had made it. When was that?

SS: I had all of these at Diaradougou. But I didn't buy them all at once, rather bit by bit.

FM: I would guess the airplane/beach backdrop dates more from the 1970s, when you were in Farakan.

MW: Can you describe the studio floor?

SS: I used a red carpet and later a checkered linoleum.

MW: What gave you the idea to put a streetlamp in the Volta Photo city backdrop?

SS: The Ghanaian helped me. I said I wanted a painting with Volta Photo visible on the second floor. I described this to him, and he drew it.

MW: You wanted the studio name to be clearly visible. Why the city and the light?

SS: It's a city growing.

FM: Maybe you saw this in a movie?

SS: Definitely not a movie—in the newspapers. But I don't remember any titles, I didn't take time to read. If you read, it's because you're interested in the papers. I wanted to make photographs. So I can't say if it's a particular magazine. But when I think of something for my studio, I hold onto it in my head.
Today, for example, when I take my color photos to the lab, I tell them if I want to change the background to one with greenery. Greenery means happiness. Then they montage the image and the background. That's something you can do today [on the computer], and people like it. You can put them in a picture, for example of Mecca. We couldn't make such changes in the era of black-and-white.

FM: You told me your first backdrop was the one with the column.

SS: There was also the neutral fabric to make ID photos. You can't put drawings in an ID photo.

MW: How many ID pictures did you make in a week compared with other types of pictures?

SS: ID photos were a lot more requested at that time than portraits. Everyone needed one, to travel for example. I made a lot.

MW: It's funny because I haven't seen so many of them in the prints you've shown me.

SS: You did—any head shot could be cropped down for use as an ID photo.

MW: I imagine you kept your backdrops when you moved the studio to Farakan?

SS: No, I gave the first backdrop—the one with the column—as a present to my assistant Sibiri Ouattara, who came from Noumoudara, a village off the road to Banfora. Along with the studio itself. The man I had been renting from died. His children met me one day to say they were looking to renovate and thought my rent was impossibly low. I was paying 7,500 francs, [and] they asked for 25,000 francs. I didn't have that much money, so I moved to Farakan. I had been in Diaradougou maybe ten years.

FM: What became of that first studio?

SS: Sibiri couldn't afford it, and he stopped being a photographer. He went into making jewelry.

MW: It seems surprising that, after paying for your own apprenticeship, you gave away one of your own backdrops to an apprentice.

SS: A friend had brought Sibiri to me; he was an orphan and wanted to learn the business. I wouldn't have taken him otherwise.

MW: Who came up with the name Volta Photo?

SS: I did.

1 This is roughly fifty current U.S. dollars. According to a global comparison of per capita income, country by country, indexed to 2008 USD, Burkina Faso residents earned $76 yearly on average in 1960. See: https://web.archive.org/web/20090220134324/ http://earthtrends.wri.org/text/economics-business/variable-638.html.

2 Known at the time as Voltaïques, the people of Burkina Faso are now called Burkinabé.

3 The Yoruba, principally from Nigeria but from neighboring countries as well, have generally been credited with establishing or popularizing studio photography in much of Francophone Africa.

4 A "brother" or "sister" in this context can be a cousin or other relative (or perhaps even a friend) with whom the speaker is particularly close. In this case Sory is referring to the cousin who helped get him the apprenticeship with Adomako.

5 According to camera collector Ivan Lo, several factories in Shanghai manufactured cameras under the name Shanghai Camera Factory no. 1, no. 2, and so forth. The oldest of these was founded in 1958, and from 1964 went by the name Seagull. In 1959 they began producing an adapted Rolleiflex twin lens reflex model; this would be the device that Sory purchased (https://vintagecameralab.com/brand/seagull). The Yashica-Mat was a Japanese twin lens reflex camera produced in many models from 1957 through the mid-1980s. See: http://camera-wiki.org/wiki/Yashica_6x6_TLR_(crank_advance).

6 A little more than $100 USD.

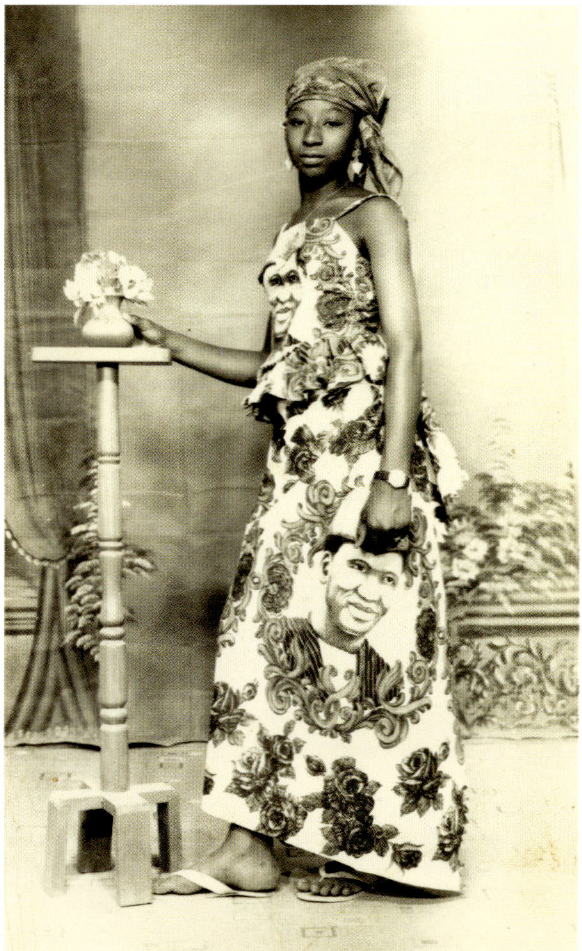

3 Kouloubi, younger sister of Yakaridjan and girlfriend of Sory at the time, 1960/65

Kouloubi wears a dress adorned with portraits of pan-African revolutionary leader Sékou Touré, the first president of Guinea.

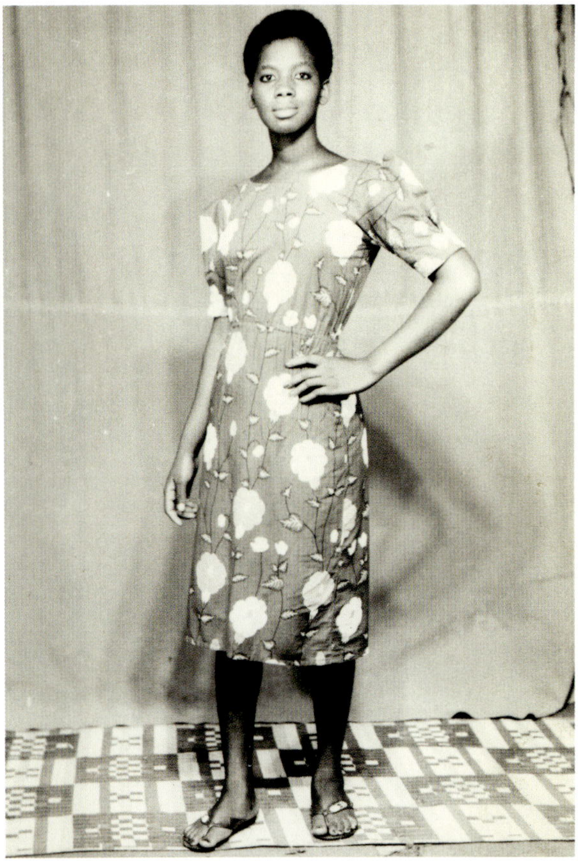

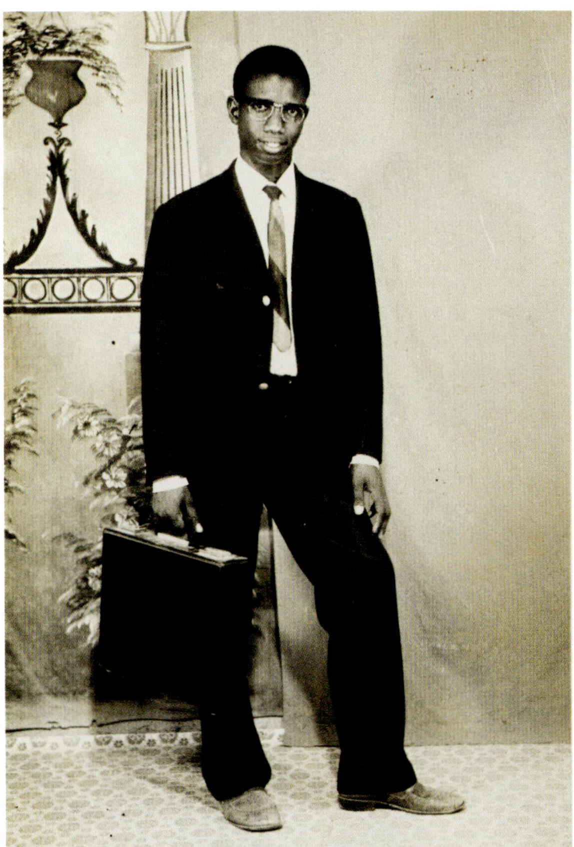

4 Untitled, 1965/75

5 Untitled (taken by an apprentice), 1965/75

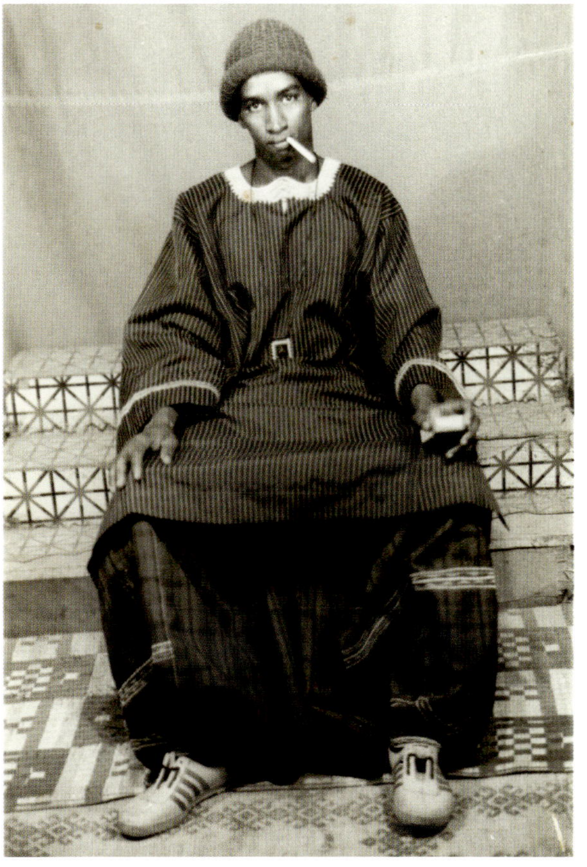

6–7 Untitled, 1965/75

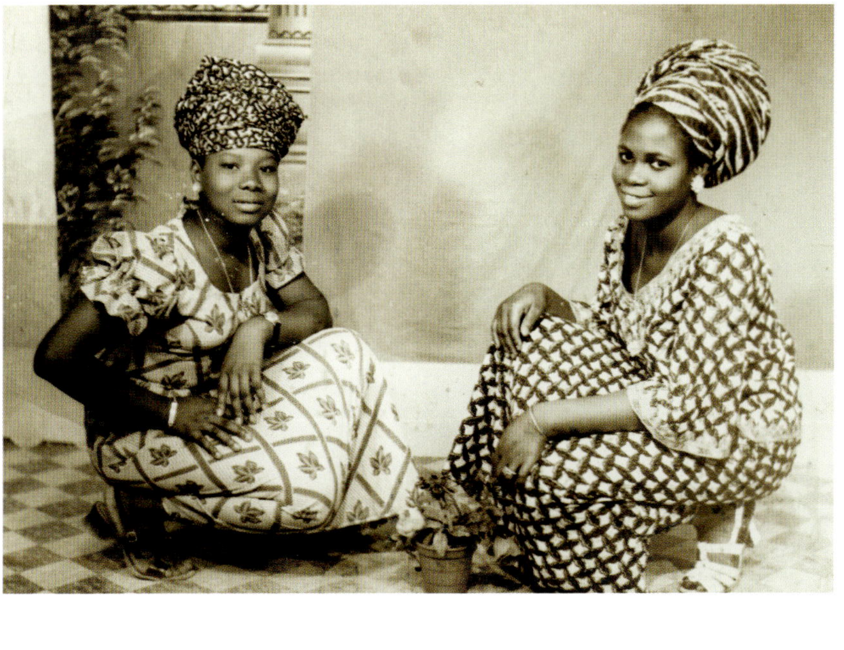

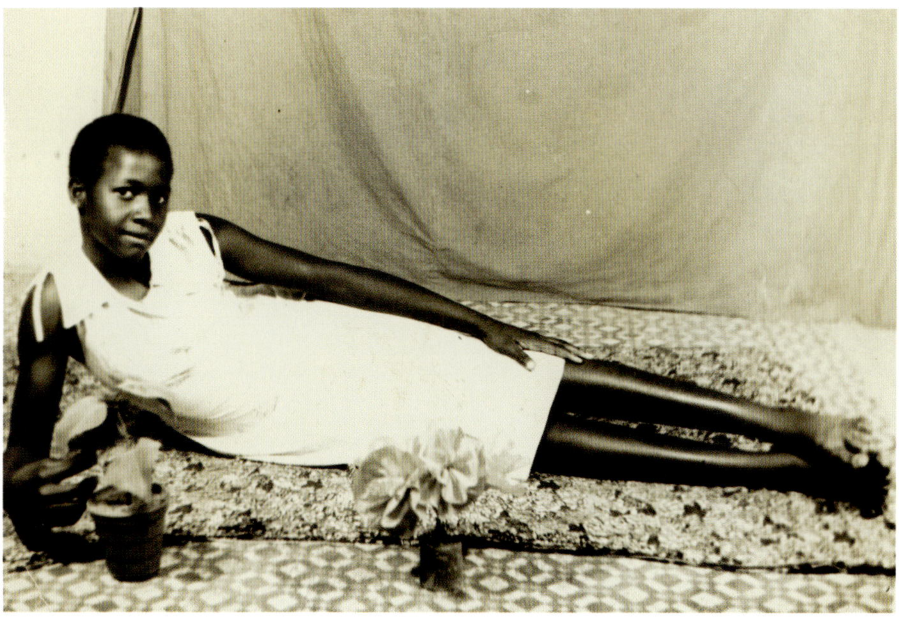

8 Untitled (taken by an apprentice), 1965/75

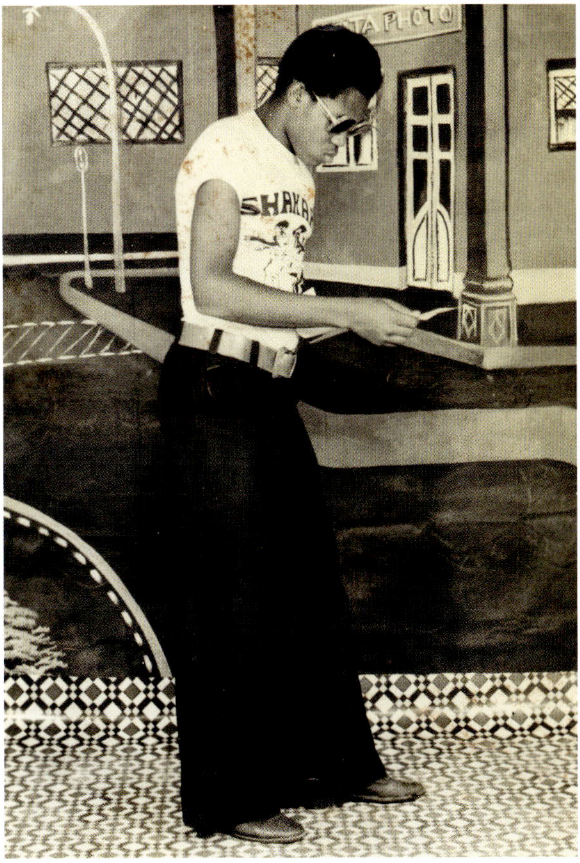

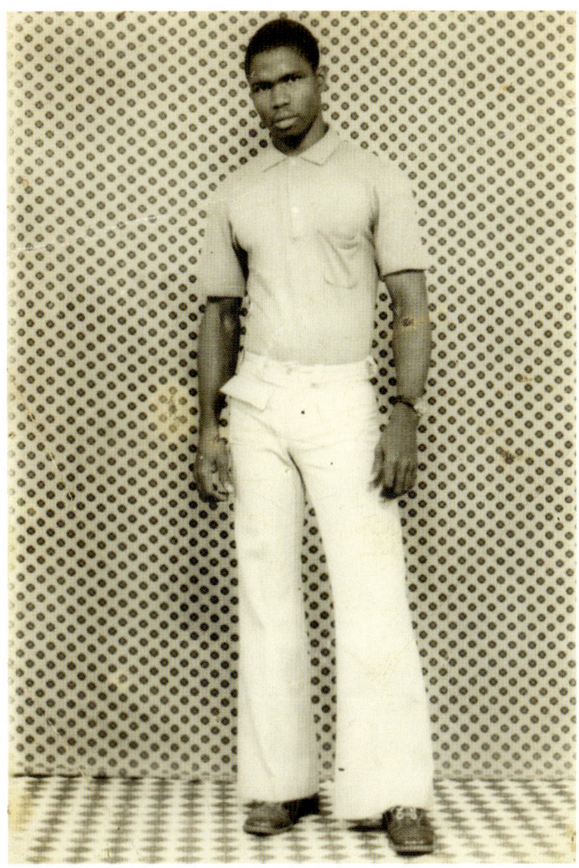

9 Yao Pelé, 1965/75

10 Untitled (taken by an apprentice), 1965/75

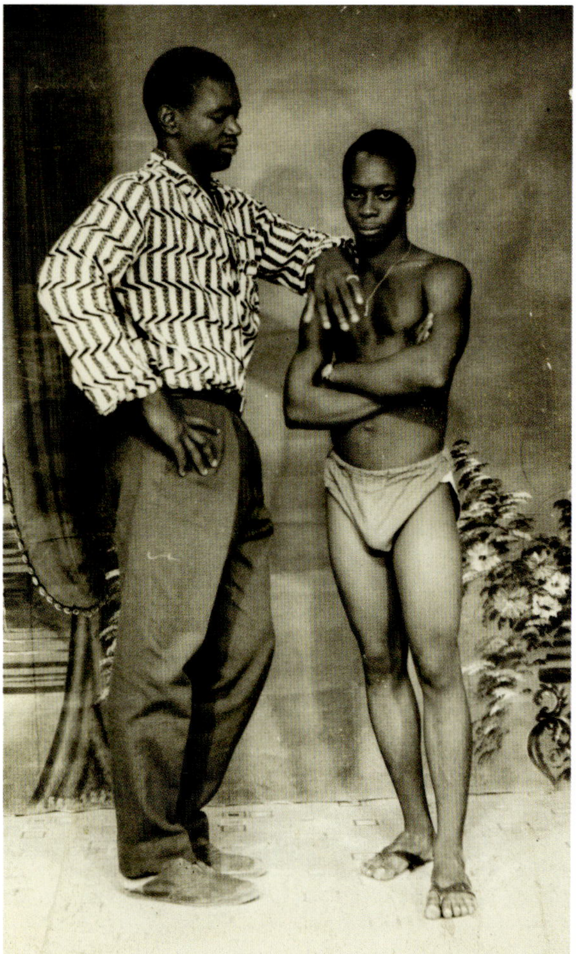

11 Sanlé Sory in gymnastic attire next to his sports trainer, Ousmane, 1957/65

This early photograph was taken in the studio of Kojo Adomako, the photographer with whom Sory first apprenticed.

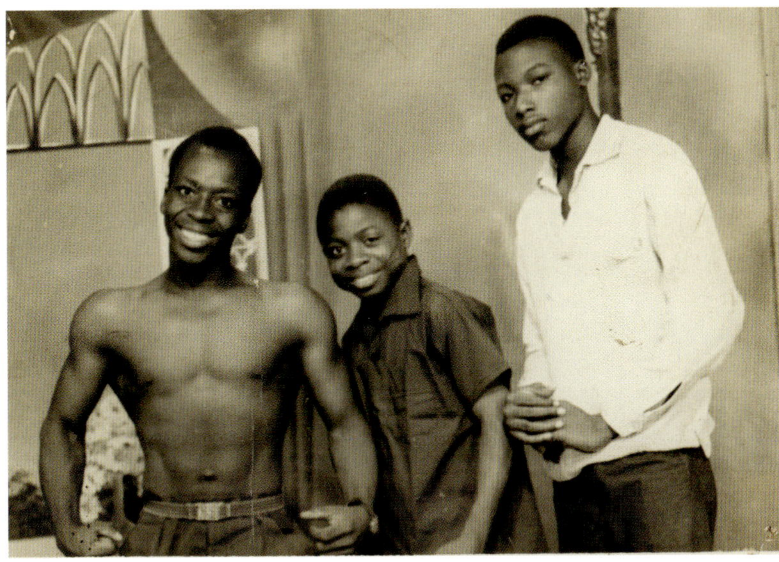

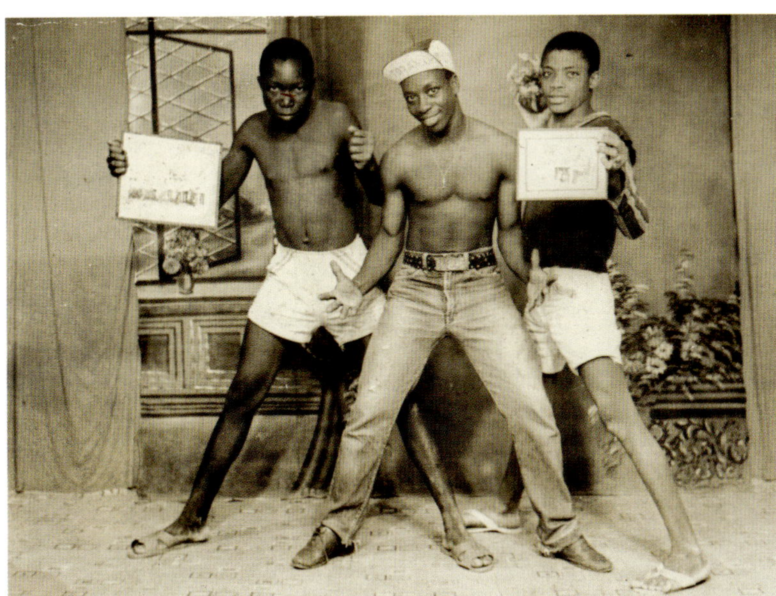

12 Self-portrait (left) with Yakini, a Yoruba youth, and Adama, a Bobo youth, 1960/65

13 Self-portrait (center) with two apprentices, 1960/65

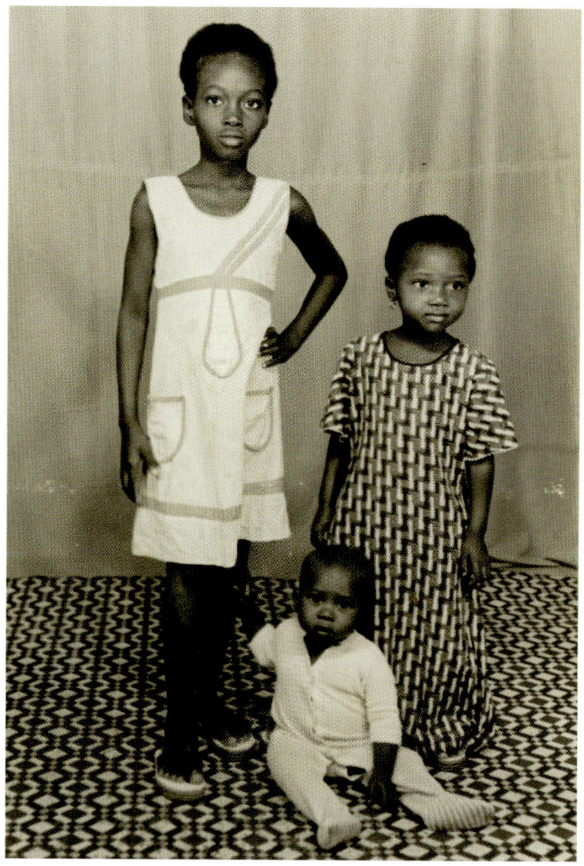

14 Untitled, 1965/75

CUSTOMERS

MW: Here we are looking at a group of men seated beneath the Volta Photo sign (plate 2). Where are we?

SS: In Farakan. That's a group of Fula.[7] They got really smashed and came to see me after. The Fula were my best clients, second only to the Malians.

AB: Why did you find it necessary to take this relatively informal picture, which is neither a studio pose nor a dance party image?

SS: These are my friends and loyal customers. They were leaving the bar, and I wanted to take a souvenir photo. They didn't pay for it. A gift shot! Or maybe a personal picture that I didn't give anyone.

AB: Did you take a lot of personal pictures?

SS: Yes, and I gave many away too. People who came often to see me also sent me other clients.

MW: How did you choose Farakan?

SS: Farakan had a lot of people on the boulevard [Boulevard de la Révolution]. But it wasn't even paved, it was a dusty dirt road when I opened my studio. People crapped behind my studio. It wasn't all set up (laughs)!

MW: Tell us what it was like to look for this spot.

SS: It wasn't easy. I had to ask all my friends if they knew a place in a well-traveled neighborhood. Today it's really difficult. Studios don't work any more in Bobo. If you find a place, it's worthless. People take cameras everywhere, phones like you have there, and they take pictures everywhere. Our customers have become photographers.

MW: Was there a market near the studio?

SS: Yes, a little one called Sankarea, near the bridge crossing the railway. It's there today—it has butchers and some ladies selling vegetables and yams.

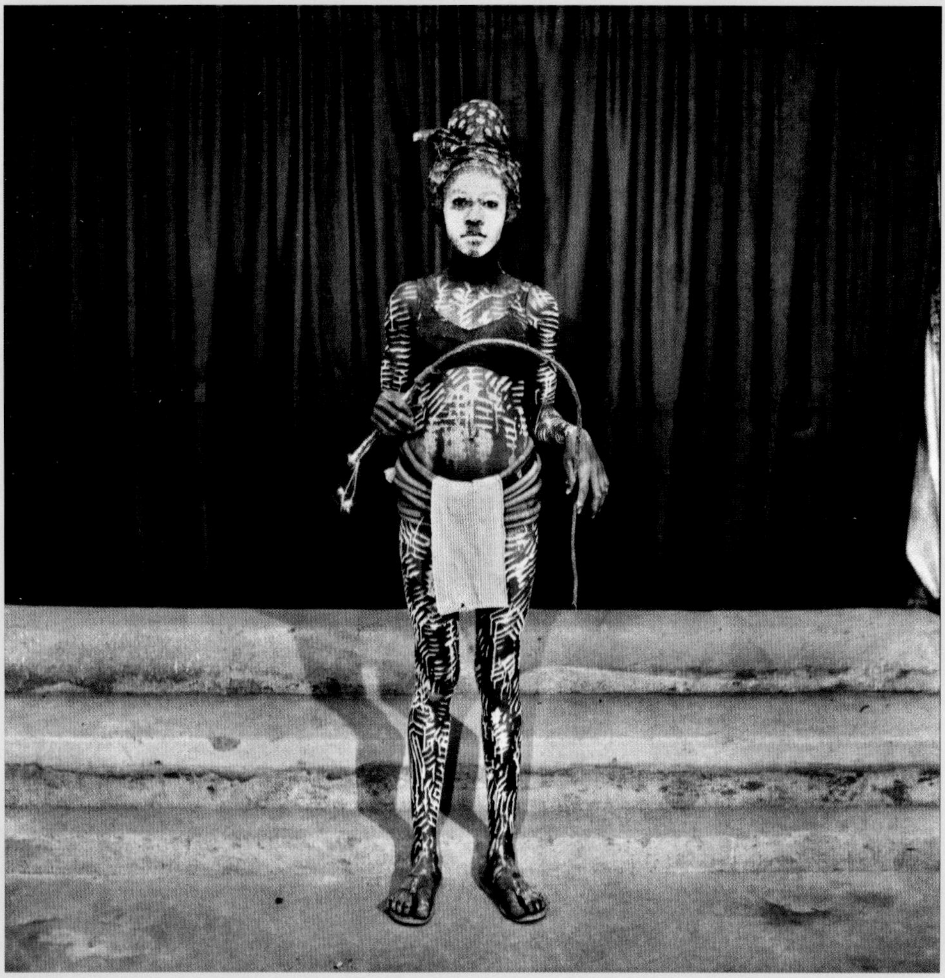

fig. 1 Untitled, 1965/75, printed 2017. 36 × 36 cm (image); 50 × 40 cm (sheet). The Art Institute of Chicago, gift of the artist and Florent Mazzoleni, 242559

FM: And the mosque.

SS: You know, people with money in Bobo get cozy with locals to open mosques. For me it's all business. A city should have two big mosques for Friday prayers. After that, it should be enough.

MW: So you didn't get customers from the mosque.

SS: They don't care. Some of them don't even like photos. The ones with beards, the Wahhabis.

FM: Looking over your negatives, however, I've noticed that sometimes you have bearded Muslims wearing djellabas.

SS: Not many. If you want to take their picture, they don't agree. You can't take their money, they say it's *haram* (forbidden). What do you mean, you say—you take a passport to Mecca, and there is a photo in it! They say that's because they have to. And they think you're dirtying yourself by working in photography. The business is broken already, and then they tell you not to make photographs. Then you can keep your cameras and stay at home.

FM: What was a typical day in the '60s or '70s like? What time did you get to the studio?

SS: Well, the apprentices slept there. Me, too, when it was in Diaradougou! I had more rooms there, two side rooms. The Farakan studio was smaller. No room for me there, so I left it to my apprentices.

MW: It's surprising that the Farakan studio was smaller.

SS: And I paid to fix it up. I'm the one who paid for plywood to remodel and make a darkroom. It was a proper store. Rent on those terms wasn't much, 2,500 francs, because I had to make the place right.

MW: Could I venture that you didn't need such a big studio if things were going so well in the villages and in town?

SS: No, I could have had three or four studios. What matters is to be in a neighborhood where it's lively in the evenings. If it's sleepy, you'll soon be closing shop. If it's a bit lively at night, until two or three in the morning, if you aren't lazy you might get lucky. But while I'm out at the parties, the apprentices were still working in the studio.

MW: Even at night?

SS: Sure, the studio ran at night! Apprentices took pictures and developed them too. Once you had apprentices, you could ride around. I had two apprentices: Sibiri Ouattara and Mamoudou Bitenga, known as Super. He's dead. His studio was Super Photo.

FM: You had only two apprentices?

SS: I trained others, but they left. They don't count. Two are in Ivory Coast; they gave up photography and bought land to grow cocoa. I've trained a lot of people, but they've gone. One left for the army and became a lieutenant.

MW: Did you look for customers at the marketplace?

SS: Right now, if I wasn't in Bamako I'd be at the market in Bobo looking for customers. I never sit still. You have to look outside of the studio. Everyone knows me, especially as I'm an old photographer. Back in the day, it was customers who came to seek *me* out. If you had a studio, people came. They wanted a photographer to take their picture.

FM: Was there a community of Bobo photographers?

SS: Not like that, but [solidarity] with other shop owners.

FM: Meaning that someone buying lace could hear about you and find you that way.

SS: Right. There were no steady customers for photography. No one told me, Sory, I can't imagine going to a different photographer. And someone might have a picture taken by you and another by Mr. Florent here, and his turns out prettier, so they show you [the other print and] ask, Sory, why can't you do better?

That's the telephone, she's pretending to make a call (plate 27).

MW: Is that why she's kneeling?

SS: She is the one who decided to kneel. I don't know who it is. You can give her a name if you like.

MW: The telephoness then (laughs). Did women come to your studio unaccompanied?

SS: It's self-serve. The married ones sometimes are not allowed. But I don't ask to know. Sometimes they come without telling their husbands. Or the couple comes to be photographed together.

7 The Fula (known also as Fulani or Fulbe; in French, *Peul*) are principally nomadic or semi-sedentary pastoralists—by some accounts the largest pastoral nomadic group in the world. They speak a common language (Fula) and practice Islam. Fula live mainly across West Africa and numbered some 20 to 25 million in the mid-1990s. See David Levinson, "Fulani," *Encyclopedia of World Cultures: Africa and the Middle East, vol. 9* (Gale Group, 1996).

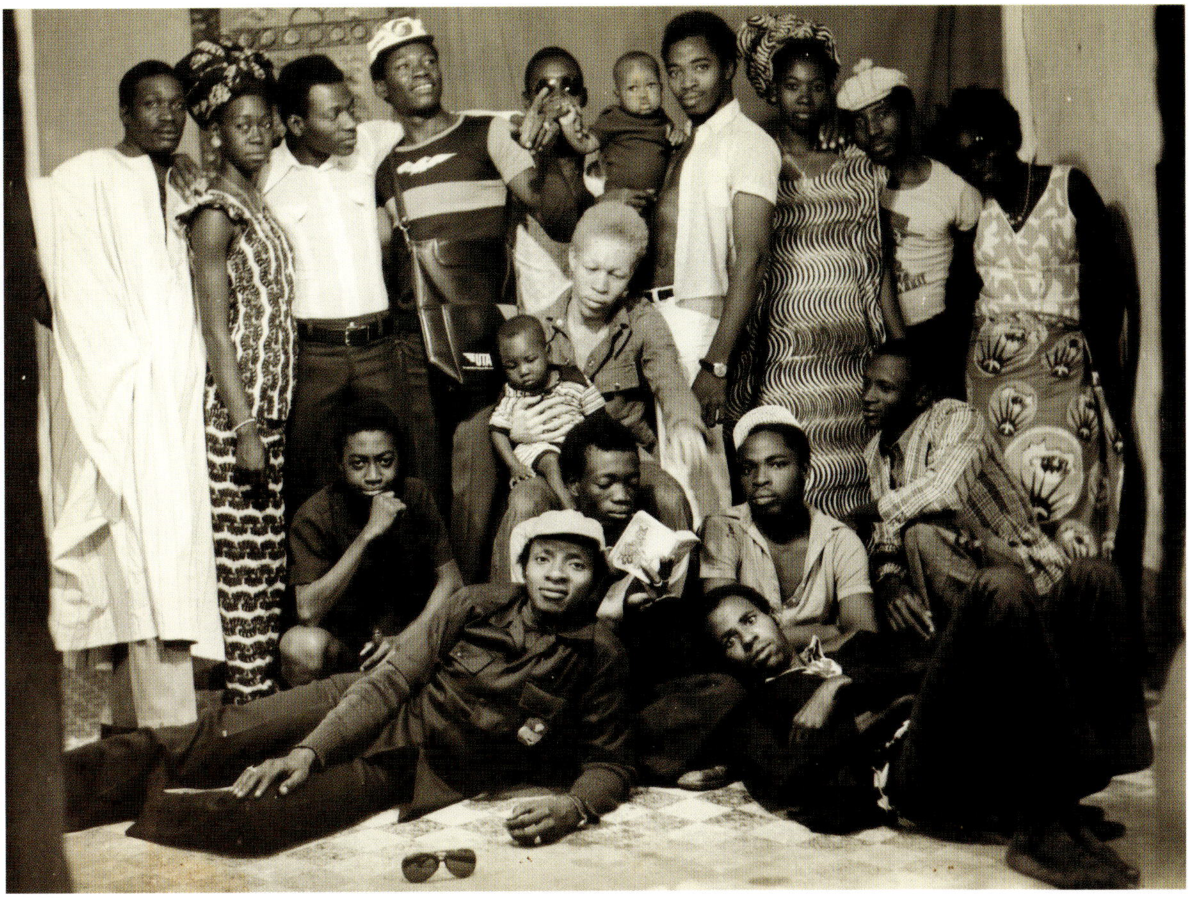

15 Untitled, 1965/75

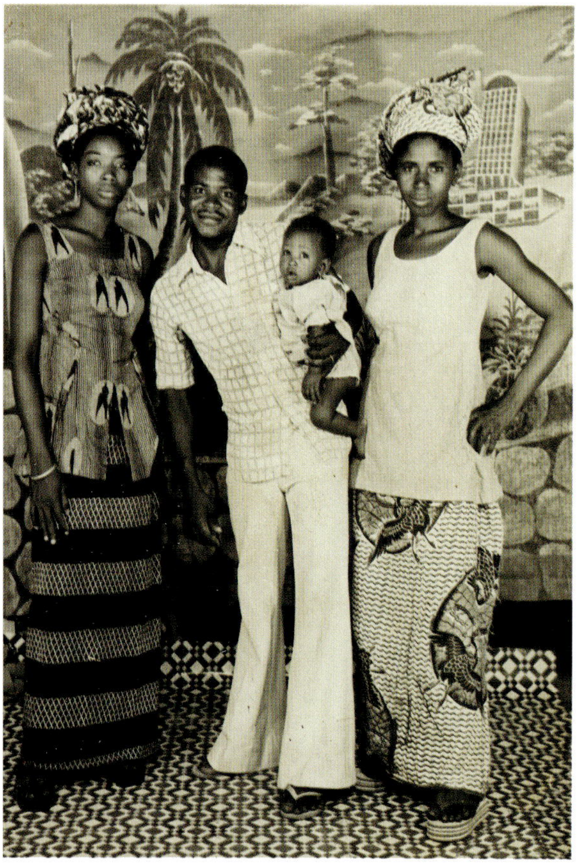

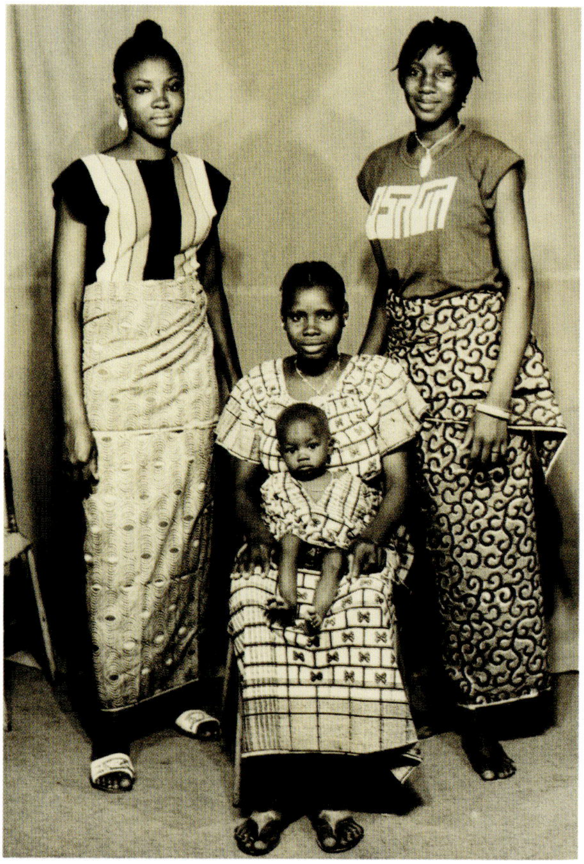

16–17 Untitled, 1965/75

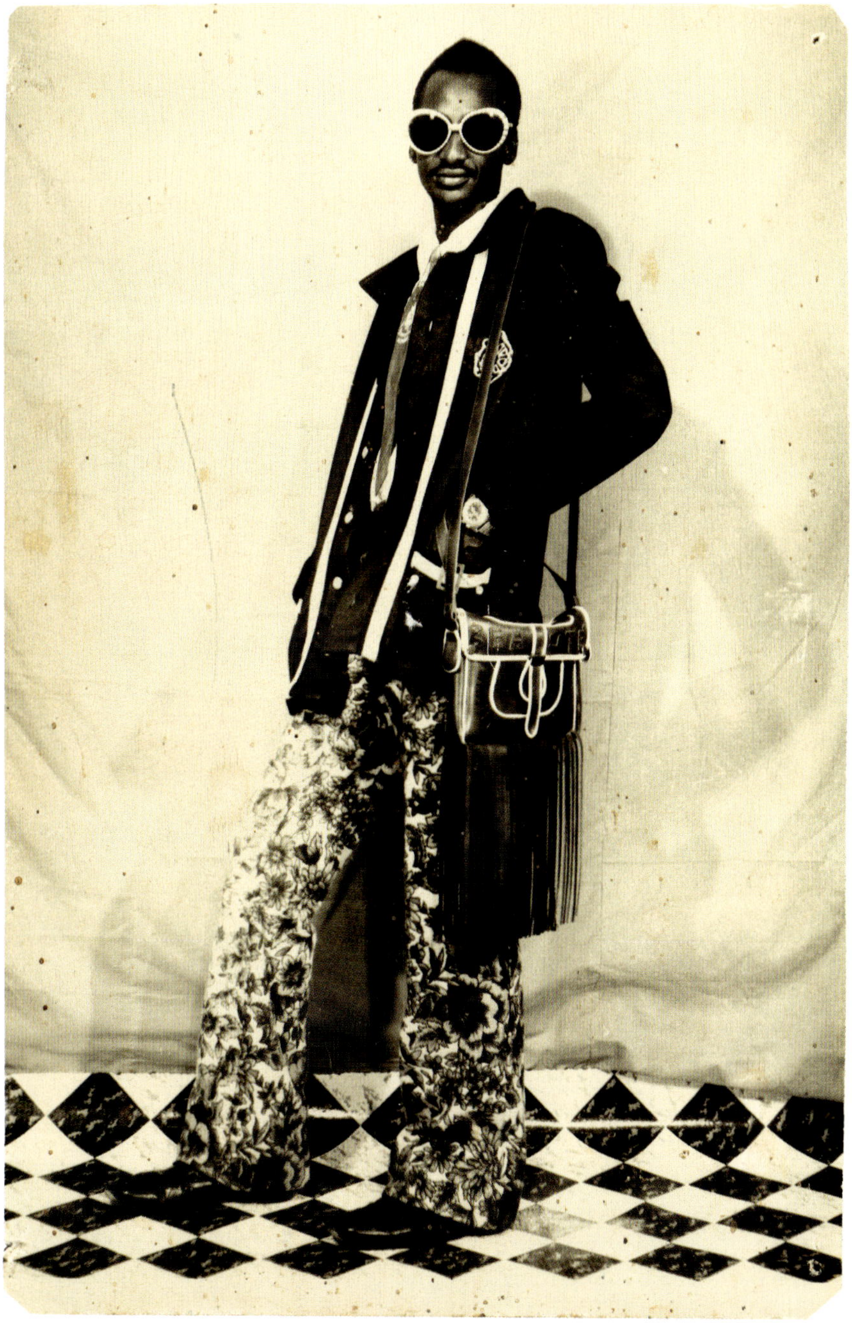

18 Fula man, 1970/80

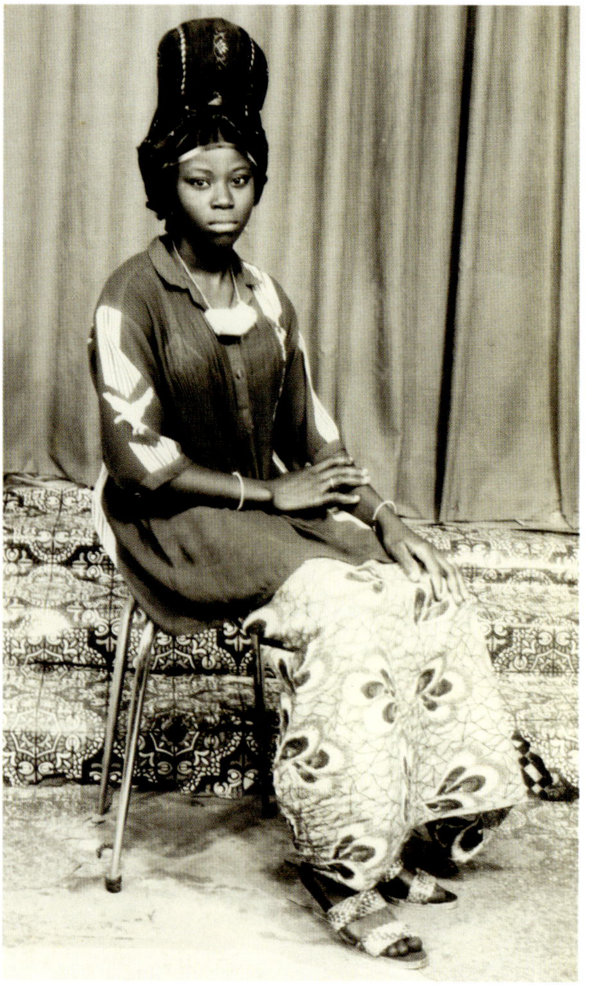

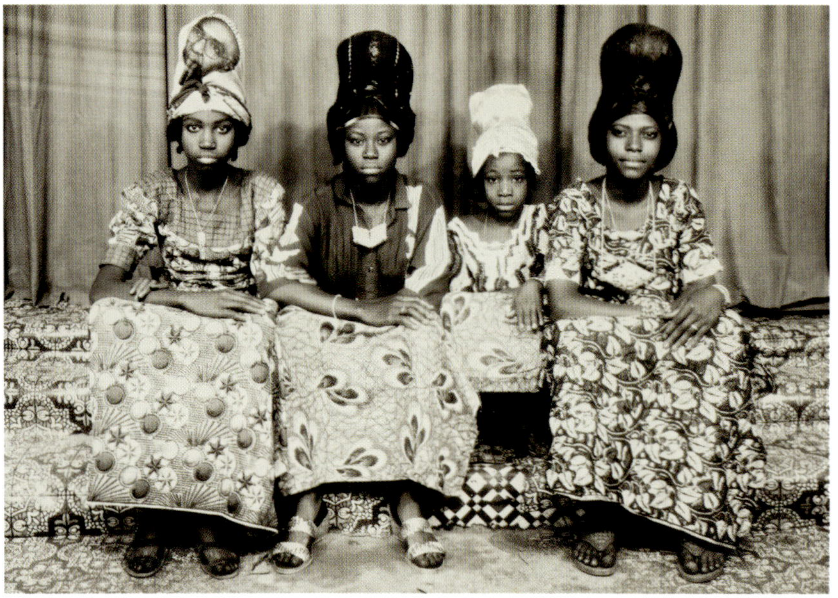

19 Woman in a ceremonial headdress, 1965/75

20 Four women in ceremonial headdresses, 1965/75

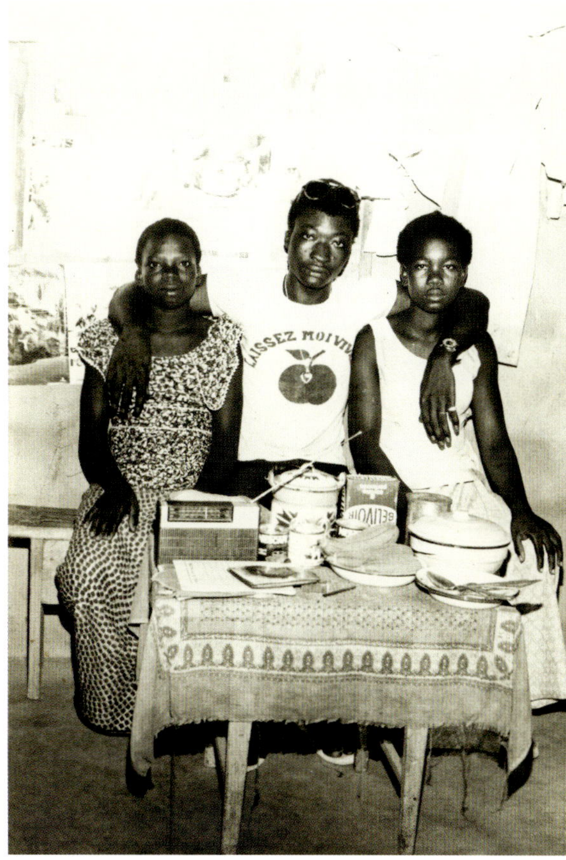

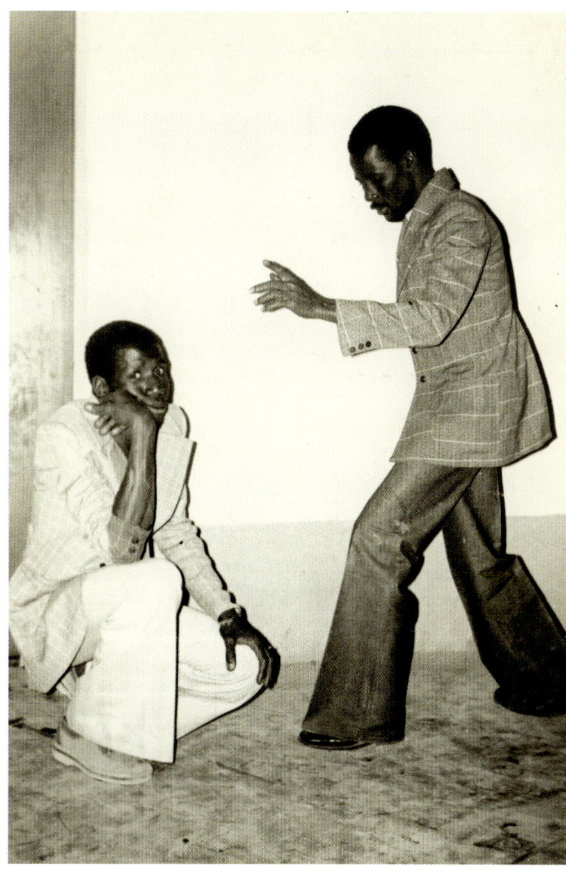

21–22 Untitled, 1965/75

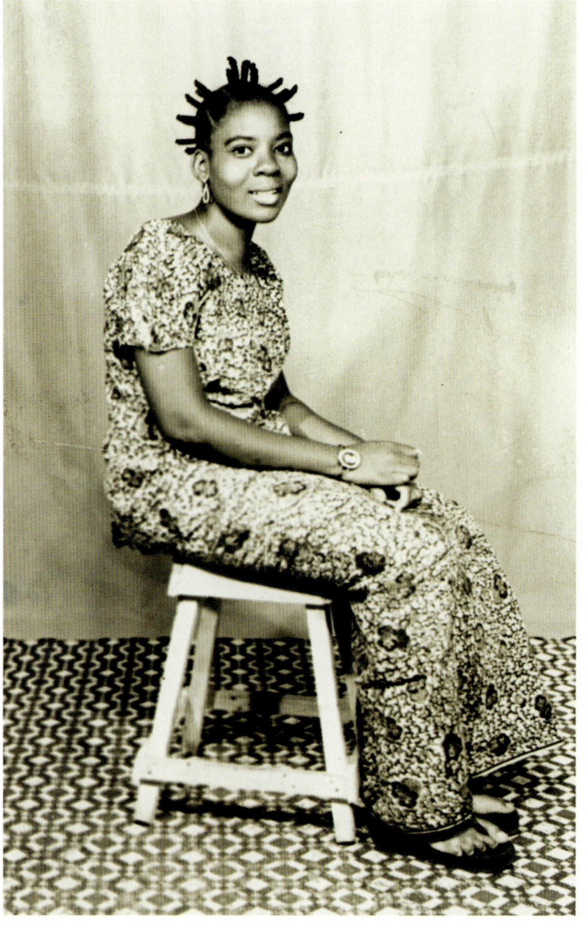

23 Untitled, 1965/75

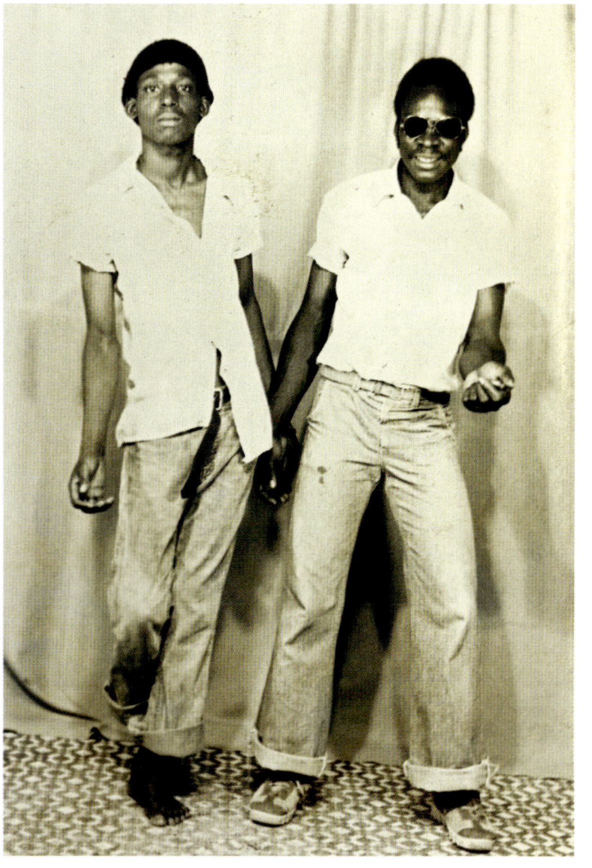

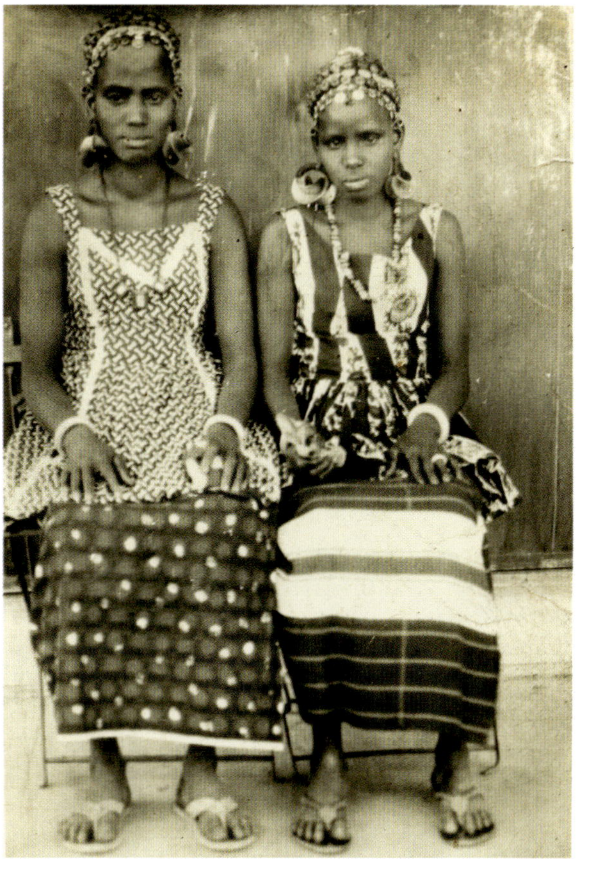

24 Untitled, 1965/75

25 Two Fula women, 1965/75

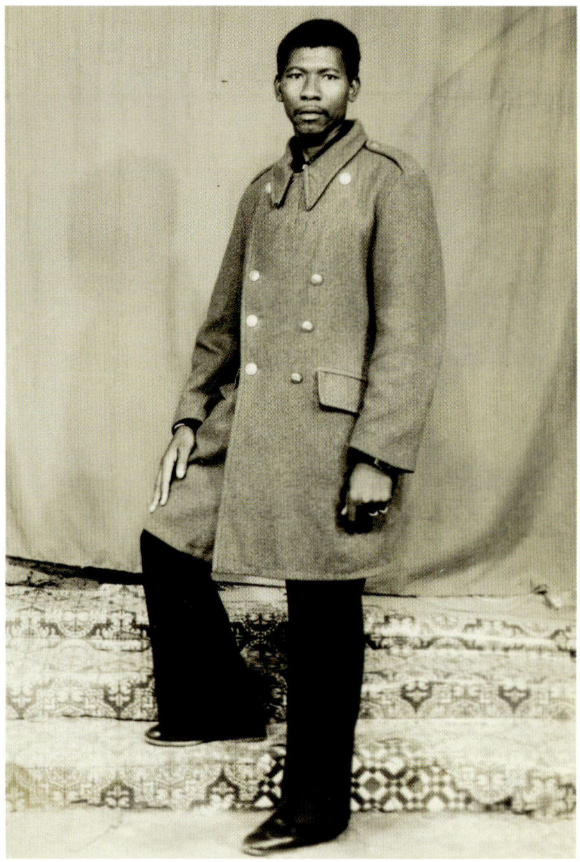

26 Untitled, 1965/75

IN THE STUDIO

AB: Why did this man, whom we see standing on a motorbike, want his picture taken in the street and not the studio (p. 145)?

SS: That guy liked my bike—it was mine. Only three people in town had one like that then: a Honda 100.

MW: Anything valuable that you bought could become a prop—everything useful could also become part of the décor.

SS: Right. My radio, the telephone, that's how it goes (big laughs).

AB: Sory, did you distinguish between work done in the studio and work done on the street?

SS: Street photos, studio photos, for me it's the same. Some customers prefer not to have their picture taken in full public view. So they come into the studio. There you can close off a space for them to change.

MW: Did you ever photograph twins or pose people as twins when they weren't? I see a fair number of pictures where pairs of sitters have gone to great lengths to dress identically.

SS: I never photographed twins. Sometimes people would dress in costume and come pose because they liked to do that.

AB: It was common to dress identically for weddings.

MW: A different example of twinning made in the camera: a single person doubled in the photograph (plate 1).[8]

SS: I did that a bunch. It's very easy. You take a piece of photo paper. In the darkroom, you take the negative and mask the paper on one side. You turn on the light for a second. Now, still in the darkroom, with the red light on, you take away the mask [and move it to the other side], and you flip the negative. Then you turn on the main light and count

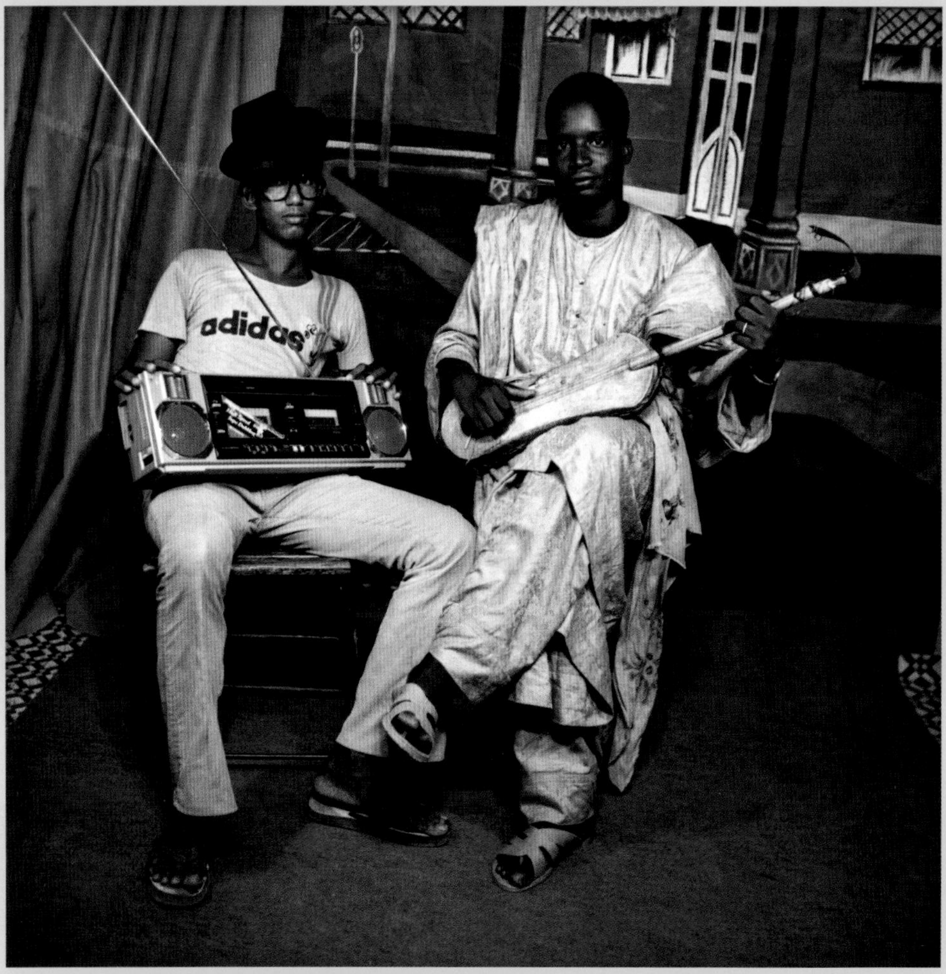

fig. 1 Untitled, 1965/75, printed 2017. 36 × 36 cm (image); 50 × 40 cm (sheet). The Art Institute of Chicago, gift of the artist and Florent Mazzoleni, 242554

the seconds again. Put that in the developer, and out comes the picture.

MW: How would a customer know you could make such things?

SS: I did it for fun, for myself. Some people liked it; I made several of them.

MW: How did you get the idea it would interest people?

SS: As you keep going with your work, you have to advance. Intelligence does that. Ah! If you don't have the intelligence, you don't do this. It's a technique.

AB: Did people pay more for this technique?

SS: Of course.

MW: When did you learn it?

SS: I don't remember. I told you I burned a lot. When you don't know the value of something, you always toss it. I didn't know it would bear fruit one day.

MW: Yet other photographers in this region numbered their images, because customers came back to ask for new prints. Did that ever happen to you?

SS: No. No one ever came back to ask me to reprint a picture. They don't need it, and they don't care.

MW: Did you ever work with a tailor, for example, during a wedding or other ceremony?

SS: No, never. The Malians dressed up for ceremonies; they would buy five suits and come see me. Or a single person would come in, take out an outfit, change, pose, change again, and get another photo taken.

MW: Did waiting customers step outside the studio to leave more privacy to those inside?

SS: No. The Fula in the photo we saw yesterday, for example, they're busy chatting. That's why they are outside. Some might come in the studio to have a picture taken. If they've sold a head of cattle they have money to lose.

MW: So those posing weren't put out by the presence of those waiting?

SS: No, people came and went at our place. Someone wanting to have a picture taken would come in, put on whatever makeup or clothing they liked, then step into the gallery area and poof—done!

AB: One of your props was a radio. But we see lots of kinds of radios in the pictures; they are not all yours?

SS: At that time the Fula, or anyone who had a little money, would have his own radio. A radio and a tape deck. The Fula put their music on. When it played—kwaa kwaa kwaa—they were happy. The Fula always brought their radios when they came to see me.

FM: They listened to nianiorou or riti, the one-string violin. It's piercing music.

SS: Yes it made the Fula really happy. If I put on a Fula tape, they'd give me 500 or 1,000 francs to get something to drink. They really liked that music in the studio. Because the rule is music like that can't stop until you give money to whoever put it on.

FM: They gave you money for the music even if you didn't take their picture?

SS: Yes indeed, that's Fula music.

FM: It relates to *djeliya*, in fact—praise. You give someone money to praise him. That's the basis of griot singing.[9] Just by putting on this music, Sory drove them crazy.

MW: Did Bobo women often have makeup at home? Or did they come see you because makeup was something special?

SS: It depends. Older women, or Malians, had everything in their bags. Young ladies needed to put everything on at the studio, because they didn't have time to go around with makeup. On the other hand, a married woman coming for a picture would take time to get herself ready.

FM: So there were two types of pictures taken: deliberate and impulsive.

SS: That's right.

MW: Did you say things to put people at ease when they arrived?

SS: No, if they've come, they're at ease. Even if it doesn't look so. Everyone poses how they want, that's what you're forgetting. I would tell certain people to pose in profile, it's prettier; but others would tell me no, they had to be photographed face on. Everyone chooses what they want in photography.

MW: Why did some people dislike side views?

SS: The Fula will never agree to be photographed in profile.

MW: Did you have seating?

SS: Yes, there were two chairs and a bench. There was also a stool.

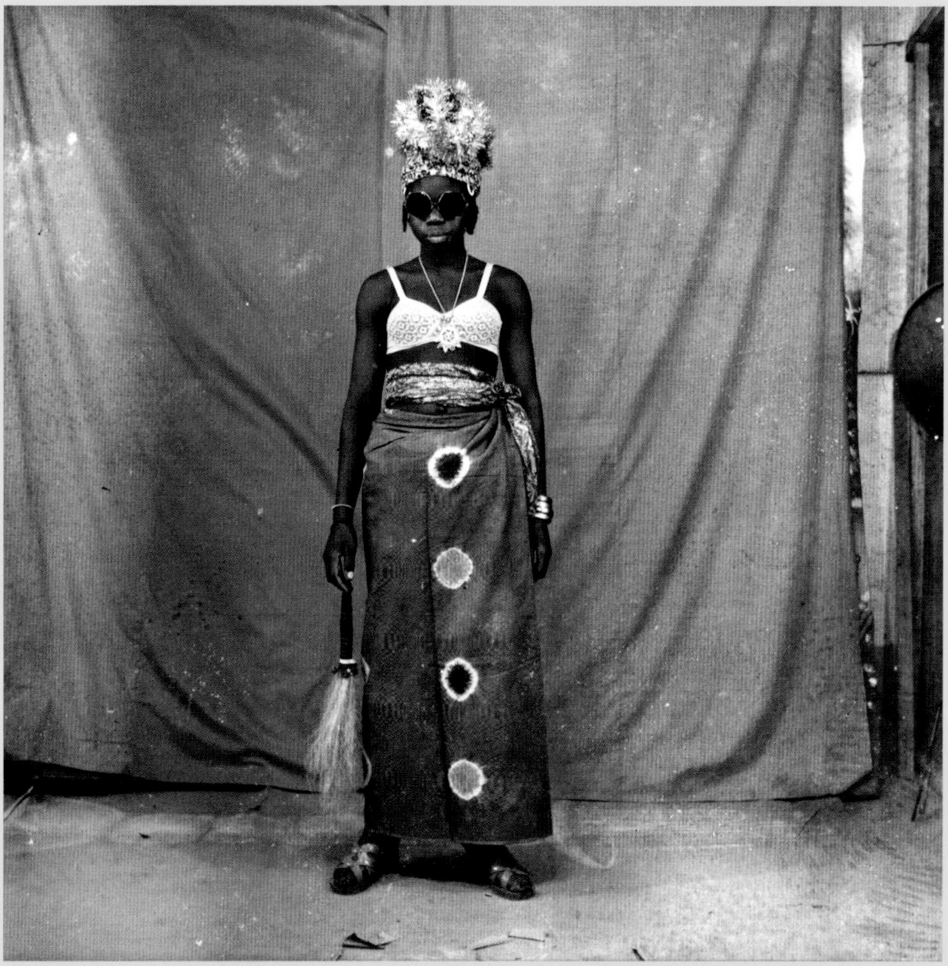

fig. 2 Untitled, 1965/75, printed 2017. 36 × 36 cm (image); 50 × 40 cm (sheet). The Art Institute of Chicago, gift of the artist and Florent Mazzoleni, 242561

This woman's attire—headdress, fly-swatter, and exposed brassiere—is associated with two annual Dioula ceremonies, known as kurubi *and* jomɛnɛ.

MW: Did you change chairs sometimes?

SS: When they broke.

MW: To change the look too?

SS: No, that didn't matter. Some people need to sit, that's one thing; others don't. Everyone makes their choice in the studio, for example if they want to kneel or stretch out.

MW: You didn't make suggestions?

SS: Not unless they asked my thoughts. I just wanted the money. That's why I opened. If someone wants to pose a certain way, I won't say otherwise. Art is their problem. I just asked them what kind of picture they wanted: ID, bust, souvenir. The choices were pinned up [at the entrance] so customers could choose. If they wanted to make changes beyond what they saw, they could do that.

That's an ID photo (p. 15). We would crop as we were printing. We put the neg up top and projected onto the paper underneath. Then we cropped as needed. For an ID photo you fold the paper in two, light one side and then the other, and put it in the developer. You get four pictures. Then you cut them up and give them to the customer.

FM: You had props as well, including a vest, an Air Afrique travel bag, magazines, the camera—

SS: Yes, I had things I took out when people asked. The motorbike, the flowerpot, the telephone, the radio. I also had a jacket with black-and-white stripes and a tie. Makeup for the ladies. Pencils, powder, a comb. Women would get ready at the front of the studio unless they needed to change. In that case they used the darkroom. But some people didn't need that. It was there if people asked. We didn't force people to wear anything. And it cost the same—we didn't charge for use of the props. It was just to draw customers.

AB: Did the women wear perfume?

SS: It wouldn't come out in the photo!

AB: Malick Sidibé once remarked that ladies would put on perfume because it changed how they felt in front of the camera.[10]

SS: Is that right? Maybe that gave them extra care to dress up well. If people were sweaty I put a little powder on their face, which looks very nice. Otherwise the skin isn't smooth.

FM: It's true you rarely see people sweating in your pictures, even though it must have been very hot in the studio.

SS: There was a mirror, too.

FM: The mirror in which you made the self-portrait (p. 24). Did everyone look in the mirror before having his or her picture taken?

SS: Certainly. The mirror was in the front room, where the sample photos were pinned up.

MW: Were the cutouts with portraits (plates 28-31) originally ID pictures?

SS: Mm-hmm. It's a bust [*pointing to plate 30*]. Same thing. He had it cut out to put inside this heart shape.

MW: But the client didn't return especially for that—it's you who reused the negative to make this image, which the young man undoubtedly used to give to his beloved.

SS: That's right.

MW: Did you make cutouts for a long time?

SS: Yes, they're useful.

MW: Did you cut out the shapes: the heart, with or without the words *Volta Photo* inside; the lion; the zigzag contour? Or was it an apprentice?

SS: I did that work. It's cardboard cut up to make fantasies. Smooth, zigzag, lion—there was also a bird, an eagle.

FM: And an antelope. Sory likes fantasy pictures.

SS: It's true.

MW: How did you get the idea of the lion, for example?

SS: As I said, you have to progress over time in your work. I made these cutouts and drawings just to make them. Because before starting in photography I made drawings. As a little boy, I watched others as they drew and said, I like this, I want to do it, too. That's how I am in general. For example, when my brothers went fishing and put the rod in the water, and got a bite, I liked that a lot and wanted to try. And then I started catching fish. I can do anything!

MW: What kind of drawings did you make?

SS: Oh, birds, people, I made a lot of drawings. Today I still take paper and pencil and draw—it's pretty. I haven't totally forgotten. If I made you a drawing, you'd say, "Amazing, he still holds up!"

MW: Did your family say something about the drawings?

SS: I kept them to myself, not to show. But I gave my drawings to village women who were stitching bags and patterned canvases. I drew on tracing paper; the ladies took it to stitch their patterns.

MW: Did they ask for certain kinds of drawings?

SS: They wanted images they could sew quickly, not too complicated.

MW: Did their customers ask for certain images too?

SS: No, it was the women in Naniagara who made the choices, and then they sold their goods.

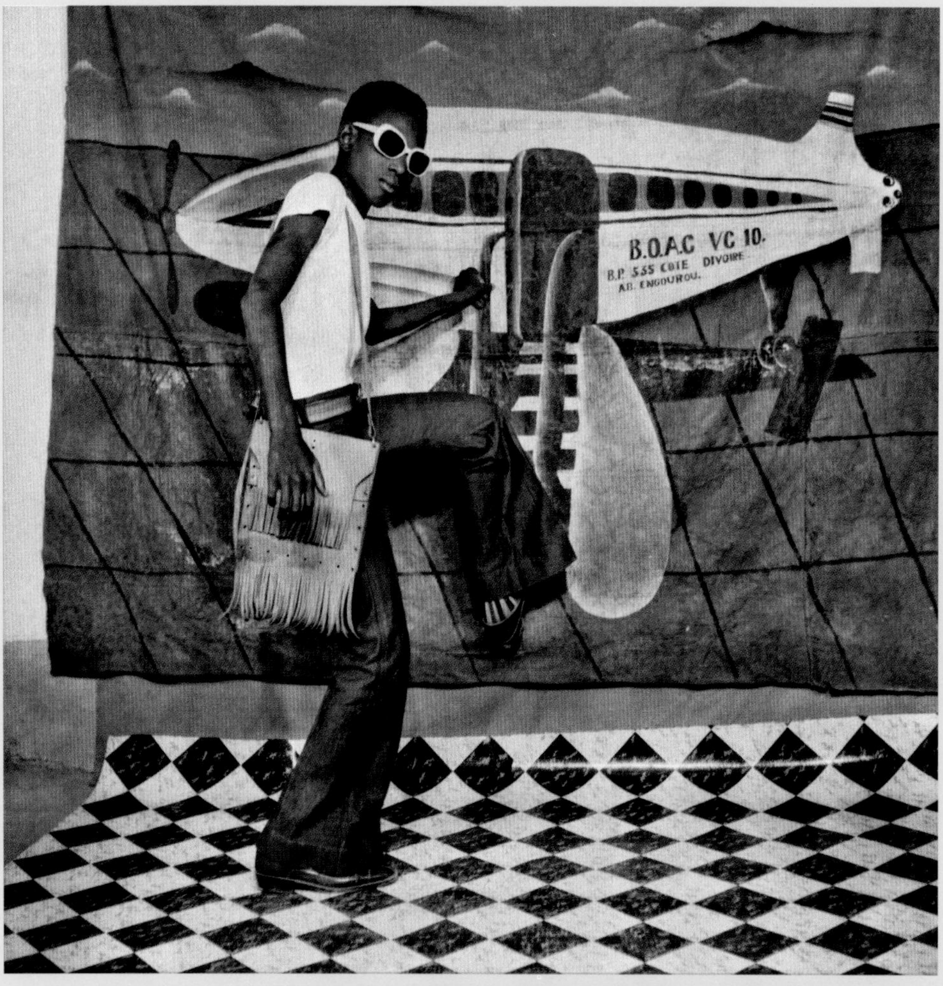

fig. 3 Untitled, 1965/75, printed 2017. 36 × 36 cm (image); 50 × 40 cm (sheet). The Art Institute of Chicago, gift of the artist and Florent Mazzoleni, 242557

AB: Did you ever color your photographs with a brush or colored pencils?

SS: I never used those things. I've never worked with a brush. I didn't think of it. You have to have a memory of something to be able to do it. I saw others working that way, but I couldn't pick it up.

AB: Could a customer ask someone else in Bobo to do that kind of work?

SS: I never met anyone who said they wanted to remake a picture of mine. My work is easy. You take the negative, put it in the enlarger. You take a match, it works like a light bulb. No red light even, just total darkness. I kept the matchbox nearby so I wouldn't have to hunt for it. I strike the match, poof, and put it out. The enlarger bulb had stopped working. And anyway the bulb was too strong for the film.

AB: On another subject, did people in Bobo get their photographs framed?

SS: People did that sometimes. Even we would cut glass and put pictures inside. Protects the image. Some people took their pictures to a carpenter.

MW: Was it relatively common or on the contrary exceptional to have a picture framed?

SS: It wasn't an obligation, but it didn't cost a lot.

MW: Did people get their frames painted?

SS: No. We don't know about that. We did trace the Burkina flag on paper and put that in a frame with a backing board and the photo on top, plus glass. I did things like that. But I never framed any photographs for myself. In my house I don't even have photos pinned on the wall; it doesn't matter to me.[11]

MW: Could studio customers see framed photos there?

SS: No. If what I had pinned up on the entry wall wasn't good enough, well…

MW: Were there small-time street photographers?

SS: There were, the Yashica people. People walked around with those at the time; when they saw you could earn a little, they got into the game. I didn't work like that—I had professional equipment. But I went around the villages with my music and my technicians, my car and everything.

8 Plate 1 is such a photograph. Others made by Sanlé Sory can be found in C. Angelo Micheli, "Doubles and Twins: A New Approach to Contemporary Studio Photography in West Africa," *African Arts* 41:1 (Spring 2008): 66-85. The picture referred to in the following comments appears as figure 15 on page 71 of that article.

9 A griot, typically a West African hereditary social function, is a storyteller who entertains and maintains historical memory through songs, poems, and dances.

10 Malick Sidibé, Michelle Lamunière, and Lia Brogel, "Ready to Wear: A Conversation with Malick Sidibé" *Transition*, No. 88 (2001): 141. Sidibé (Mali, 1936–2016) is regarded as one of the preeminent studio photographers of postcolonial West Africa. A near contemporary of Sory, Sidibé photographed the stylish youth and partygoers of Bamako, among other subjects.

11 A photograph showing Sory's table and guitar also includes a number of his photographs prominently pinned on the wall (p. 170).

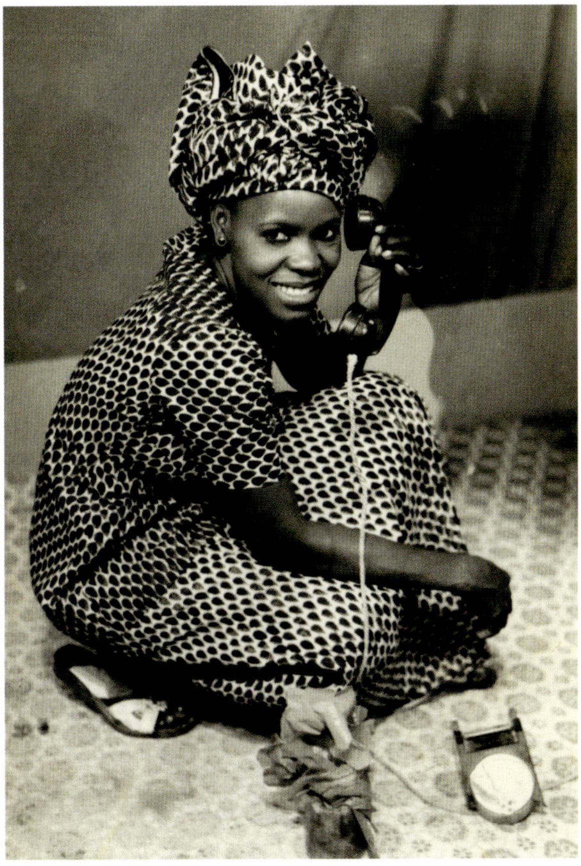

27 Untitled, 1965/75

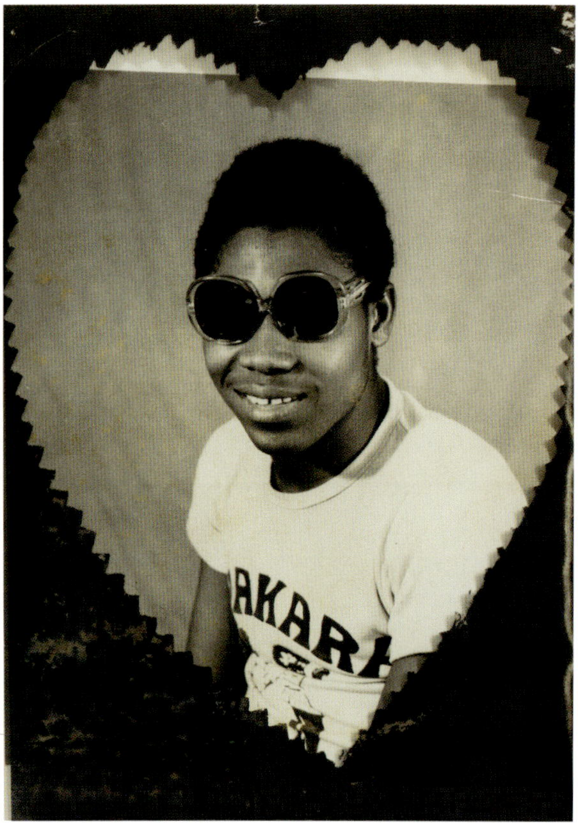

28 Yao Pelé, an apprentice who later joined the army and became a lieutenant, 1965/75

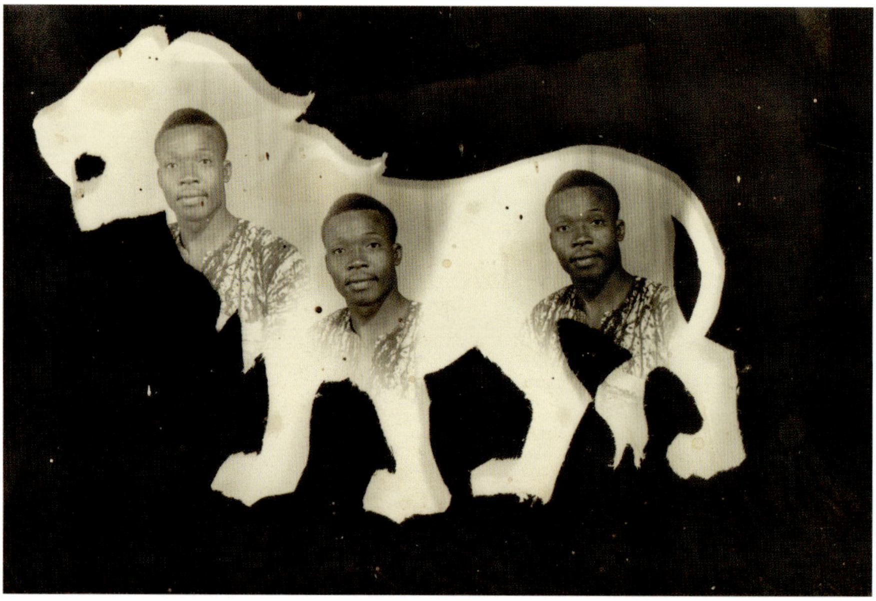

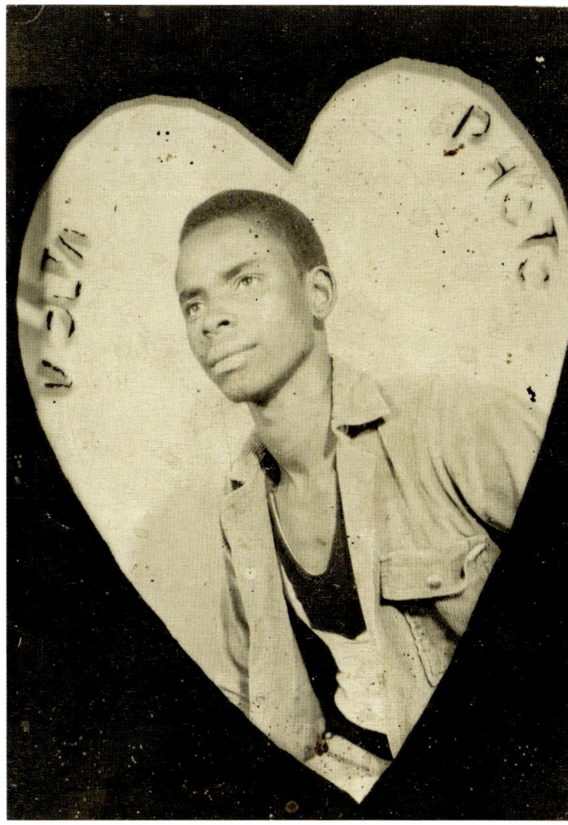

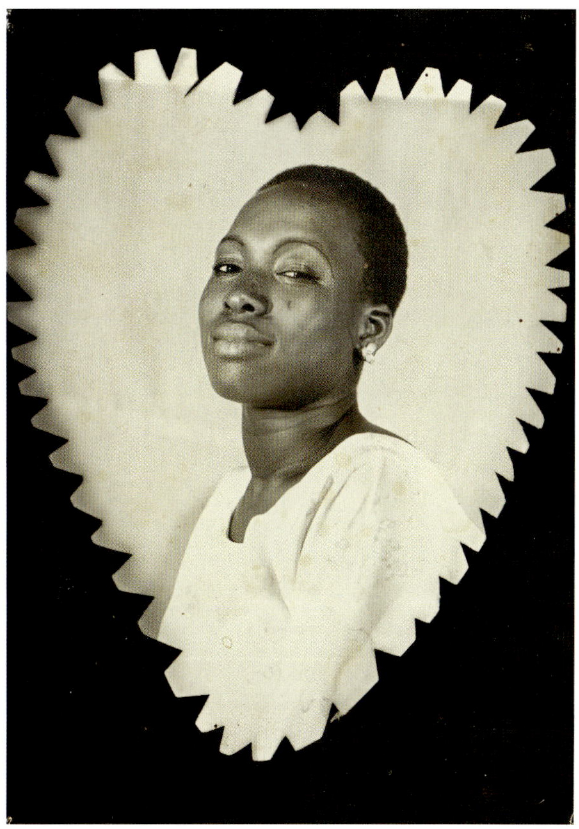

29–31 Untitled, 1965/75

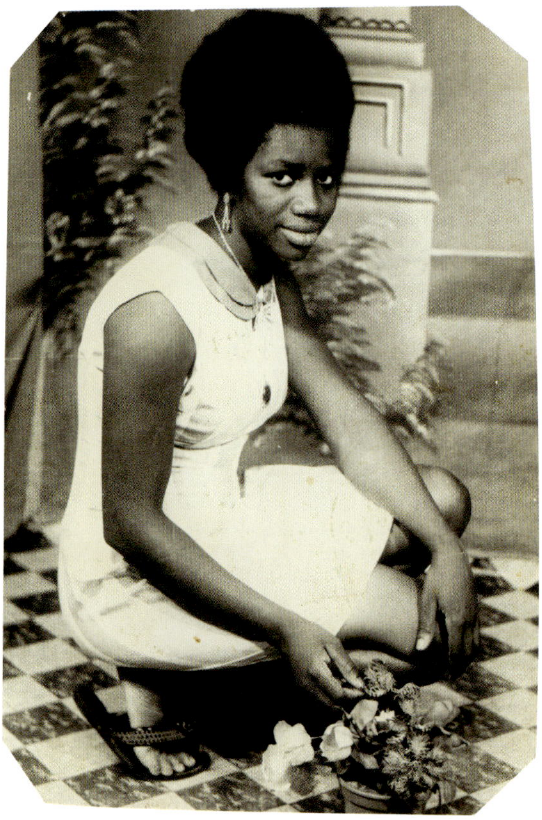

32 Untitled, 1965/75

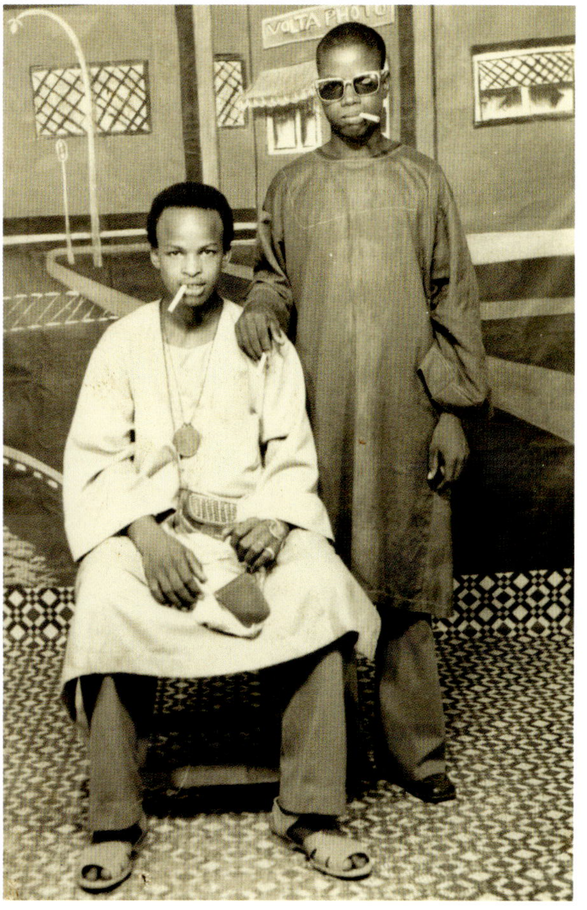

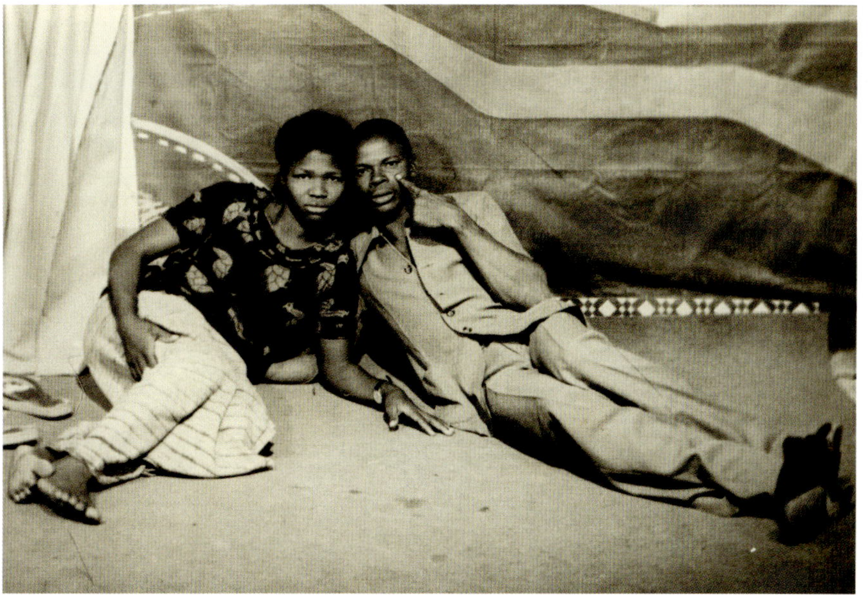

33–34 Untitled, 1965/75

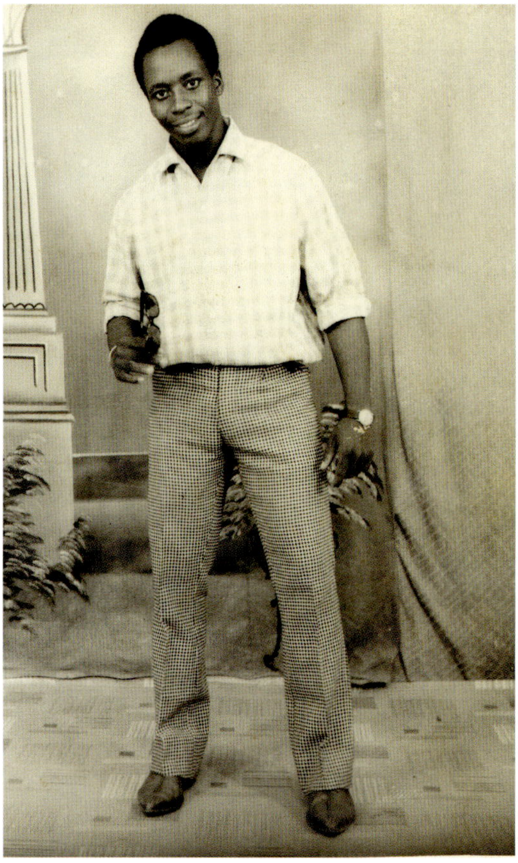

35 Self-portrait on postcard stock, addressed on reverse: "SORY X. Director of Photography. Bobo B.P. 139," 1960/65

36–39 Untitled, 1965/75

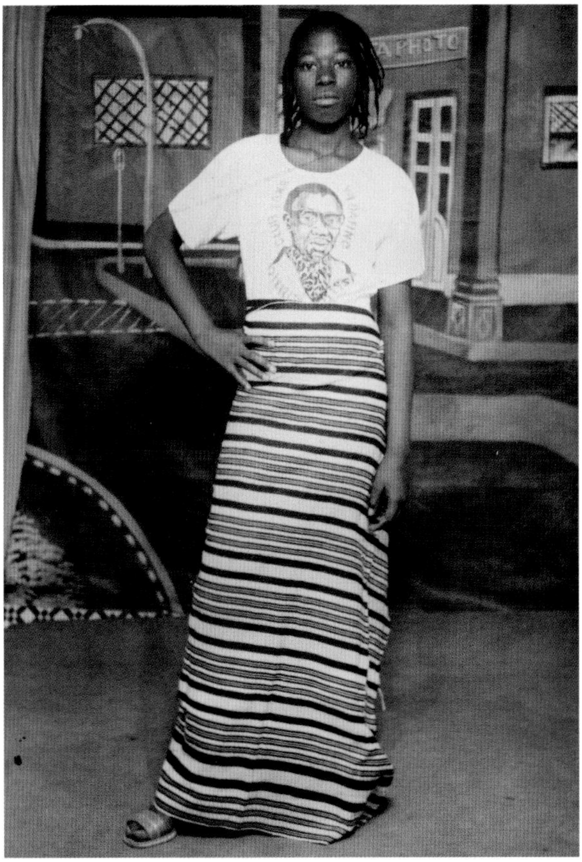
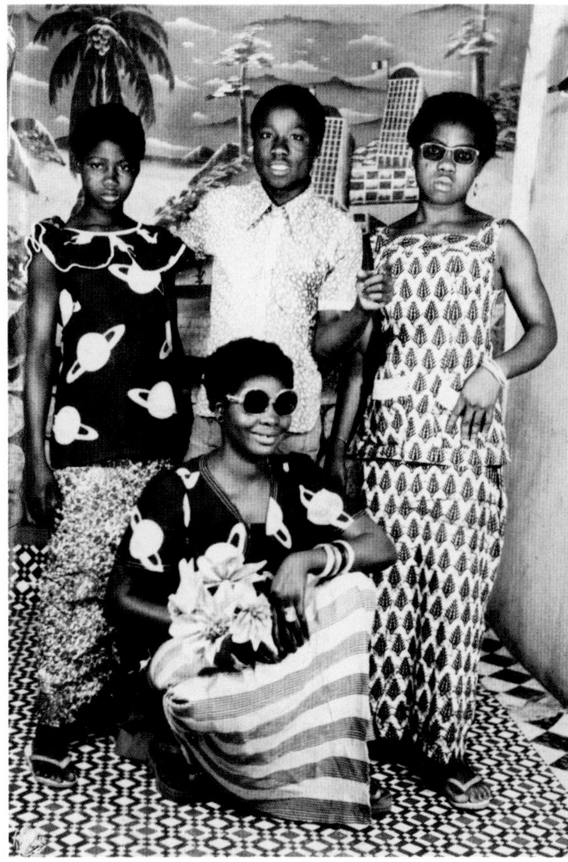
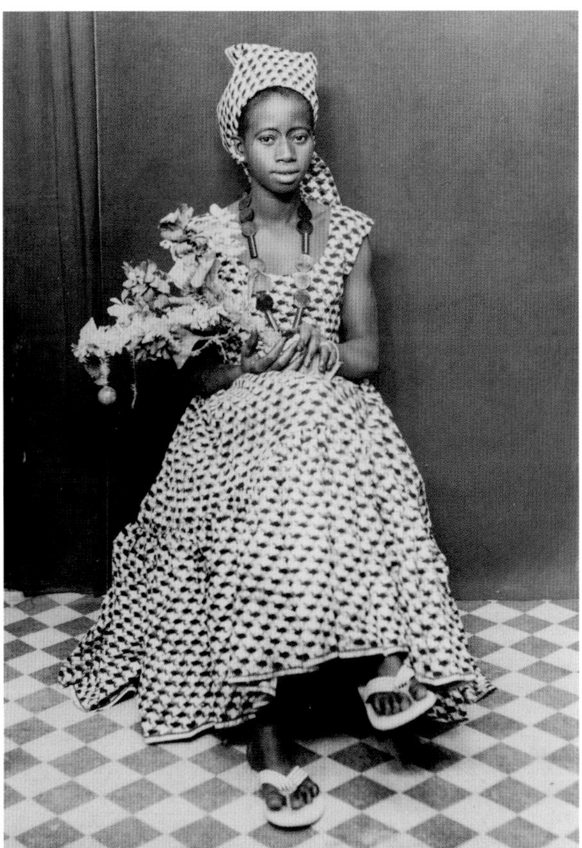
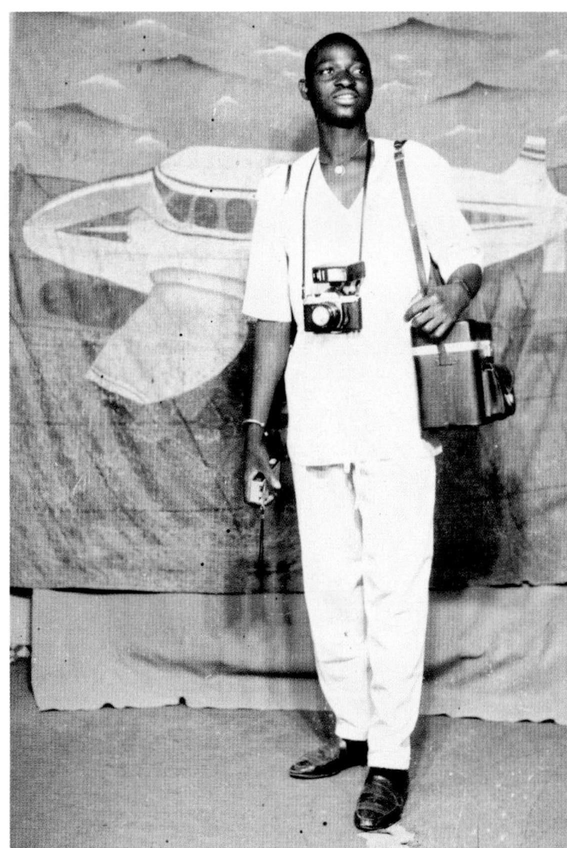

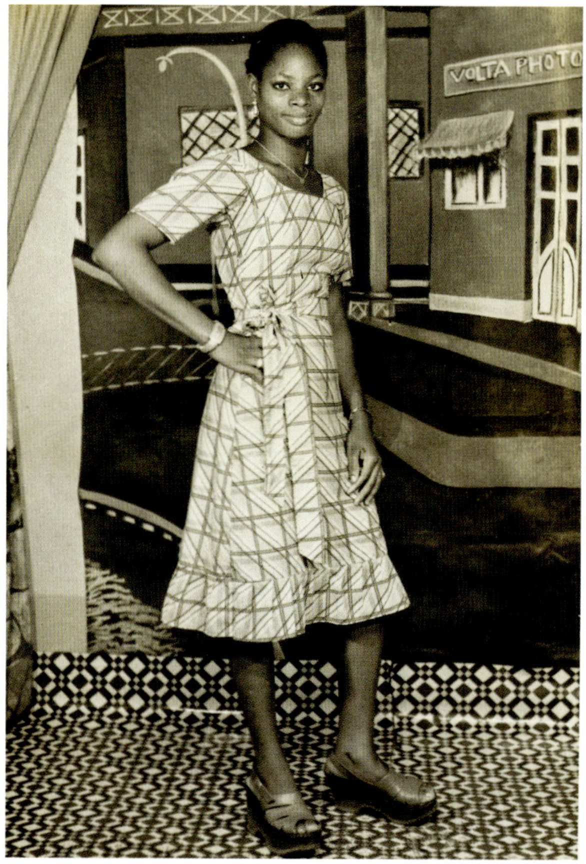
VOLTA PHOTO

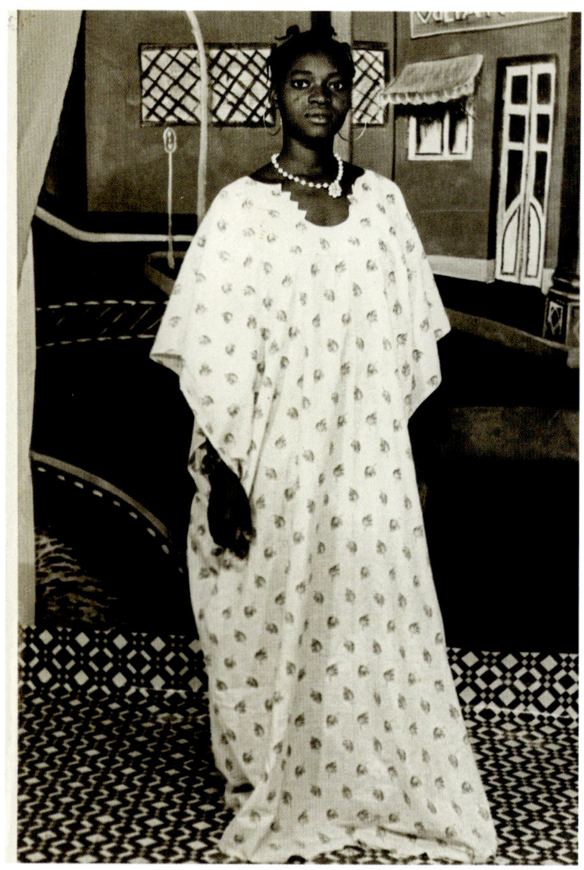

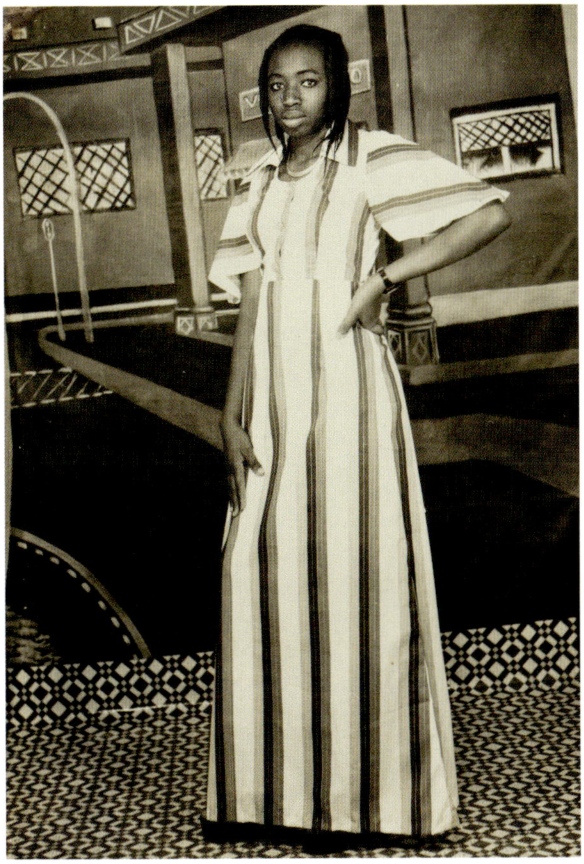

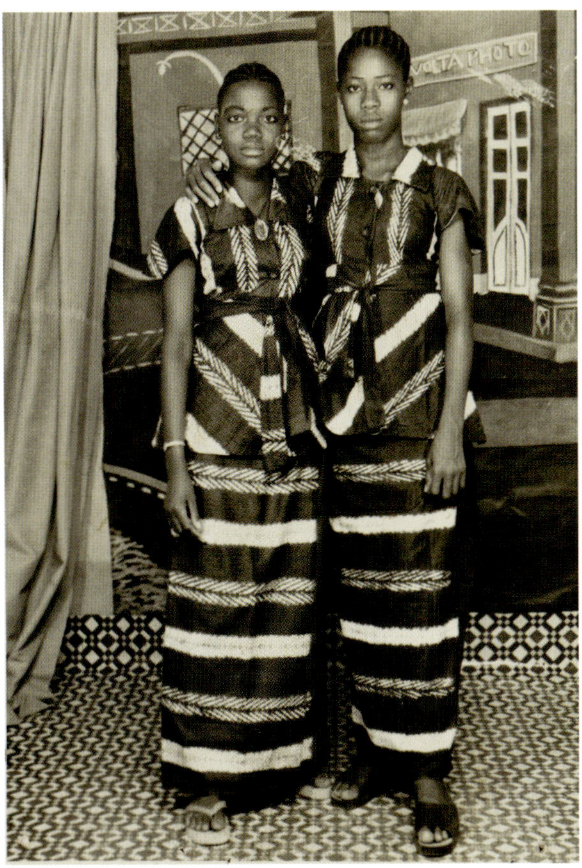

40–43 Untitled, 1965/75

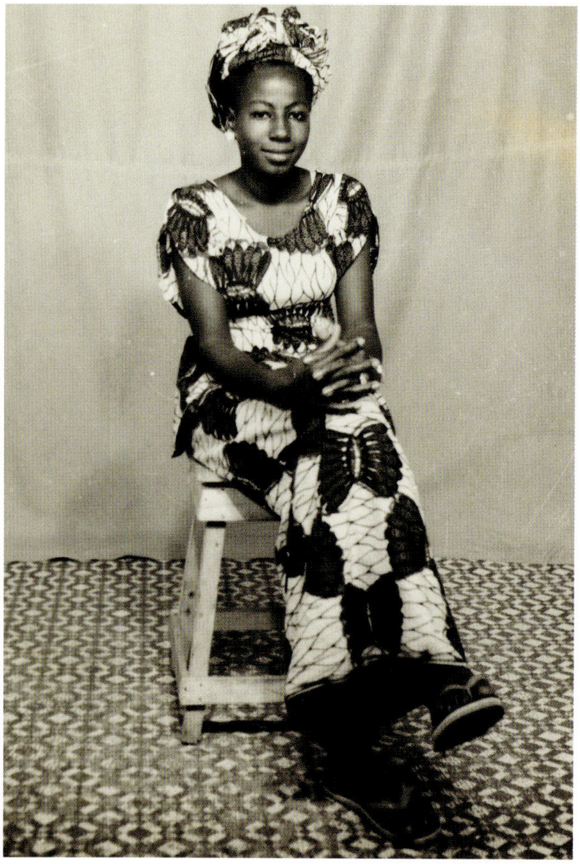

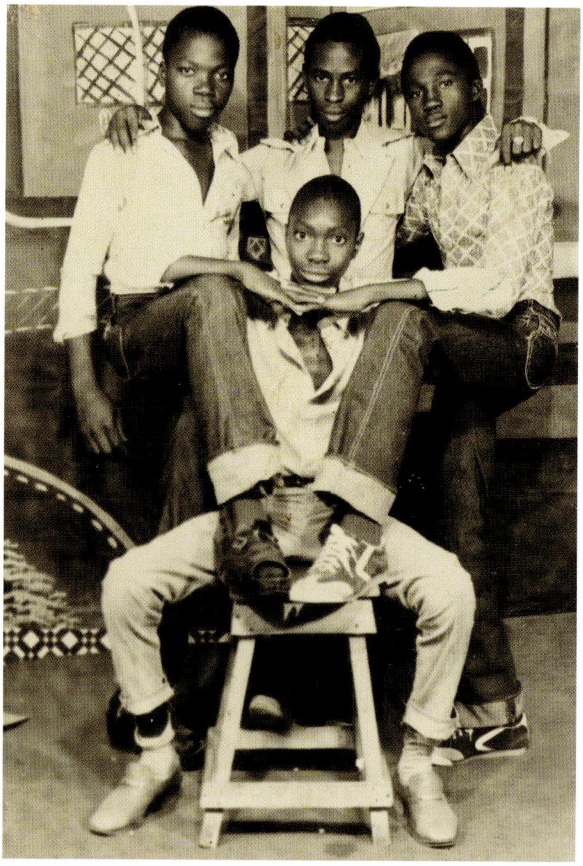

44–45 Untitled, 1965/75

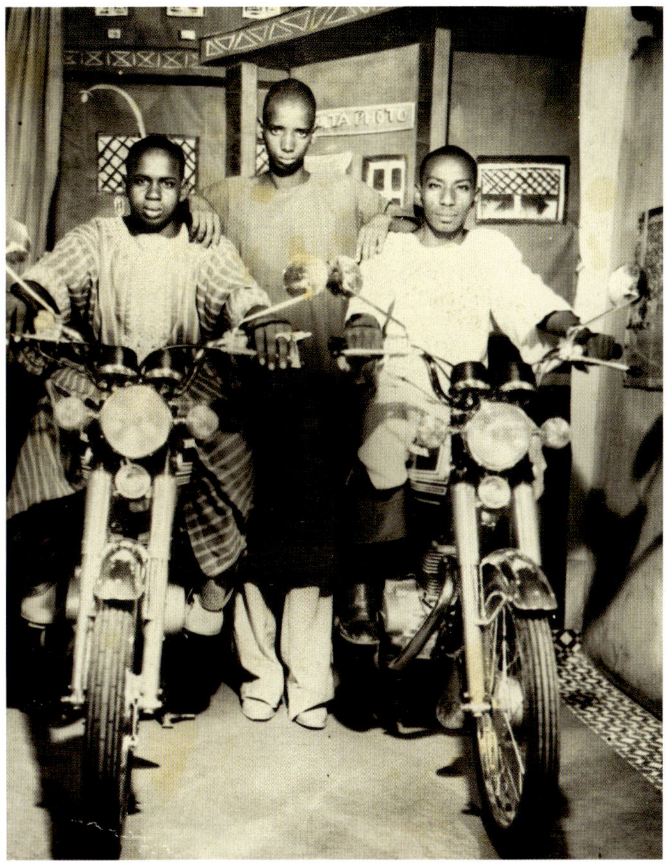

46 Untitled, 1965/75

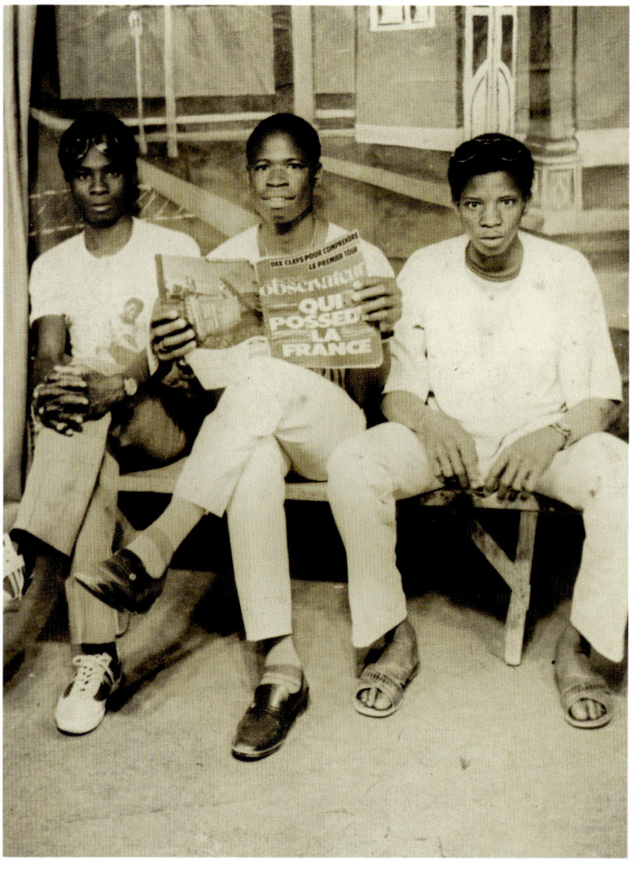

47 Untitled, c. 1983

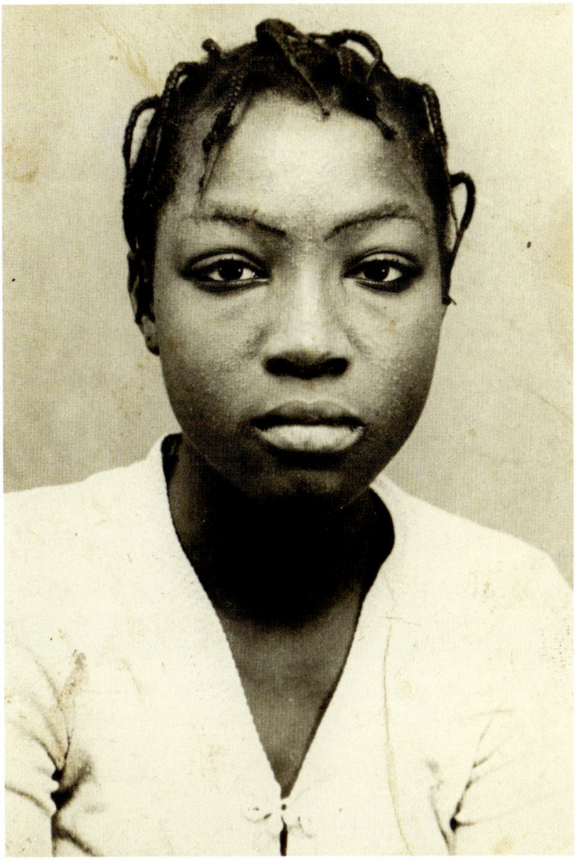

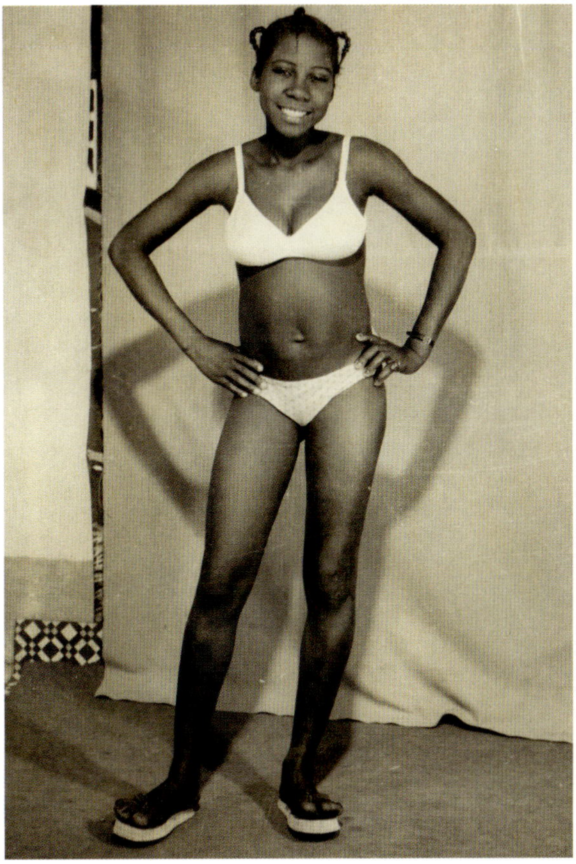

48 ID photo, 1965/75

49 Untitled, 1965/75
This photograph was taken by one of Sory's apprentices. It shows the apprentice's girlfriend, also pictured in the image above.

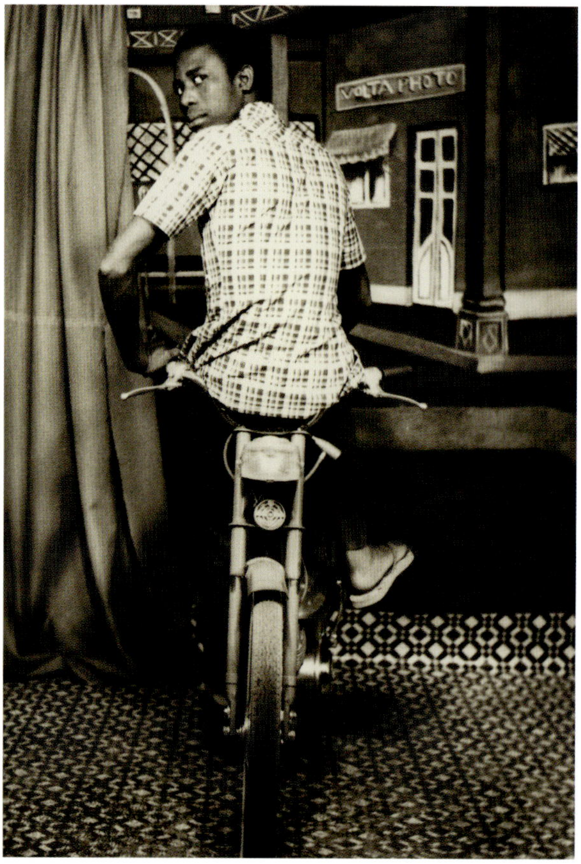

50 Untitled, 1965/75

PUBLIC LIFE AND PRIVATE PICTURES

MW: How would a customer know which backdrop to choose?

SS: The pictures that were on view. In the various tableaux [pinned up at the studio entrance] you could see pictures everywhere. And if anyone saw a tableau and said, I want this backdrop, we pulled it out right away. Then, poof, the guy stops in front of it, and there you go.

AB: Did customers also respond to the people they saw in these various photos?

SS: No, it was only the backdrop they wanted.

MW: No one said, I'd like to look as handsome as so and so?

SS: A customer would say, "My head's big and the other's is small"; so I reframe, and the two heads look the same size.

MW: Were there famous people in your pictures? Musicians, politicians?

SS: Oh no. If I took a picture of a politician, I wouldn't put it up in my studio room. People don't care, and the politicians don't need it. Also, taking photos of politicians in their cars means you have to run after them, and they don't pay you. You have to make out an invoice and send it to their administration. Anyway, people don't get that excited by pictures of other people. Today they don't even need a photographer. Everyone has their own cameras and takes their own pictures. It's everyone for himself and God for all.

MW: I get the sense you mistrust politicians.

SS: I don't like politics. I've always said so. I'm not lettered, for one; I'm caught up in politics but don't have any money, for another. What good is it? I've never worked in public service.

AB: Do you know of the RDA?[12]

SS: That's Ivory Coast, and Maurice Yaméogo.[13] I was a young man, and we were paid to march in rallies (laughs).

FM: There are pictures of Sory in shorts and shirt, marching for his country, with the crossed flags *à la française*, black, white and red, showing off the pride of Voltaic youth.

MW: What did you think of this?

SS: We were innocent and didn't know anything. We were used, that's all.

AB: What magazines were widely read at the time? *AfroMusic*, *Bingo*?

SS: I didn't know who was who in records, so I looked for music that would please customers. I liked Tabu Ley Rochereau and Guinean records: Bembeya Jazz.[14] Of our own people, well, Tidiane Coulibaly and Dafra Star.

MW: Were there any magazines you cared for in particular or set out in the studio?

SS: People brought their own magazines. I didn't put anything out for people to spend time flipping through.

FM: And what about *Salut les copains*, as posters from this magazine can be seen in some of your pictures?[15]

SS: That's in people's homes, not in my studio.

FM: Posters of James Brown, for example, were in your studio.

SS: The apprentices did that.

MW: Did you read magazines?

SS: I didn't have time.

AB: But a general culture of images in Bobo—billboards, advertisements—did that register?

SS: There weren't so many. Today you see billboards and this, that, and the other, especially at the entrance to town. None of that before. Those things cost money! Except for big companies, people won't pay for that.

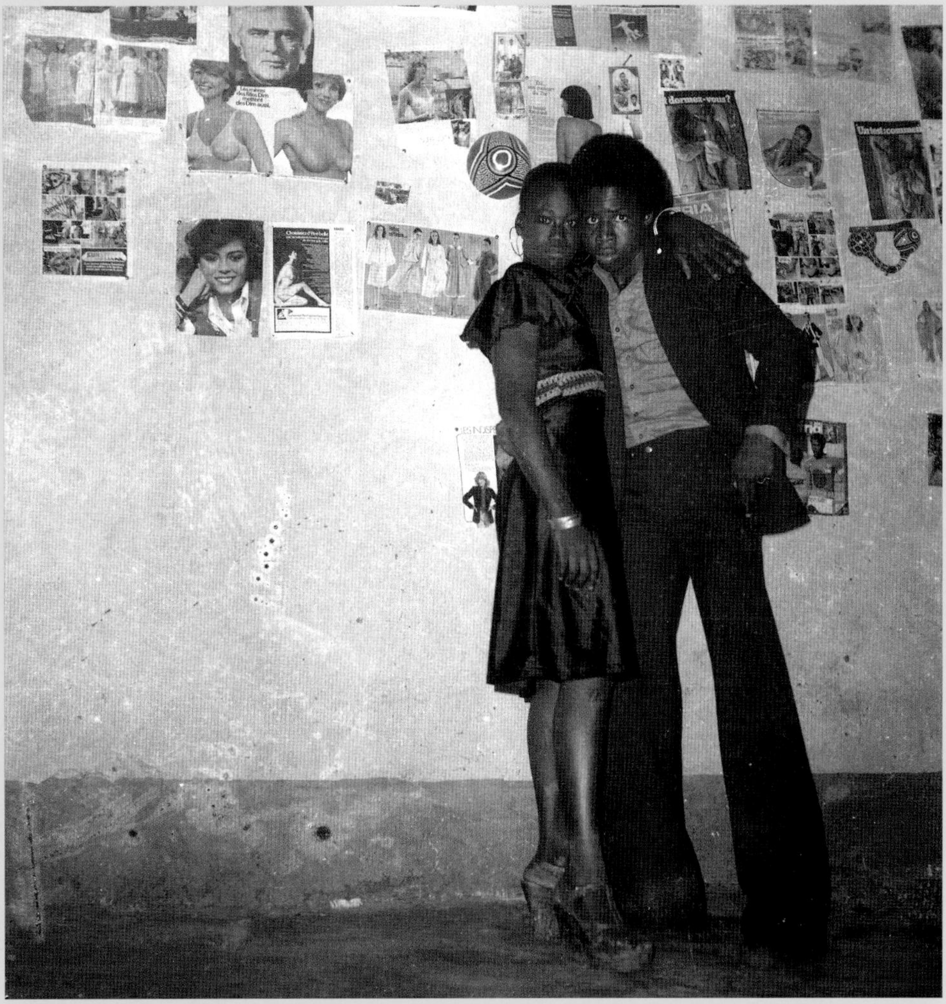

fig. 1 Untitled, 1965/75. Illustration from 6 × 6 cm negative. Courtesy Florent Mazzoleni

FM: Stores didn't ask you from time to time to make photographs for them? I've seen in your pictures some photos of home appliance places, or Peyrissac, the local hardware store that Volta Jazz also celebrated in a song. You made photos for them; in one there are lots of motor scooters in front, and the store name is visible.

SS: That's not an ad picture. The person called me because he worked there. You can stand in front of a car that doesn't belong to you and have someone take your photograph.

MW: When you photographed the partygoers, did they worry about being rendered so visible?

SS: Most of them liked photos then. Some would tell me to take their picture only in one spot and not to follow them

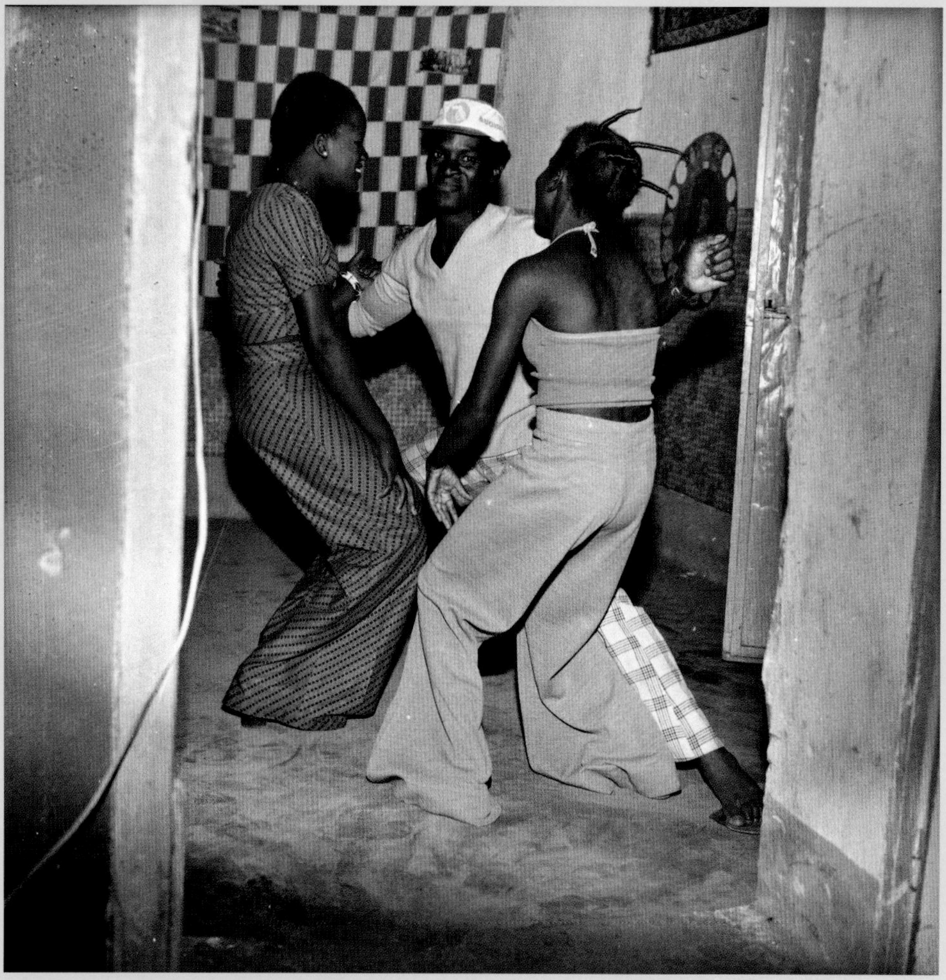

fig. 2 Untitled, 1965/75, printed 2017. 36 × 36 cm (image); 50 × 40 cm (sheet). The Art Institute of Chicago, gift of the artist and Florent Mazzoleni, 242555

around; they didn't want everyone looking. I'm the photographer though; they can't hide from me (laughs). I'm the witness. If they hide, I'm there; indoors or out, I'm there. I can do lots of things. People who have lost their parents ask me to take a picture of the corpse. At the burial, at the grave, I take the picture. I've done that. But [in those cases] the family keeps the negative—it's private.

This one is in the bush (p. 17). A little village called Dandé. That's where I was given the hunter's portrait to recopy, the same day as I made this picture. I was going to emcee a party, and since night had not yet fallen, I was driving around looking for customers.

MW: How did you go about that?

SS: I'd park, [and] the kids would come and tell everyone the photographer had arrived. That's how I managed to enter this young lady's home. She didn't want to be seen in public. It embarrassed her to be exposed like that. She said she'd rather pose indoors.

MW: Did other members of her family come to have their picture taken?

SS: She was the only one. But as I walked around, other villagers asked for ID pictures. We carried the one-color cloth in a bag. That worked well, and it still does today.

MW: So this is an ID photo?

SS: No, it's a souvenir photo.

MW: She wouldn't get her print right away, unlike today.

SS: I asked people to come the next evening to my studio to pick up their prints.

MW: Even the young lady?

SS: In that case, I'm the one who went back, it's sixty kilometers [37.5 miles] from Bobo. I returned the following week. As I said, I went out often to the bush to make parties. Usually I went on market days. Otherwise folks would be in the fields—you couldn't find them. On market day people brought their goods. I also had things to sell! Anyone who wanted an ID picture came to see me. Or someone would say, "My old man can't move," so we would go see him, and I'd take the picture in the man's home, in the courtyard. For example, someone whose bell is about to ring—that means he's going to die—and the family wants a picture.
I photographed an old man that way one time. They invited me in, I entered, and the setup was kind of strange. I had to enter through the roof. I was a little scared, but they said to come in, so I did. Everything was white; his skin was like a mask. They asked me to arrange the pose. "Oh?" I said. But I worked things out anyway. There was a kid on the roof, to open it. There was a *canari* [a jug to collect water] over the hole. I've seen some funny things, right? Well. I took the picture, went back out, and when I was back on my bike I was relieved.

FM: How did you show pictures to your customers when you went to see them? Did you keep them in a box?

SS: Yes, we used the box for the papers and put it in a bag to carry pictures to the villages. You could simply go see the village chief and leave finished prints with him. Everything was prepaid. If a picture didn't come out, we retook the shot.

I didn't take that picture; I just made the copy (plate 52). He had died a long time before. His children came to ask me to reprint this picture. I don't know where the man had it taken originally.

FM: Probably a Wassoulou hunter from southern Mali?

SS: I don't know. Put what you like.

FM: No, we're not just going to put whatever we think!

SS: Sure sure, I gave you the green light. Everyone takes the position they want.

12 The RDA, or Rassemblement Démocratique Africain (African Democratic Assembly or African Democratic Rally) was a party of Francophone African unity and leftwing resistance to French rule. It lasted from 1946 until 1958, building a platform for socialist, pan-Africanist political views. Splintering thereafter into national parties, the RDA and its successor movements played a significant role in the transition from colonial to autonomous government in West and Central Africa.

13 Maurice Yaméogo (1921–1993) was the first president of an independent Upper Volta (declared on August 5, 1960) and interim prime minister since 1958. Yaméogo worked to create a union with Ivory Coast, extending dual nationality to citizens of both countries. He was also a dictator who eliminated political opposition even before independence. Yaméogo was peacefully overthrown in 1966, ushering in a period of relative prosperity.

14 Tabu Ley (or Tabuley) Rochereau (1940–2013), born Pascal Tabu Ley, was an internationally renowned Congolese singer who came to prominence in the 1950s and 1960s, when he joined or founded a number of bands that operated, like Volta Jazz, as syntheses of Afrocentrism and international modernism: African Jazz, African Fiesta Flash, and others. Bembeya Jazz, an Afropop formation created in 1961, was the most visible of several bands brought into being by order of the first President of Guinea, Ahmed Sékou Touré (see also note 18).

15 "Salut les copains," a popular music program on the French radio channel Europe 1, generated an offshoot publication of the same title, launched in 1962 and soon available in several languages. An anniversary concert the following year led cultural critic Edgar Morin to coin the phrase "the yé-yé generation."

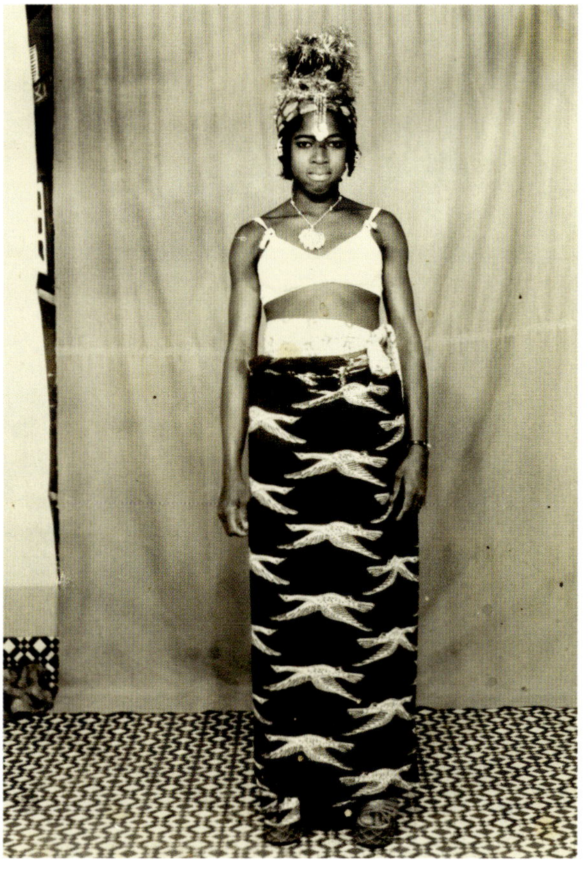

51 Bobo woman in a ceremonial headdress, 1965/75.

52 Photographer unknown
Hunter, perhaps from the Wassoulou region
Reprinted by Ibrahima Sanlé Sory, 1970/80

Sory was asked to rephotograph and print this picture by the man's children in the village of Dandé.

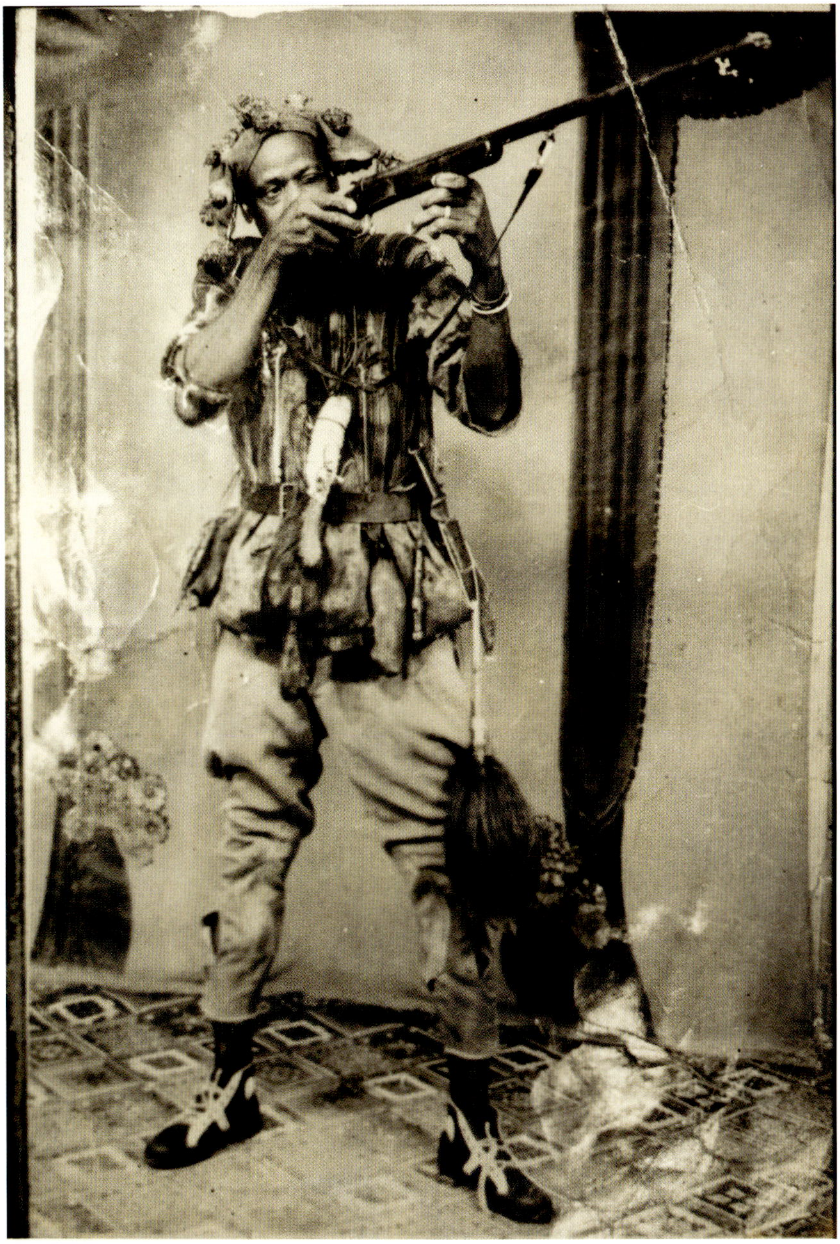

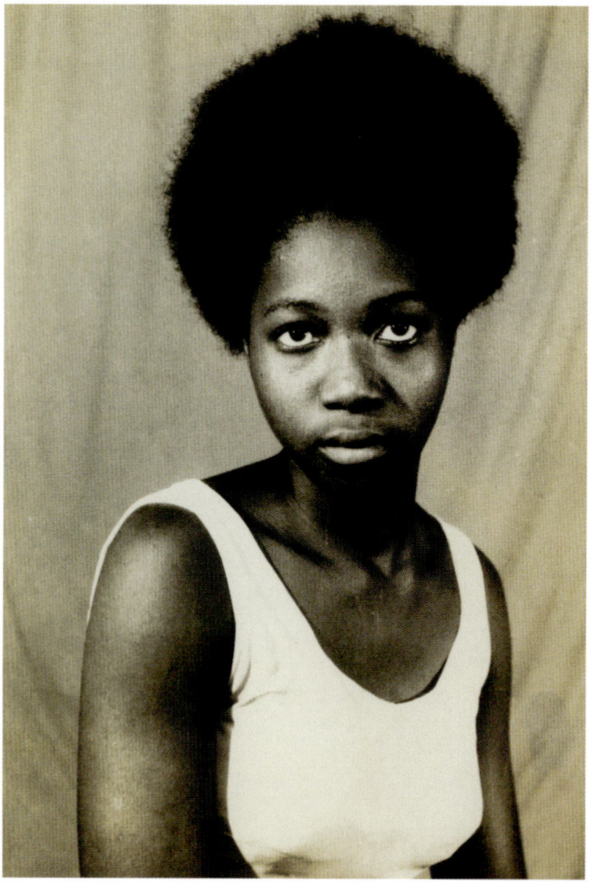

53 Untitled, 1965/75

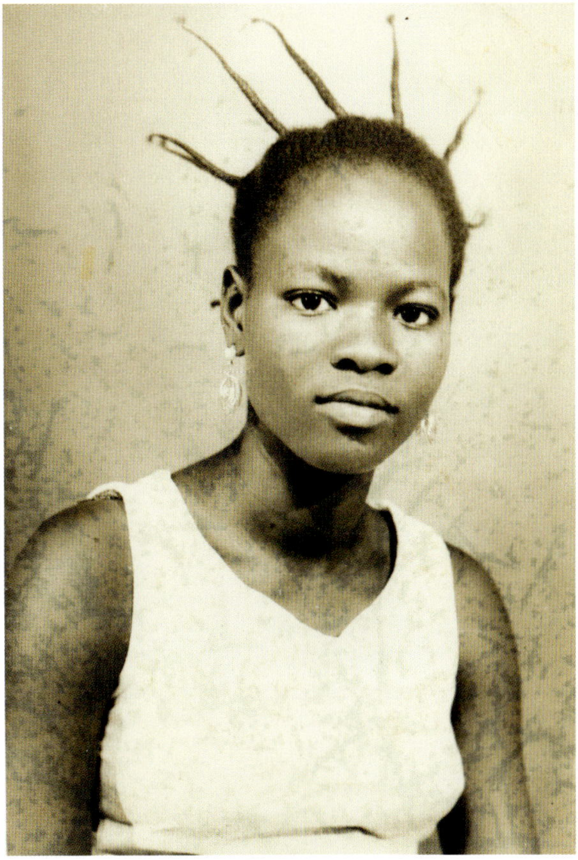

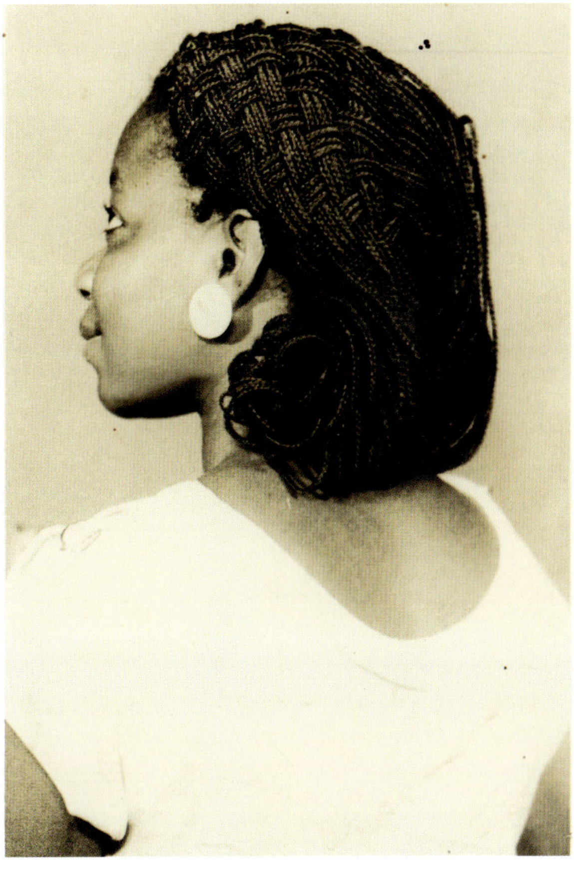

54 Untitled, 1965/75

55 Untitled, c. 1980

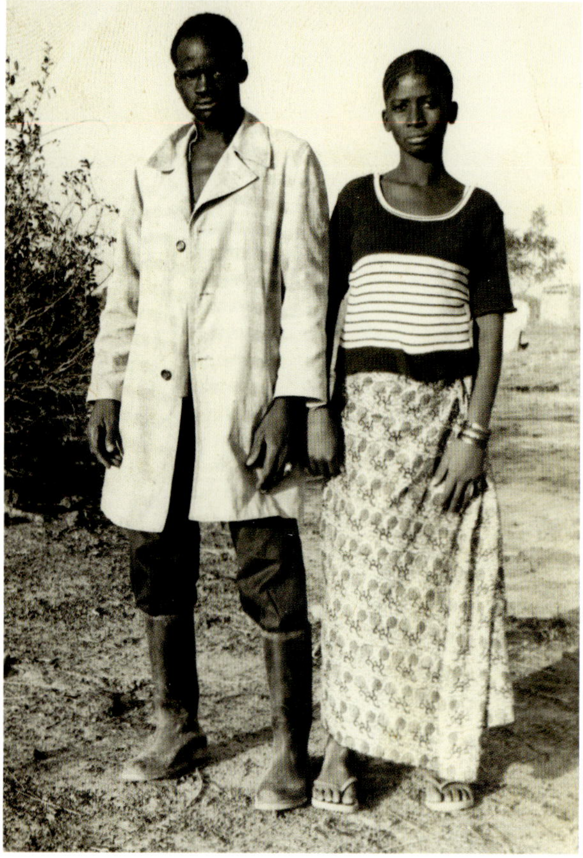

56 Untitled, 1965/75

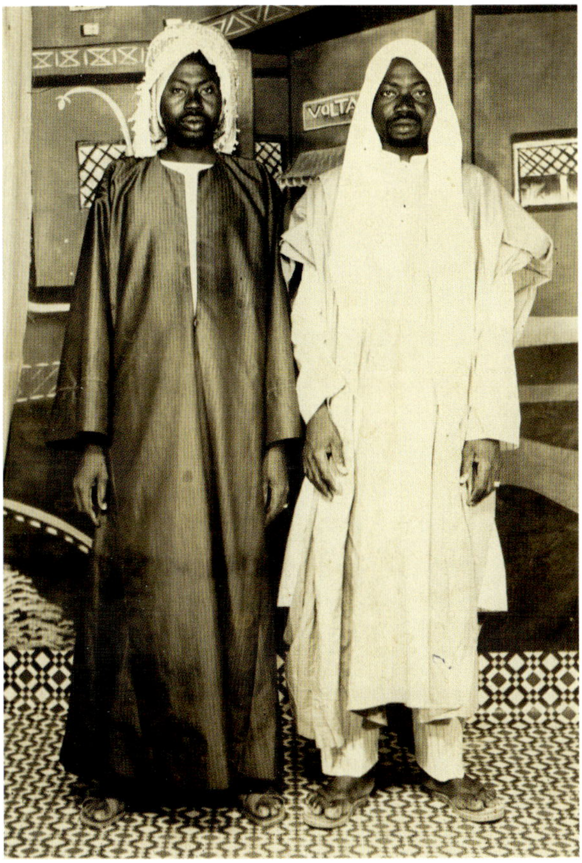

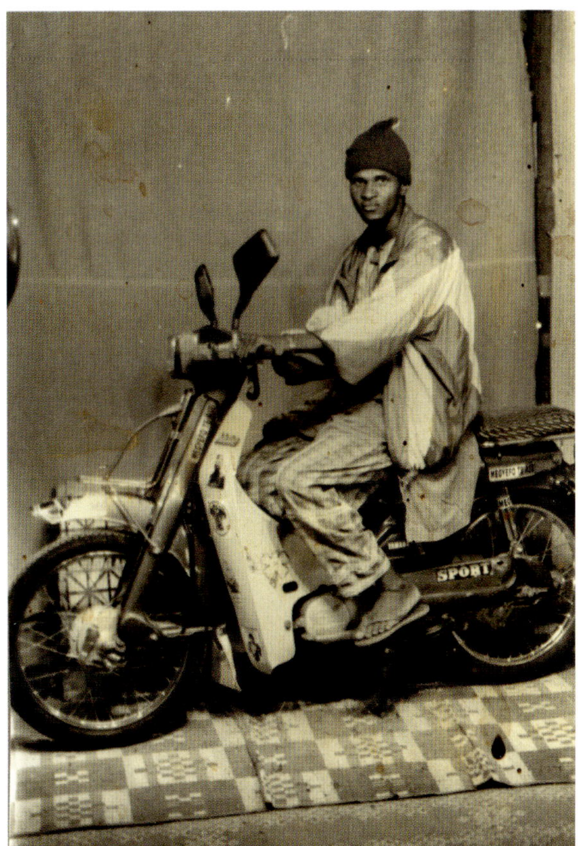

57–58 Untitled, 1965/75

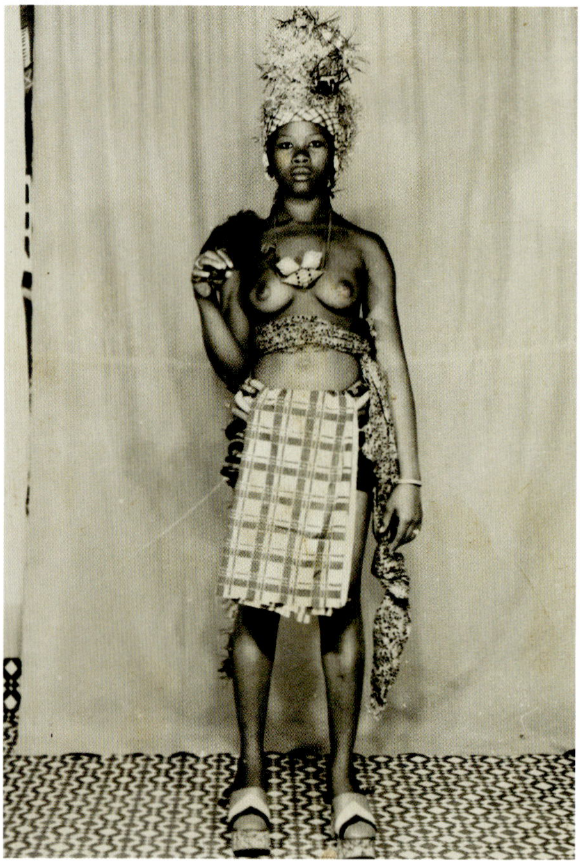

59 Untitled, 1965/75

As in the image on p. 57, the dress and exposed upper body here are associated with the Dioula ceremonies kurubi *and* jomɛnɛ.

MW: When did you start your village tours?

SS: I worked with my music box for a long time, beginning with Diaradougou.

FM: I can date certain Volta Jazz record covers with Sanlé Sory photographs to 1967.

MW: Putting together a music evening, though, is different than photographing a music band.

SS: The two things are totally separate. Party pictures are my *reportage de nuit* (nighttime journalism). People would invite me. They would come to the studio and say, "Sory, we're dancing tonight. We're going to celebrate, there's food, we're getting a sheep, some chicken—"

FM: He received invitation letters sometimes—

SS: They had their own music setup, and I only took the photographs. When I made dances it was with cassettes. You can't play records in the bush because of the dust. We recorded on tape the songs we wanted, put them in a tape player, with speakers, and made a party. People danced until the dust rose high like that (laughs).

FM: They had an expression for open-air dancing: *bal poussière* (Dust Ball).

SS: Yep, you water the ground a bit and start dancing. Until dawn. And I would use this activity to make my photographs.

AB: After you took photos at the village parties, did you return to sell them?

SS: At that time, people who wanted photos paid up front. They even paid ahead for the film. They would say, "I want at least two rolls" (meaning twenty-four shots). Then they'd ask you to check that they were well posed, looking good with a lady at their side, you didn't even need to talk to them. You had [the requests] in mind, and you calculated how many pictures to take. So when you saw them dancing, you went click-click. All prepaid.

MW: Tell us how you would set up a dance party.

SS: Suppose it's Ramadan tomorrow. I'm going to emcee your party. Clear a spot for my equipment. Tickets are this much, let's say 100 francs. I arrive and set up. I put one of my three technicians at the door to collect money. Another takes care of the music, and the third handles the generator. Using this to make photos, that's what it was about. For me it was a way to get the young people together.

FM: To have them contained in one place.

MW: Was it all recorded music? Did you ever bring musicians?

SS: It was all tapes.

FM: When you photographed musicians it was in town.

SS: Right. But I could be in town tonight, and tomorrow I'm called to the bush to emcee. I was driving everywhere. Saturdays and Sundays I was in the bush. Sometimes I stayed in town on the weekend if it was lively. But things were better for me in the bush than in town. In town I wasn't the only one. But it was just me in the bush. I was the only photographer doing that.

MW: So people partied, you snapped pictures, and then you came back—

SS: —especially on market days when people showed up. On other days everyone was off in the fields.

MW: Did you pay the people who found you party spots?

SS: They paid me. These were pub owners. I brought them business. When people dance they have to eat and drink.

MW: Were the technicians different from the apprentices?

SS: The apprentices didn't go the villages with me.

AB: Tell us about the sound and light installation.

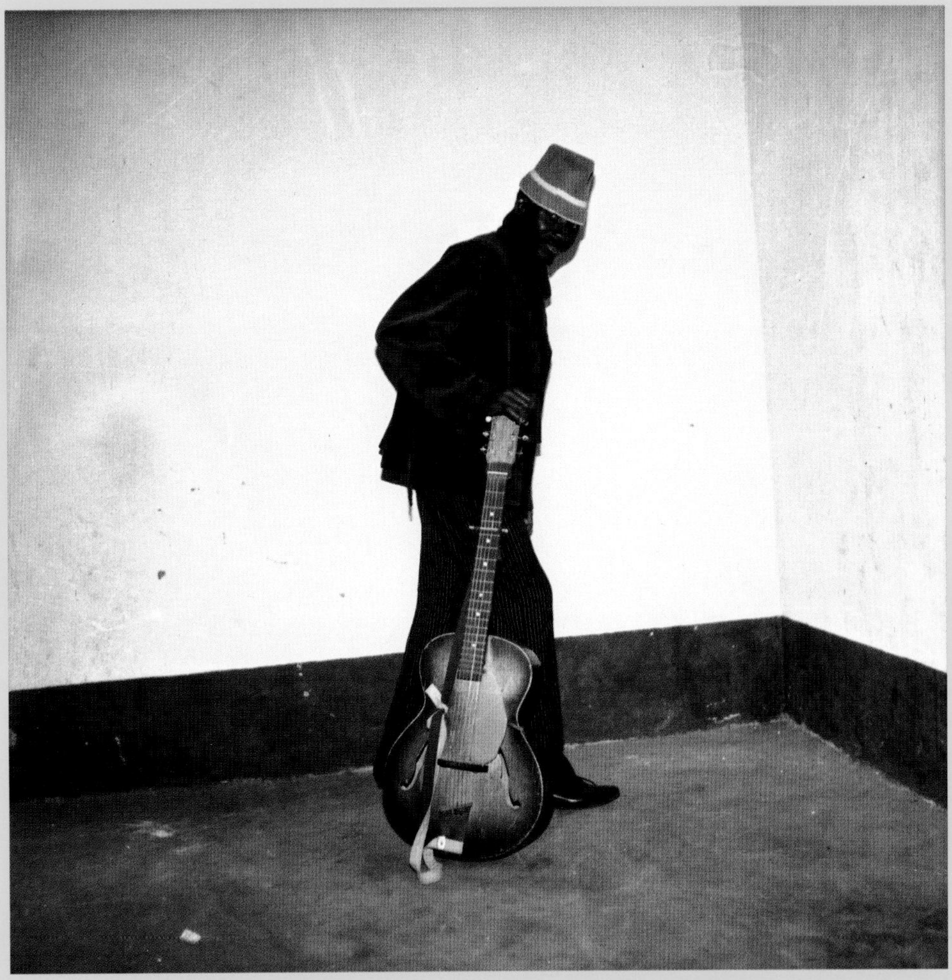

fig. 1 Untitled, 1965/75, printed 2017. 36 × 36 cm (image); 50 × 40 cm (sheet). The Art Institute of Chicago, gift of the artist and Florent Mazzoleni, 242565

SS: I had two speakers with loudspeakers. We called them funnels. I had my amp and tape deck. And then I came and talked. I'm a big talker (laughs)! The technician is there, but he can't do my talking for me.

MW: So talk to us.

SS: "Anyway do your best to show up, lots of you, I came from Bobo to emcee, so you have to do your best to keep me happy. It's a beautiful night. I'm here to keep you dancing 'til dawn. I take pictures too, hey ladies, that's what you need (laughs)." That's what I said. And then I talked about the barman—"He's here to serve you." I talked him up. He was supposed to give me some money, too.

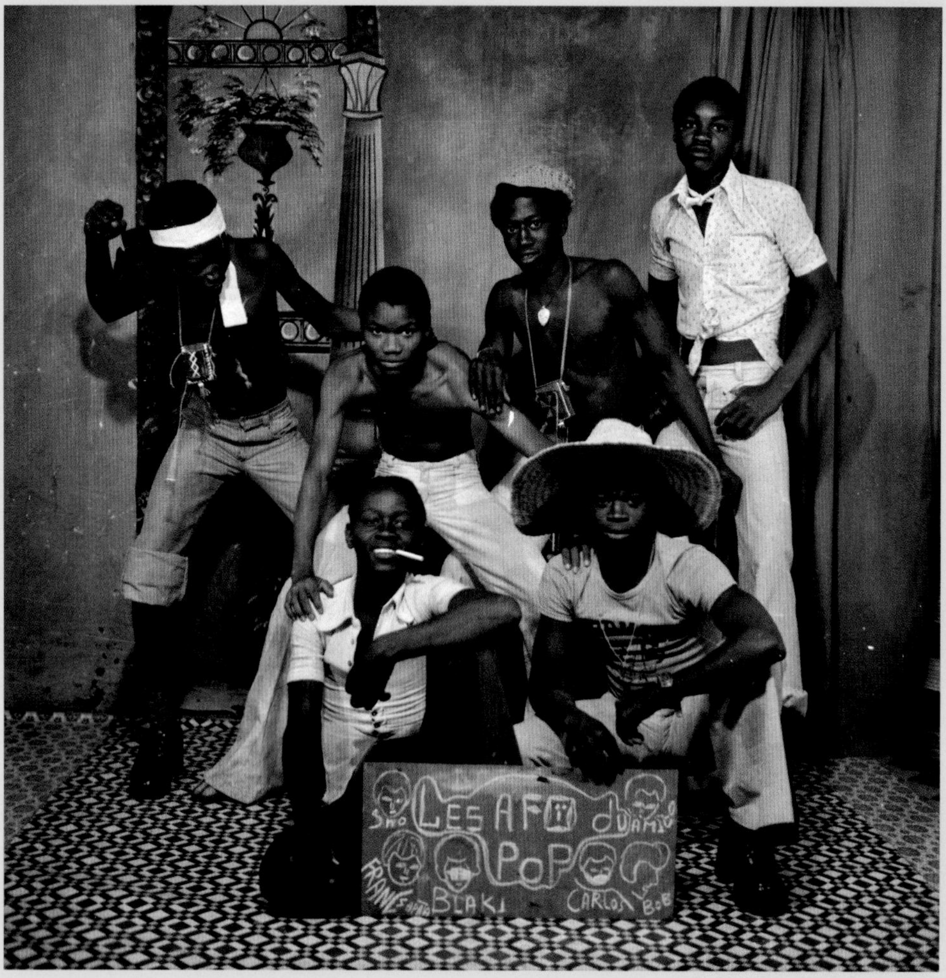

fig. 2 Les Afro-Pop, 1965/75, printed 2017. 36 × 36 cm (image); 50 × 40 cm (sheet). The Art Institute of Chicago, gift of the artist and Florent Mazzoleni, 242560

So we would stay until six or seven a.m. From eight p.m. until seven in the morning. If I said I'd stay just until three a.m., they'd say "No!" If I said my generator was low on gas, they'd go find me gas to keep the dancing going. If you go to the bush today, I'm better known there than in town.

AB: How did you pick places?

SS: Where there was a lot of growing, especially in the Kou Valley: rice, bananas, especially cotton at selling time. If cotton is selling—ooh!—farmers have money, and they're coming to see me. All I need is a bit of land, and I'll do my setup. But I'd say, "I can't stay over, I've got family in Bobo" (laughs). They would want me to emcee every night!

When they had money, they didn't know what to do, so they drank.

MW: What years were these?

SS: Around 1971, 1972, through the eighties and nineties. I kept it going. That's why I remember a lot more about the bush [than the studio].

MW: Sounds like in the end you weren't so often at the studio.

SS: No, I was. But not in the evenings, when I went to dance halls to chase customers. I'd quit the studio at eight, leave it to the apprentices, and comb all of Bobo.
I got around by scooter, looking for music and customers. Sometimes people would invite me to surprise parties. If those weren't on, I went to the dance halls. I could handle anything, and I got in everywhere, no problem.

MW: What kinds of music did you play in the villages, since these were your parties?

SS: Every kind of thing!

MW: And where did you find all these kinds of music?

SS: There were record sellers who made tapes for us, like Drabo, who is today the only record seller left in Bobo.

MW: How many tapes did you have at the time?

SS: Hundreds. I had lots of things: Ernesto Djedjé [Ivory Coast], Rail Band [Mali], Bembeya Jazz [Guinea], Youssou N'Dour from Senegal, Moré music from Burkina.

FM: You had Congolese too, Cuban, and [Nigerian] High Life…

SS: Oh yes. And reggae. All kinds of music. Because when the customer asks for it, I need to do everything I can to put it on.

MW: Was there any European music?

SS: Where I'm from they don't like tunes that don't heat you up. They like it hot. Then they sweat. They're cold, so they dance and take their shirt off (laughs). They dance, and they're saying "You're killing me I'm so hot!" It's too much. They dance and dance without stopping. Back then the old village ladies would make crepes. People bought those, ate them, and started in again.

FM: You had quite a little business: barman, cook, technicians, yourself—

MW: Did you like to dance?

SS: I'd raise my hands to encourage them (laughs). I heated people up. If you're caught napping, you pay a fine! You're not here to sleep. And at the end you buy a drink to get back in shape. Drinks weren't given away—you had to buy them.

FM: What he's saying is important; it was a way of showing one's social status. There were people who earned well in the countryside, growing rice and cotton. They never bought drinks for the others; they would pour the drinks on the ground, to tamp down the dust but also to show their status. If the others want to drink and have fun they need to work.

SS: Right, that's what I'm saying. I would ask them, Why aren't you buying the drinks and they would tell me, If you give away drinks people stop working. So everyone pays for himself. It's the same with the photographs: they aren't expensive, but if you don't have money—if you bought a ticket to the dance but you're not buying drinks, no way you'll be getting a photo. To go to these parties at the time, you needed at least 500 or 1000 francs.[16]

FM: Sory, I never saw tapes at your place either.

SS: When I stopped, because my wife fell ill in the mid-1990s, we chucked the whole setup: the speakers, everything. My little brothers came from the bush, and I shared out all the tapes. Everything went to the villages.

FM: Did you put Malian songs on one tape, Congolese on another?

SS: It was mixed. No separate tapes country by country. And you start a tape as soon as the last one is done.

MW: Who made the compilations?

SS: When you went to the [record] store, for instance to Drabo, you would ask for this or that theme, and he made the mix.

FM: How many record stores were there in Bobo?

SS: A lot: Carrefour du Disque, Intermusique, Music Hall, Etablissements Antoine D'Albin (from Benin), Black Soul Music, and Amadou Diallo's Voix de l'Afrique.

FM: I think they sold records at the Normandie, too. I've counted around ten record stores in all.

MW: Did you have a way to keep the music going at the parties?

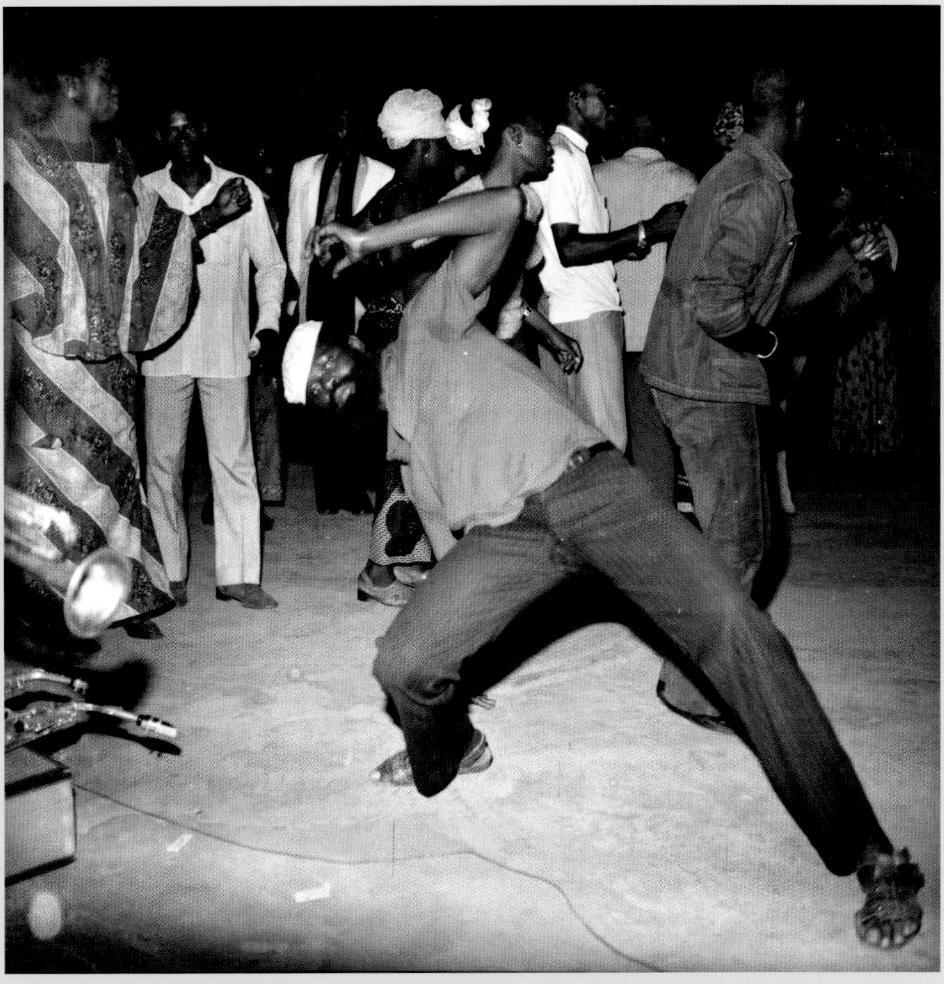

fig. 3 Yacouba Zéro, 1965/75, printed 2017. 36 × 36 cm (image); 50 × 40 cm (sheet). The Art Institute of Chicago, gift of the artist and Florent Mazzoleni, 242558

SS: You have to have two tape decks. One is running, and you line up the tape in the other one. But it's the funnels that bring people. When the funnel's going, even fifteen km [nearly ten miles] away, man, you heard the music and came.

MW: Is this image (fig. 3) taken in town or in the villages?

SS: That photo is from a dance hall—Dafra Bar, I think.

FM: There were several dance halls and clubs: The Calebasse d'Or (Golden Calabash), Volta Dancing, Normandie, Dafra Bar, Bois d'Ebène (Ebony), the Lion d'Or, and Chez Samy.

SS: There were lots of bars, and the musicians made the rounds. You could invite them, too, they'd get the neighborhood youth dancing and then move on. Volta Jazz, Echo del Africa, Dafra Star, Les [Imbattables] Léopards... They went all over town to get young people dancing. And I went along to make pictures. I made my own reputation among the musicians. They rented my generator, we fed them, and people danced until dawn.

MW: To go back to the "bush parties" for a second: your role at the parties makes me think of American big band jazz, where the drummer is the bandleader; he sits up high, like a chief, surrounded by his drums. It seems to me that at the parties, you were the drummer. The role of deejay, so important today, belongs in your parties to a humble technician, whereas people flocked to see the photographer, like the drummer long before.

SS: Yes, because people came, and if the room was full, when people were at the door I went "peep" with the flash; that lit them up, and they said, "Hooray, the photographer is there, it's gonna be good." You have to set off the flash.

MW: Exactly: the party grooves to the rhythm of the flash.

SS: It's the flash that tells you the party's started. I had that idea. [Instead of] speaking into the microphone, I went "peep peep peep" at the door.

MW: At the parties, did you tend to take a lot of pictures in quick succession, or did you spend time choosing each shot?

SS: For the portraits, if the spot is well lighted you don't need to waste time. You hold your camera at a good distance and when you see the guy—it's all about framing. Photography is framing. And sensibility. If the guy is in the middle, you click. You're not going to spend all night focusing—too many people. So you set the camera on three meters [ten feet]. Framing is what matters. If the flash goes off, it'll be good.

MW: Yes, your flash is your percussion, it sets the party beat.

SS: That's my Citroën Deux Chevaux truck, with my wooden sign (plate 93). I stacked in there my funnels, the amp, two tape decks, at least two cameras—Yashica-Mat and Rolleiflex—and my Multiblitz flash. When you saw the truck arrive, you knew Sory was there.

MW: A handheld flash, then.

SS: Yes. With a fully charged battery you could shoot up to two hundred pictures with it. It helped draw customers. The room is full, but everyone's sitting down, so you enter and go "peep peep peep"—not even taking pictures—and people say, "The photographer's here." Free of charge! It's a kind of advertising.

AB: Did the bands pay you to come take pictures?

SS: No: first the customers paid to get in—maybe around 100 francs. Then they paid me to take their picture. And I paid the band so I could be there.

AB: And the musicians?

SS: If Tidiane wanted a photo, he could buy one, or I could give him one.

FM: If you earned well, you gave the musicians pictures, is that it?

SS: Yes, as a thank you. For the pleasure. To be a photographer is a pleasure.

That's the one who stopped photographing and became a lieutenant: Yao Pélé, one of my apprentices (plate 61). He trained as a photographer but quit. He's still alive.

AB: The T-shirt he's wearing was very popular.

SS: Yes, the shakara olé olé.[17]

FM: The dance came from Nigeria but was quite popular in West Africa. You danced buttock to buttock and thigh to thigh.

AB: And the T-shirt?

SS: You could buy it at the market. Even now, people who form an association, for example for dancing, they'll make a T-shirt and sell it at the market.

The one in the back is Amadou Diallo (plate 62). He had a record store and emceed at parties. That's what he is doing there. It's in Bama, in Kou Valley.

This one is my party (plate 65).

MW: Why is he holding a record?

SS: It's for show. He's chosen someone's preferred record.

FM: It's a Guinean record from 1972, *Miri Magnin*, by Kélétigui [Traoré] and his Tambourinis.[18]

SS: Is that—yes, that is Amadou Diallo holding the record. He was a tall guy.

MW: Amazing memory!

FM: We'll find out the name of his record store. I'll check my Bobo records, because some are stamped with the store name, which is incredible.

MW: Were you invited to photograph the musicians?

SS: A photographer never got invited by the musicians. When we heard the sound of a concert, we went to see if we could drum up customers, that's all. Musicians don't need any kind of photographer.

MW: Who would buy a picture of a singer, then?

SS: The singer might want one, if he has kids, to show them he used to be a singer.

MW: Not to sell records?

SS: No.

Aren't those the guys in Echo del Africa (plate 64)?

FM: I think so, too. Youssou Diarra isn't there. But Antoine D'Albin was in the band. Is that him on the right?

SS: I'm not sure.

FM: I'd put the date in the late 1970s, with the lamé outfits.

MW: What are these "Five Jamaicans from Bobo-Dioulasso" doing (plate 70)?

SS: They are music fans. They don't make music themselves.

FM: Youth clubs: Le Club de Malick, Les Flambeurs, Les Gentlemen, and others.

MW: What does such a club do?

SS: Since they look happy, they've paid their dues, and now they're going to listen to music, dance, and have fun.

FM: Did they pay dues to buy records?

SS: They don't need records; they don't care about that. They were going to dance parties. And they don't play music. I love music, too, but I'm not a musician. I don't write songs, and I don't have an instrument. But the sound of music makes me happy.[19]

MW: It's a whole culture built around music. And dancing isn't all one does. Did people get together to listen to music?

SS: Yes, they liked to listen to music.

MW: They gave themselves a made-up band name.

FM: It's like Los Beatles. That explains also the name Volta Jazz, which referred to the United States and black American music. The Five Jamaicans gives an Anglo-Saxon feel. Jazz is very important and goes back to Mali in the 1950s. There was Renaissance Jazz first, then Ségou Jazz, in 1949 and 1953. After that came O.K. Jazz, in Congo, from 1956.

MW: Where are they posing?

SS: It's in Farakan, next to my studio, on the boulevard.

MW: When people on the street saw these young fellows posing so theatrically, did they make comments?

SS: Some things people did to attract attention from those around them. Sports, weightlifting—I could lift 70 kilos [155 pounds]—people stopped to watch that. But people making a photo was no one's business, and no one cared. People walked right on by. And it doesn't take long.

MW: Did you help them pose?

SS: They made the decisions. They are the ones who arranged themselves like that and then had the photographer shoot the picture. One of my apprentices made

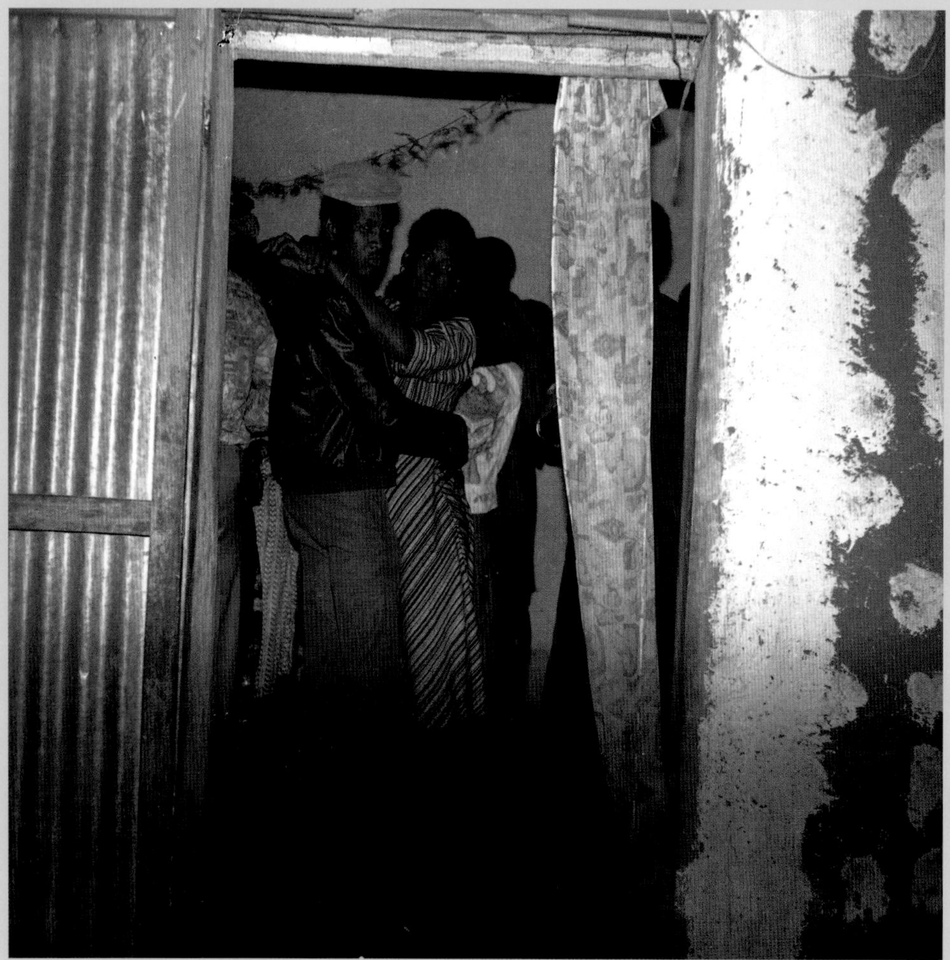

fig. 4 Untitled, 1965/75. Illustration from 6×6 cm negative. Courtesy Florent Mazzoleni

[this image]. That fellow [in the picture] is one of my music technicians.

AB: Was the Five Jamaicans club perhaps responding to the aesthetic promulgated on the cover of a record such as those released by Volta Jazz? Were group portraits for the orchestras becoming a look to be imitated?

SS: I couldn't know that. I told you that I didn't make the pose, they decided among themselves.

That's my little brother Bamoussa again, with my technician Adama Sawadogo (plate 60). He's the one who put on tapes [at the parties]. That's my turntable, and they're playing around to make the picture.

MW: So you did have a turntable?

SS: Yes, but it all went away later, it was all handed out in the villages.

MW: This is obviously not a commissioned picture—your brother wouldn't pay you. Who decided on this pose?

SS: This is my blood brother. He wasn't a driver yet at the time, so he worked in the studio developing the pictures. This is my technician, and Sibiri was probably there, too. I guess Sibiri took the picture. When you have children, you can't wear them out by trying too hard to keep them in line: "Big brother doesn't let us take any pictures." Also, my apprentices aren't going to dare tell me, "Boss, come take my picture." A little respect. They are embarrassed in front of me; I'm the man in charge, they won't bother me over their pictures. So they do it behind by back, and then I see, and I don't say anything.

MW: But maybe you were there when it was taken?

SS: No, I told you I moved around a lot.

MW: When you got back, maybe Bamoussa offered you a print as a present?

SS: Not at all—he didn't even want me to see the picture! It's a secret photo. He should have told me he wanted to take it, but he didn't. But they made a souvenir, and it's very lovely.

16 This is approximately $1 to $2 in current United States dollars.

17 Fela Anikulapo Kuti (1938–1997), the charismatic dissident Nigerian musician and political activist, released the album *Shakara* in 1972; his band was called at the time Africa '70, and his music merged Afro-American funk and jazz with a mixture of African musical forms. "Shakara Oloje" is a 13 ½-minute song about posing and bravado (*shakara* in Lagos street slang). The lyrics, sung partly in a mixture of Yoruba and Lagos slang, and partly in pidgin English, describe aggressive encounters featuring the titular braggart and another man, on one hand, as well as a woman.

18 Saxophonist and keyboard player Kélétigui Traoré (1934–2008) was one of a number of musicians brought to prominence by the Guinean president Touré. Touré accorded funds for performances by several orchestras, as the bands were called, and also provided them with a recording facility as well as distribution for the records they produced.

19 This is not entirely true. The photograph mentioned in a footnote to section 4 (p. 170) shows a guitar resting on the left. Pressed about this, Sory said that he did play guitar "for my pleasure."

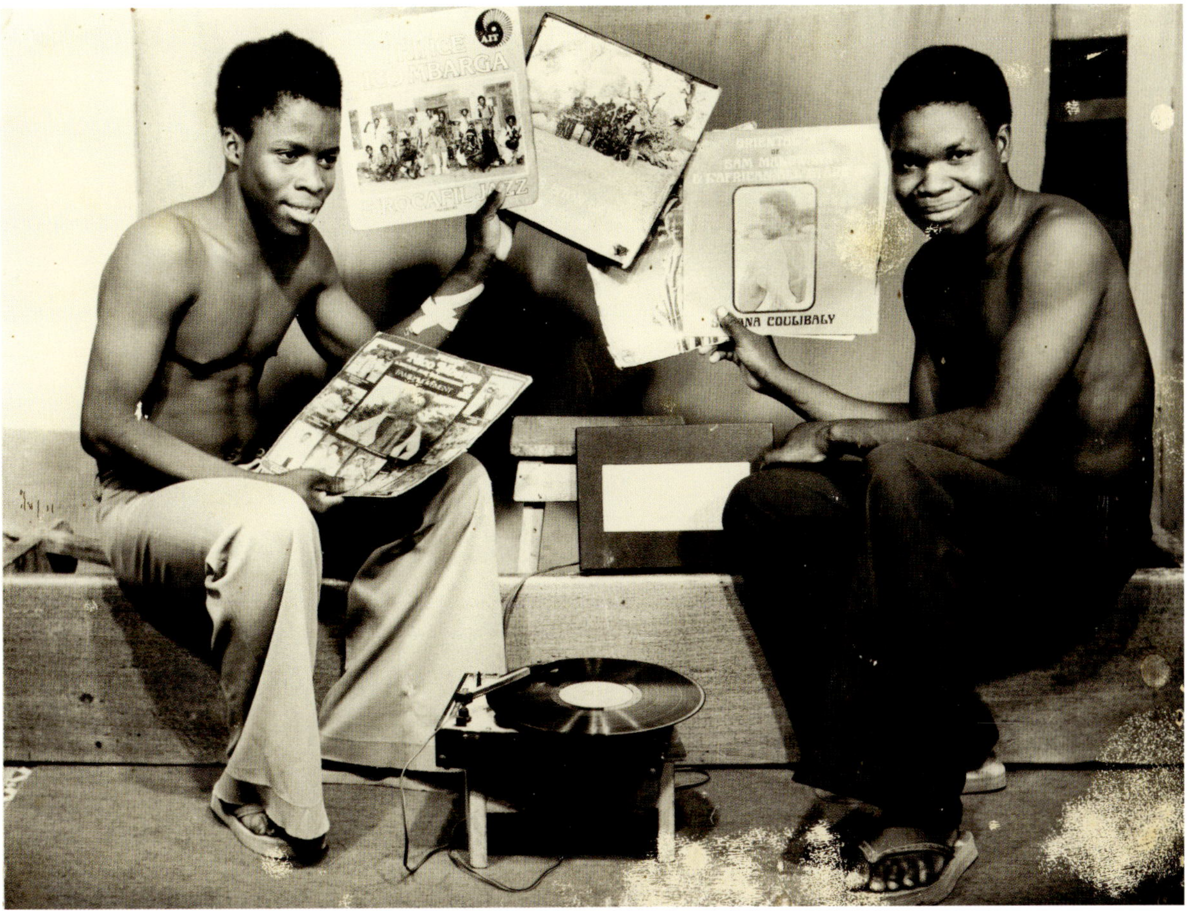

60 Untitled (taken by apprentice Sibiri Ouattara), 1979/84

Bamoussa Sory (left) printed photos in the studio; Adama Ouedraogo (right), a Mossi youth, DJed parties with Sanlé Sory. They display records by Prince Nico Mbarga, Sam Mangwana, and Le Super Biton de Ségou, which, along with the record player, belonged to Sory.

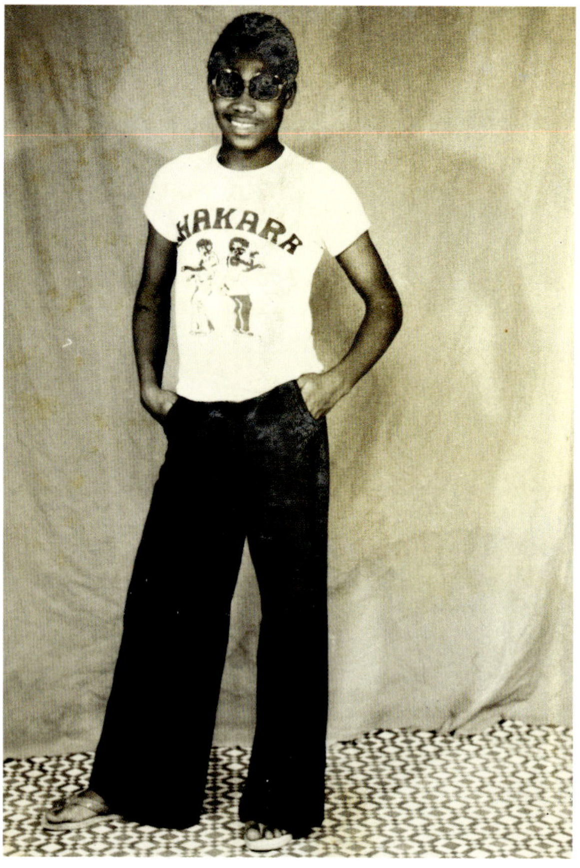

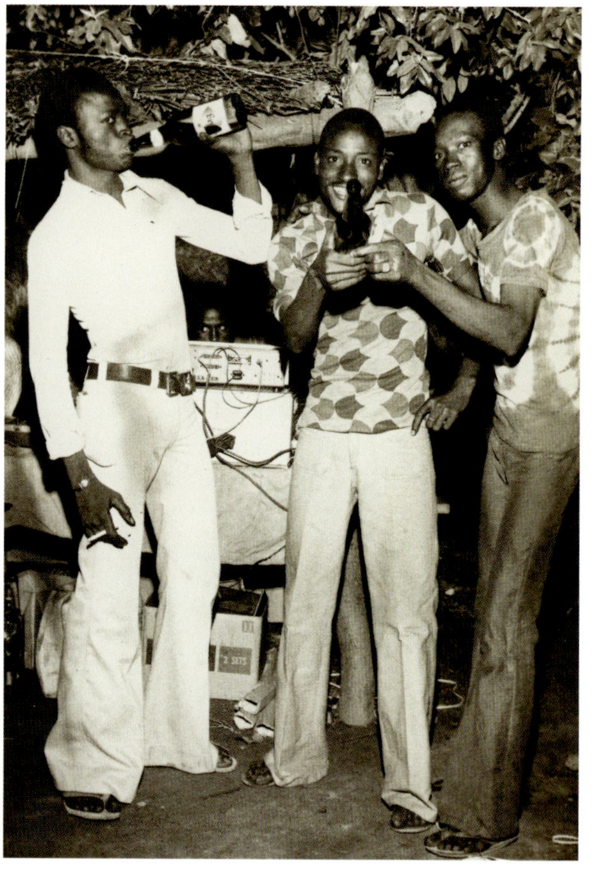

61 Yao Pelé, 1965/75

62 Village party in the Kou Valley, 1970/80

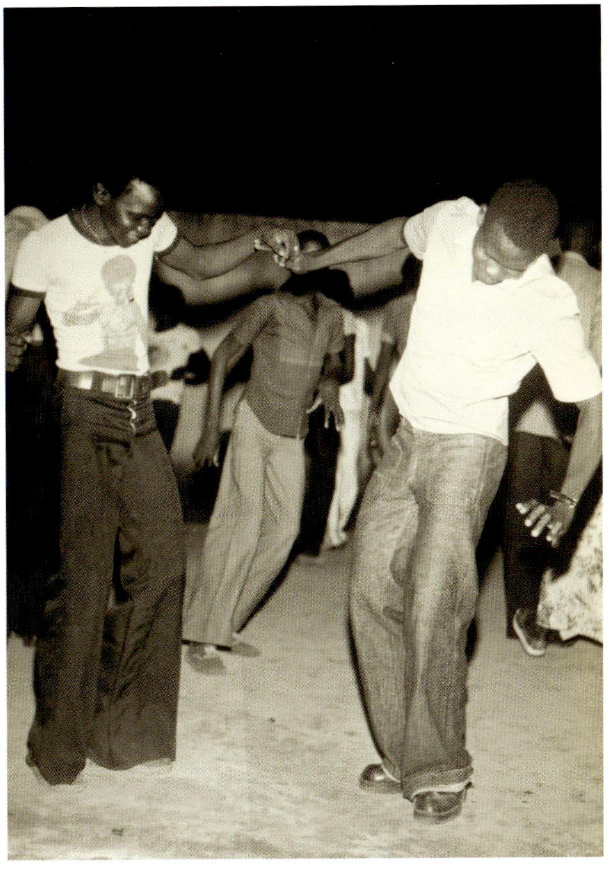

63 Village party in the Kou Valley, 1965/75

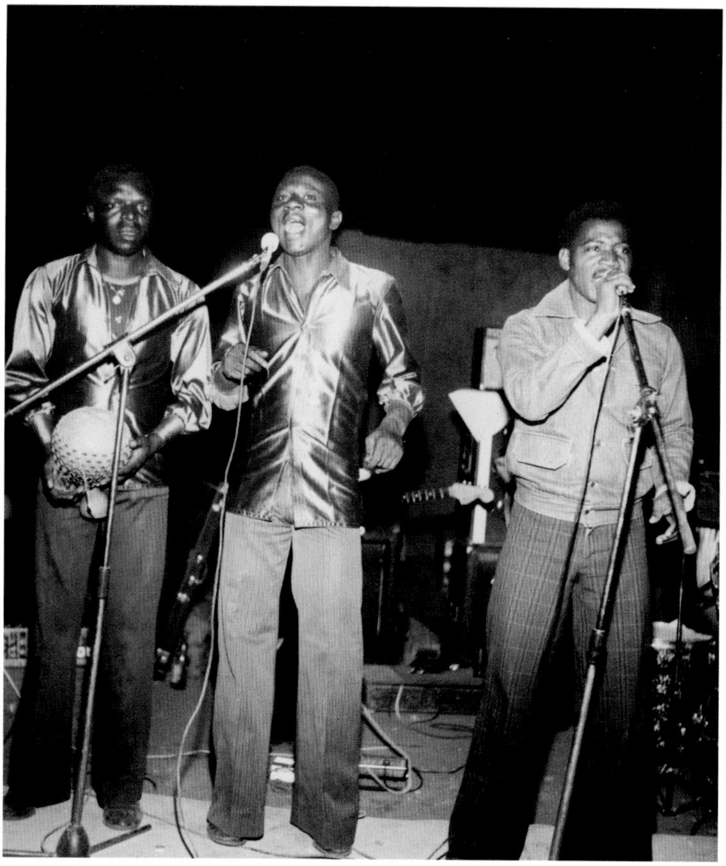

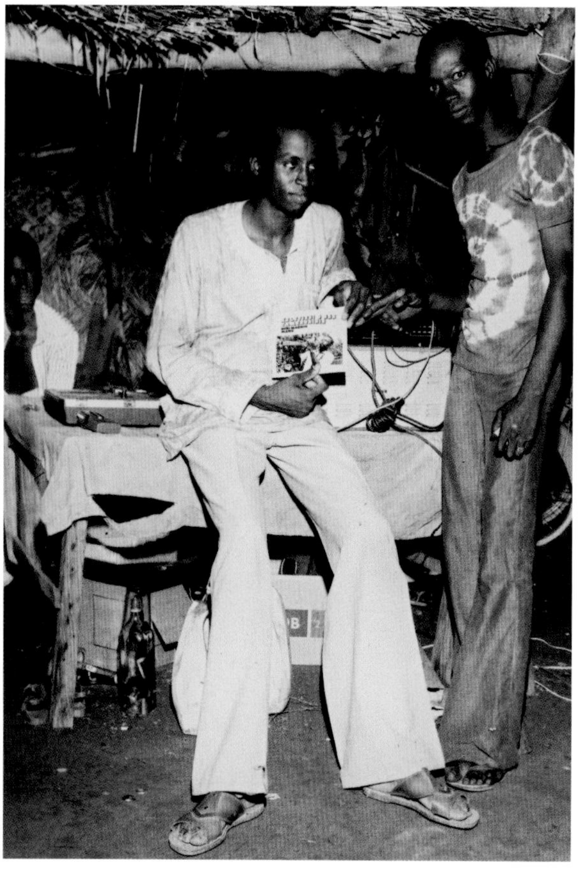

64 Echo del Africa Nacional in concert, 1975/1980

65 Amadou Diallo (center), record seller and party organizer, 1970/80

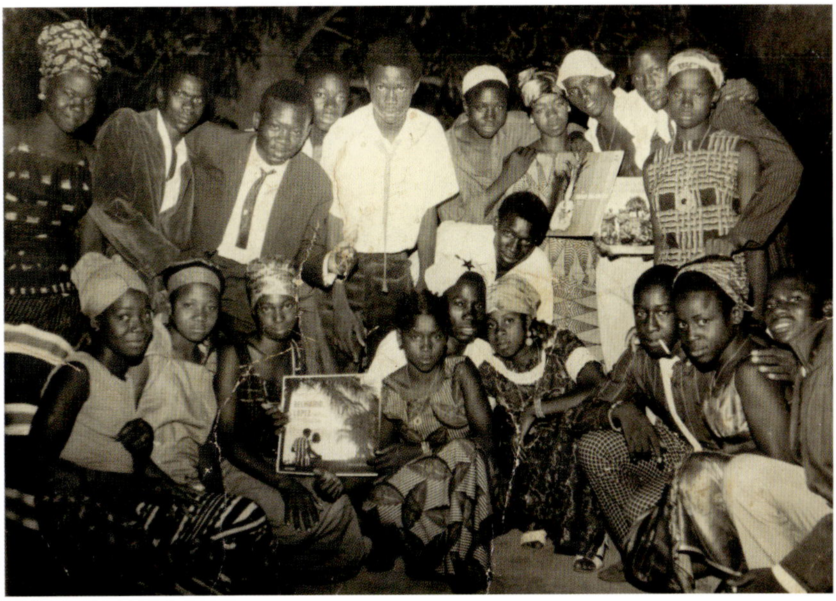

66 Fans of Cuban music holding a record by Belisario López, May 16, 1967

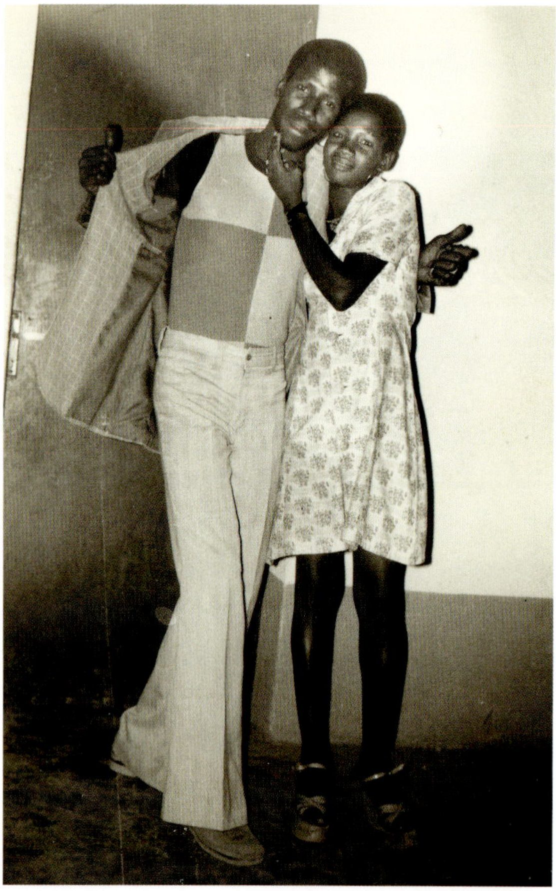

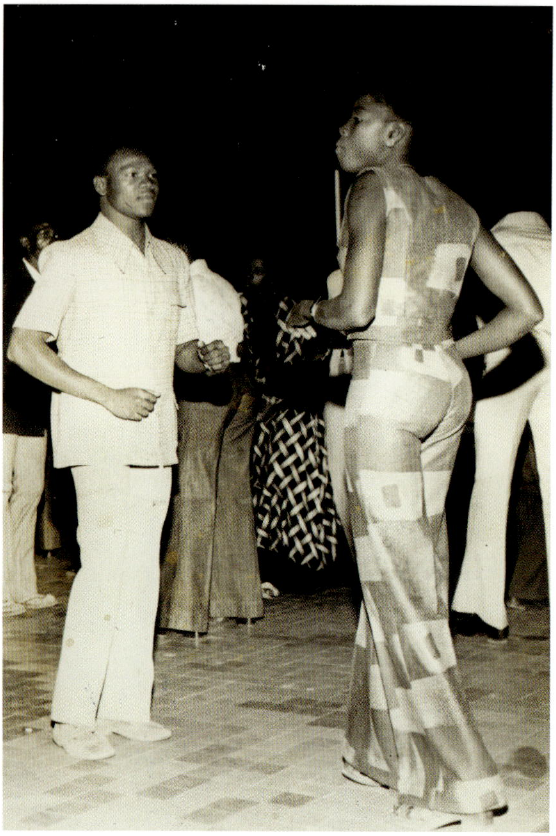

67 Untitled, 1965/75

68 Party at the Messe des garnisons (Officers' Mess), 1965/75

The Imbattables Léopards usually played at this venue, located across from Radio Bobo (see map p. 8).

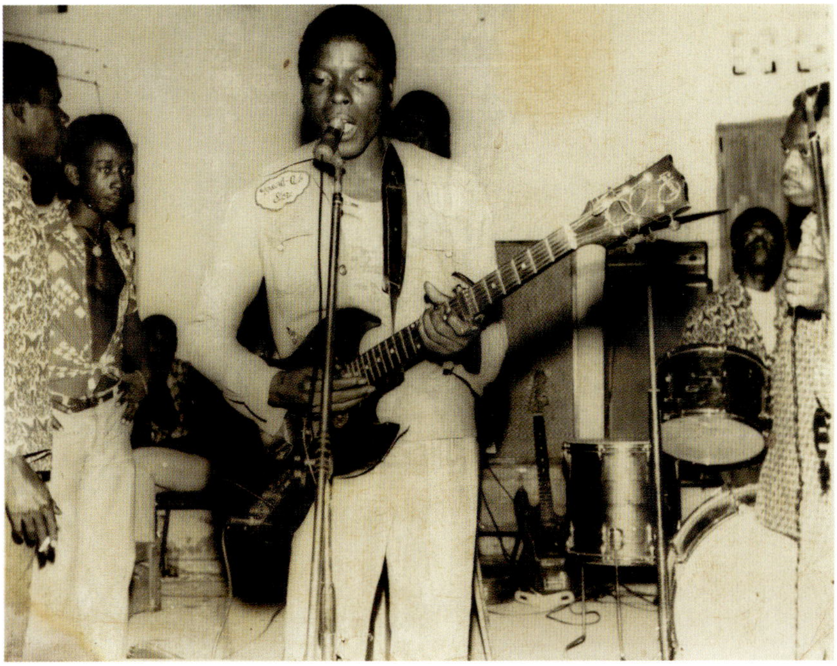

69 Untitled, 1965/75

70 The Five Jamaicans of Bobo-Dioulasso, a reggae fan club, 1965/75

Included are Bamoussa Sory (second from right) and several tailors. Photograph taken on the boulevard next to Sanlé Sory's studio in the Farakan neighborhood.

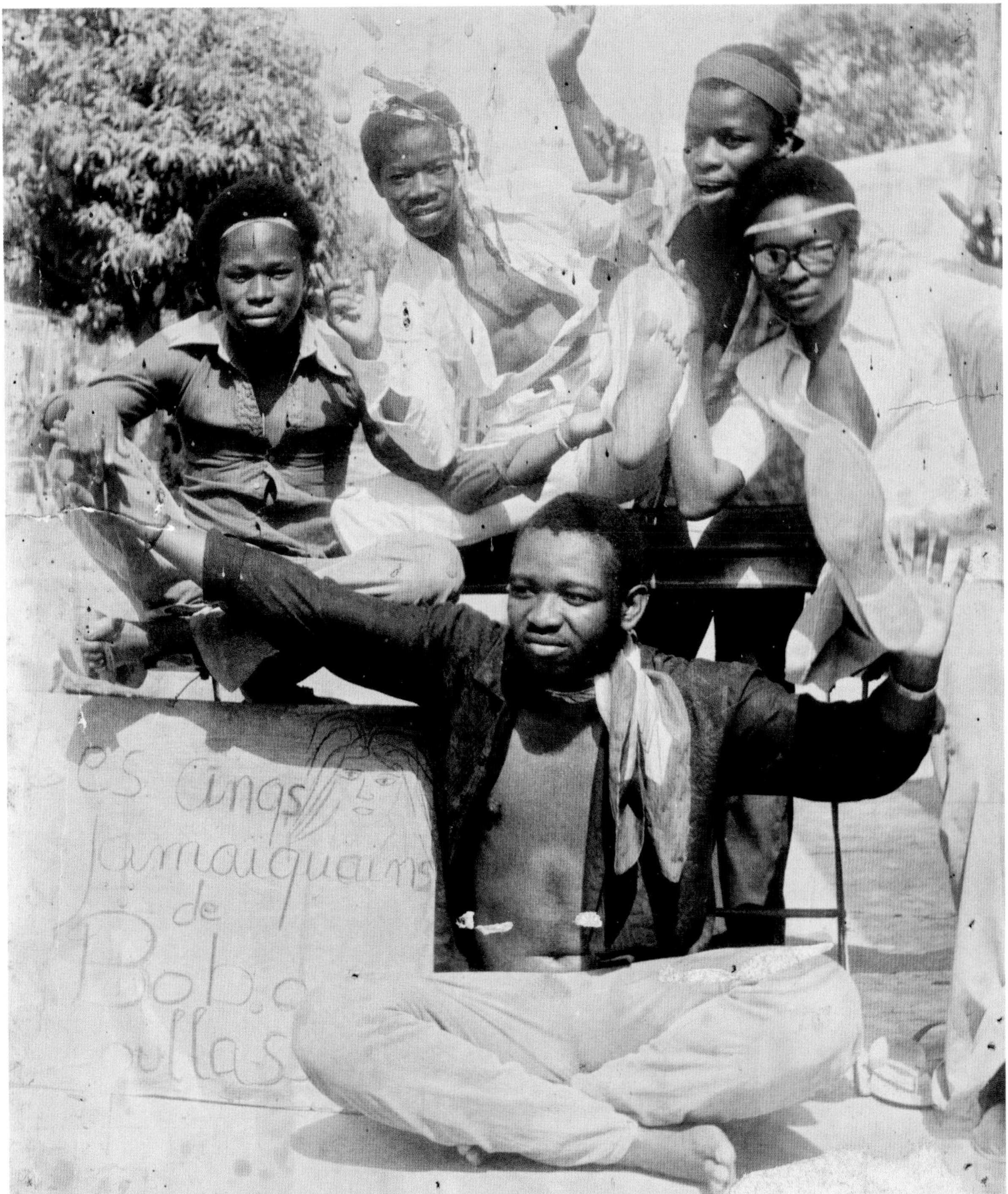
es Cinqs
Jamaiquains
de

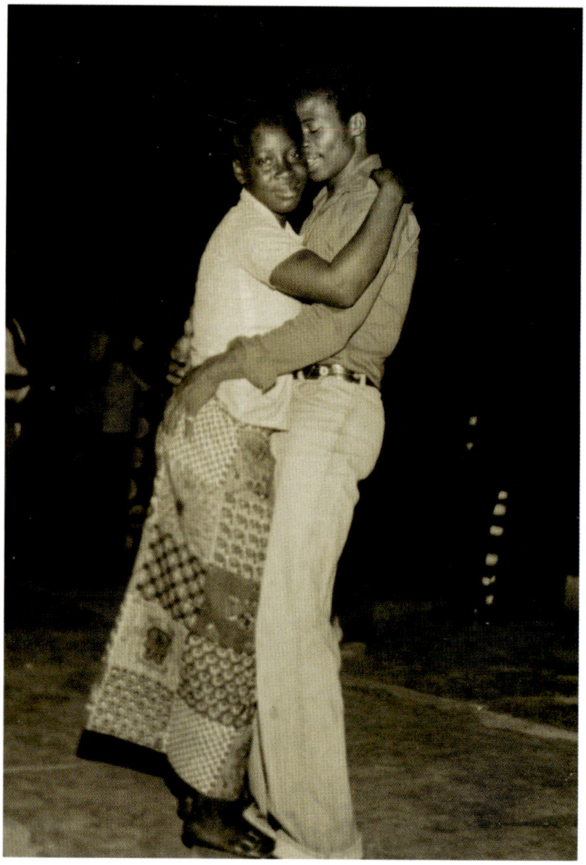

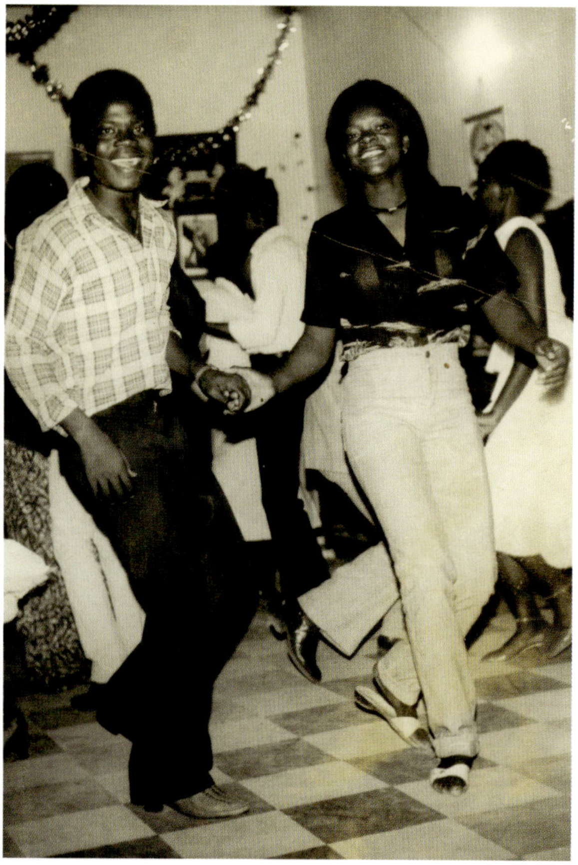

71 Dancing the blues, perhaps at Volta Dancing, 1965/75

72 "Surprise party," 1978/1980

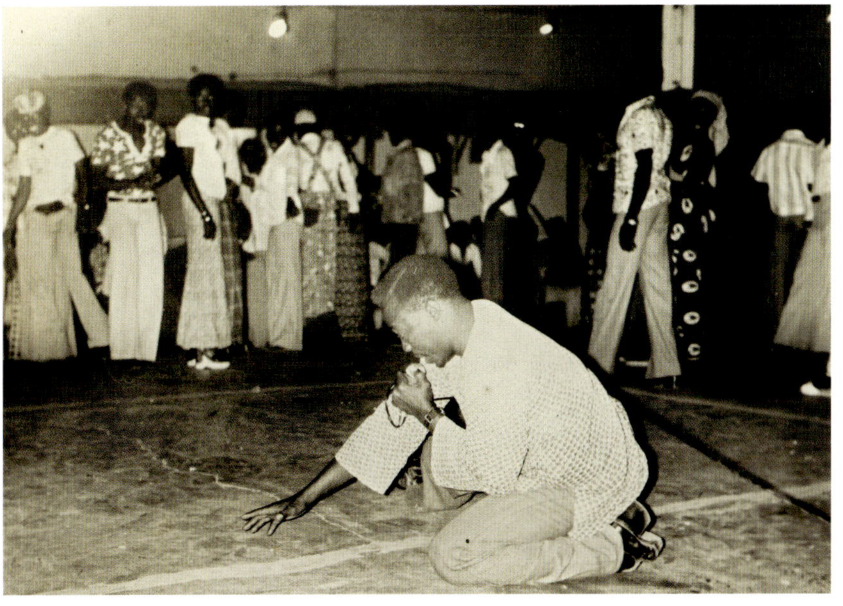

73 Tidiane Coulibaly performing at Volta Dancing, c. 1976

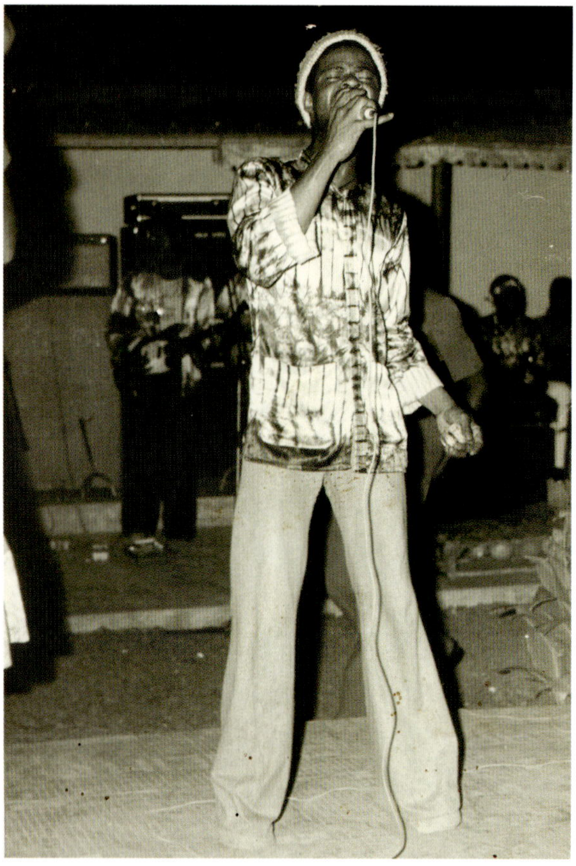

74 Untitled, 1965/75

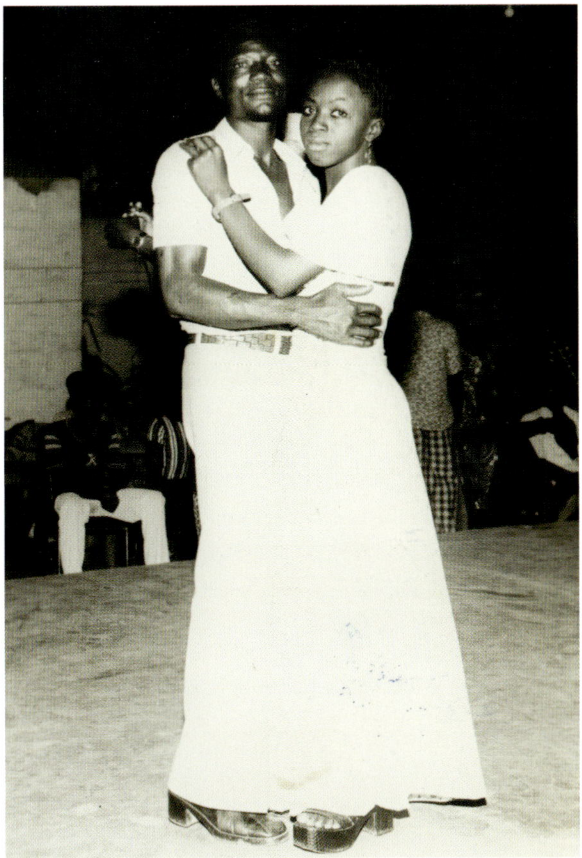

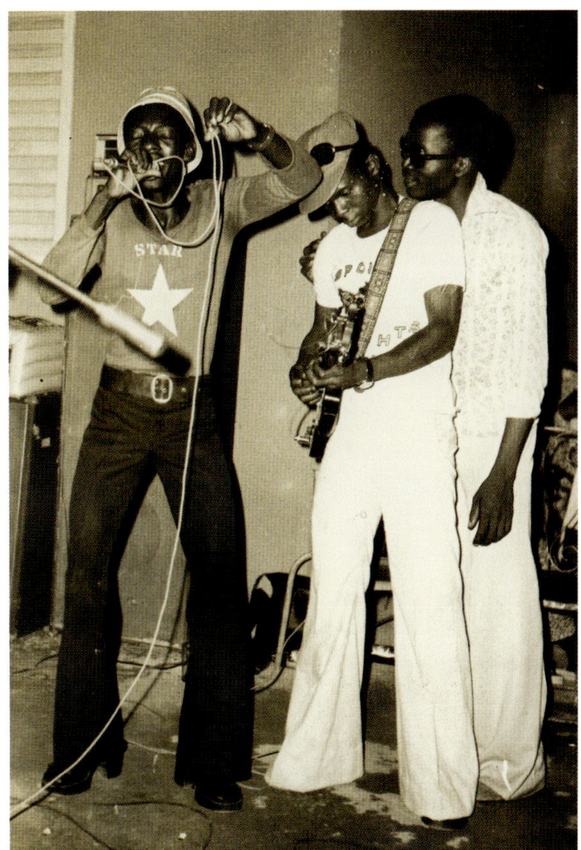

75 On a garden terrace in Bobo, 1965/75

76 Untitled, 1970/80

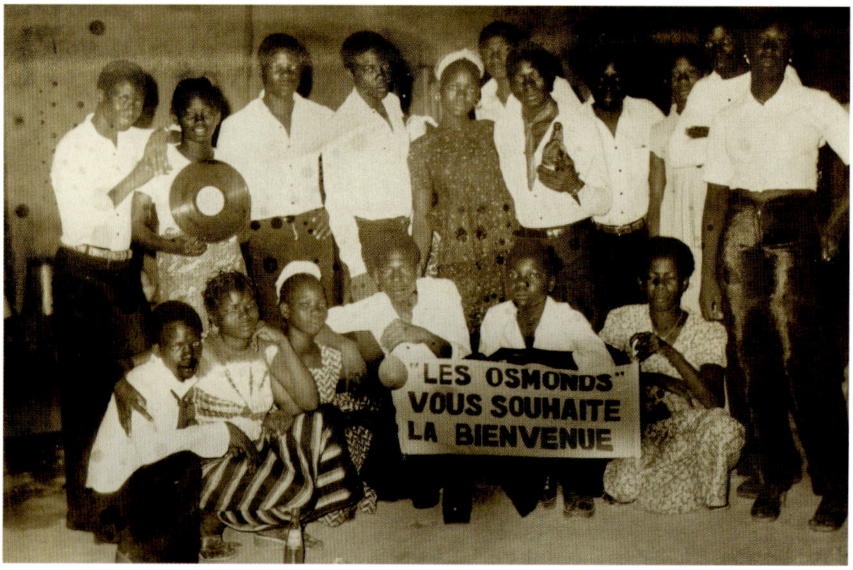

77 The Osmonds, a fan club in an outlying Bobo neighborhood, 1971/72

VOLTA JAZZ: A BAND AND ITS RECORDS

MW: I suppose you know who this is (p. 160).

SS: Myself. And Abou Traoré, trumpeter for Volta Jazz.

MW: For once you are not the photographer.

SS: Mamoudou [Bitenga] Super, one of my apprentices, took the picture.

FM: On another, equally ruined photo from this set, we see singles by Volta Jazz. That print is marked on the back *Disques France-Afrique*—the record label used by Volta Jazz. So I think it was a promo evening for Disques France-Afrique. You can see *super African production* written lightly at the top. And look here, in fact this picture also shows all the Volta Jazz records.

MW: What are you holding in your hands, Sory?

SS: A little stick. It's to point to the records.

MW: This we agree is an advertisement for Volta Jazz; it was used (in color and in black-and-white) as a cover for two records (p. 161). Who decided on the pose?

SS: Idrissa told them to do it like that. I made all the Volta Jazz photos, but Idrissa chose the locations, and he gave me the [color] film too.

FM: Why is it in black-and-white, when the album image itself is in color?

SS: Well, you could photograph in color and print in black-and-white.

MW: You said once that all the cover photos for Volta Jazz seven-inch records were taken in a single day.

SS: Yes, for the sake of the musicians we shot a full film roll in the Bobo Zoo.

MW: All the pictures in one day? With what frequency did the singles come out?

FM: I think it was around one per month over a two-year period.

SS: This picture was taken at the Théâtre de l'Amitié (Friendship Theater).

FM: The one that's on the big boulevard as you enter Bobo, before the Institut Français?

SS: That's right. For the color photos, we took all the pictures at once, and then sent them for processing to Abidjan [Ivory Coast]. I had no way to print them at my place.

MW: And then the records came out serially, as you've indicated, Florent. One might say that the number of records was set according to the availability of the photographs! Making the records to fit the pictures.

AB: However, I noticed that some images were reused as alternate covers for other records.

MW: Did the musicians' outfits belong to them, or were they rented?

SS: The bandleader ordered them. They were sewn for the musicians and belonged to Idrissa Koné.

MW: So the idea was to take advantage of having all the musicians together and finishing the roll (also to simplify long-distance processing).

SS: Correct. The musicians were all in Bobo. But they didn't put on these outfits every day. If it's a holiday and they want to be recognized as part of Volta Jazz, they might wear them. Or if they're really happy, they might suit up on a regular day. Also maybe if they're going to play somewhere specific, they might think it's better to wear the outfit. It's kind of a service uniform.

FM: To explain about the one yellow jacket: Volta Jazz operated for a time as a repertory ensemble, democratically, with the lead musician changing monthly and wearing the yellow jacket. I find that truly extraordinary.

MW: So the film was processed and the prints made in Abidjan. What about the sleeves?

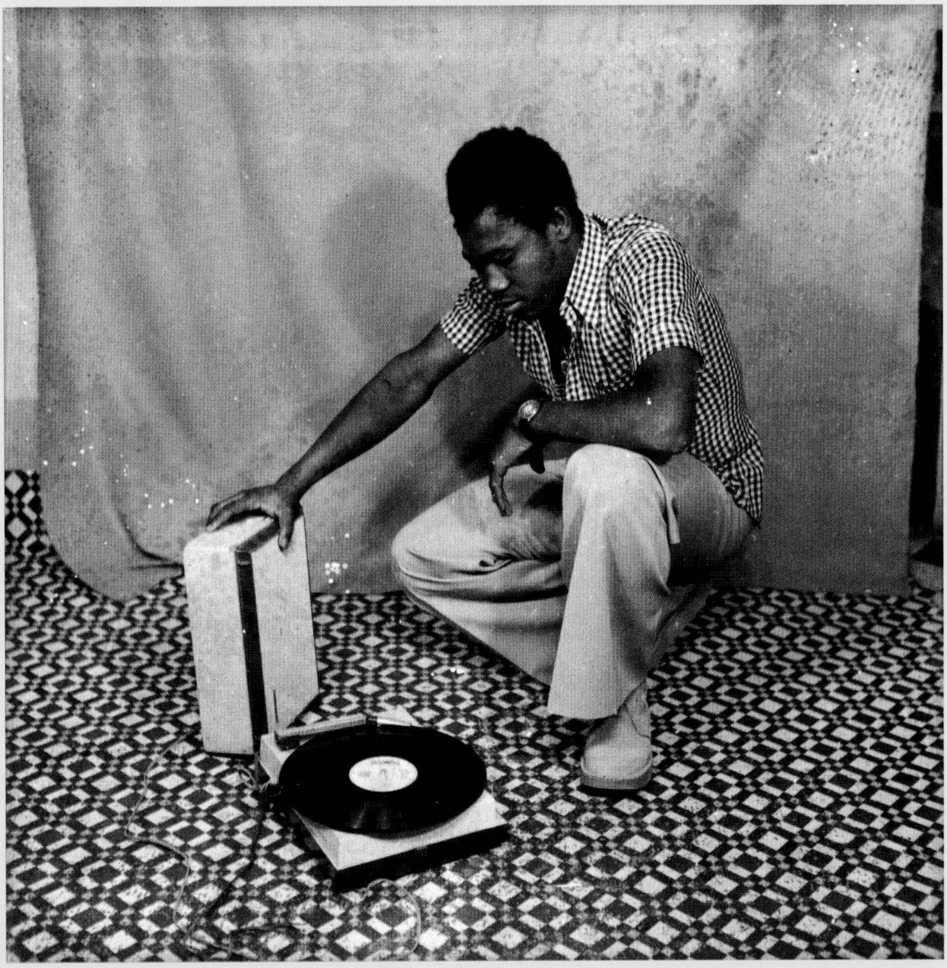

fig. 1 Yao Pelé (taken by an apprentice), 1965/75, printed 2017. 36 × 36 cm (image); 50 × 40 cm (sheet). The Art Institute of Chicago, gift of the artist and Florent Mazzoleni, 242563

FM: In Italy. An Australian friend found me a dead stock of records in an Italian factory—that's what gave me this idea.

MW: Meaning you couldn't check the image quality either during printing or in reproduction.

SS: My job is to take the picture.

MW: This is Tidiane Coulibaly (plate 73), and what's the place?

SS: Calebasse d'Or. It was also known as Volta Dancing, it was the same property. The owner was an African woman named Madeleine.

MW: Which years?

FM: I'd say 1976-77, he has platform boots. That was when he had left Volta Jazz and was singing with Dafra Star.

SS: In the background of this picture (p. 19), on the right, that's a traditional outfit.

MW: Is it typical for the region? Did people wear this in the street?

SS: Yes. An outfit with black-and-white stripes.

MW: The Volta Jazz musicians wore similar outfits. You said before that you also had a jacket with black-and-white stripes among your props. Did it look like this costume?

SS: Yes, my [studio prop] jacket resembled a traditional costume—called a *faso dan fani*.

MW: The band seems then to have had two outfits: the service uniform and a fabric with black-and-white stripes that evokes local tradition. The contrast between the two strikes me as significant.

FM: I think the striped outfit came at a time when Idrissa had organized a contest in Bobo called the Black Farmer Contest (Coupe Paysan Noir). The "service" outfits by contrast seem almost [like those worn by] Houphouët-Boigny.[20] Idrissa Koné's changing politics in the 1970s led him to stress social engagement and Volta heritage. That's what I take from the striped clothing but also the choice to put a Mossi [traditional] building on this particular sleeve, whereas the Volta Jazz records in color give off a lovely air of modernity. It was the same [with 1960s bands] in Congo (OK Jazz, African Jazz), Ivory Coast (Les Eléphants Noirs, Yapi Jazz) and Guinea (Orchestre de la Paillotte, Orchestre du Jardin de Guinée, Bembeya Jazz).

SS: Yes, that's true.

20 Félix Houphouët-Boigny (1905–1993) was president of Ivory Coast from the time of its independence in 1960 and before then a member of parliament in France. A modernizer who saw close ties with France as the key to economic success for his country, Houphouët-Boigny dressed in bespoke double-breasted suits when many West African leaders appeared by preference in tunics or other traditional clothing.

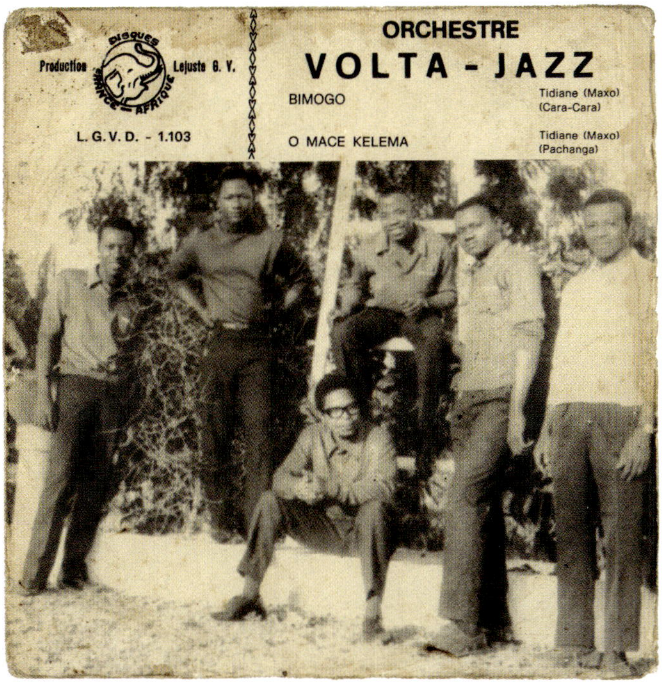

78a Disques France-Afrique / L.G.V.D. Productions

Volta Jazz 45-rpm record sleeve
Photograph by Ibrahima Sanlé Sory, c. 1968

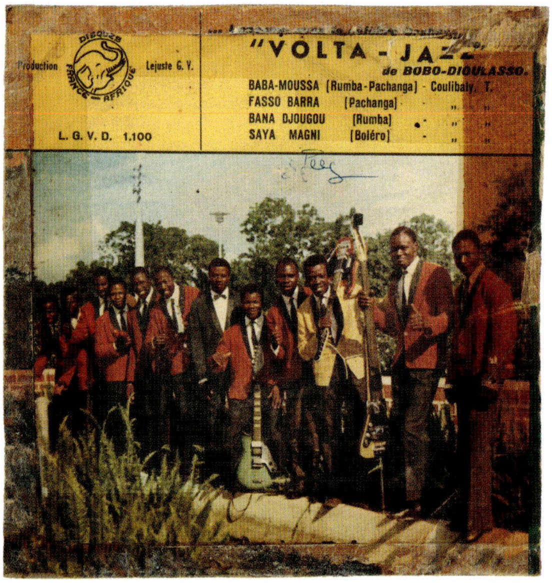
Production
DISQUES FRANCE-AFRIQUE
Lejuste G. V.
L. G. V. D. 1.100
"VOLTA - JAZZ"
de BOBO-DIOULASSO
BABA-MOUSSA [Rumba-Pachanga] - Coulibaly. T.
FASSO BARRA [Pachanga]
BANA DJOUGOU [Rumba]
SAYA MAGNI [Boléro]

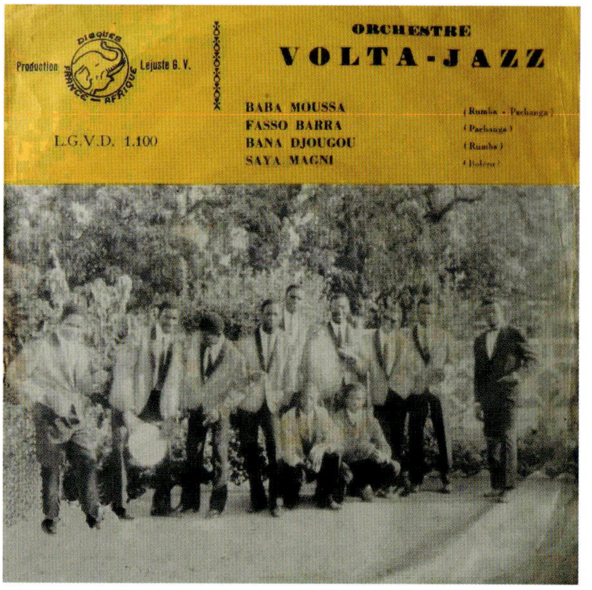
Production
DISQUES FRANCE-AFRIQUE
Lejuste G. V.
L.G.V.D. 1.100
ORCHESTRE
VOLTA-JAZZ
BABA MOUSSA
FASSO BARRA
BANA DJOUGOU
SAYA MAGNI

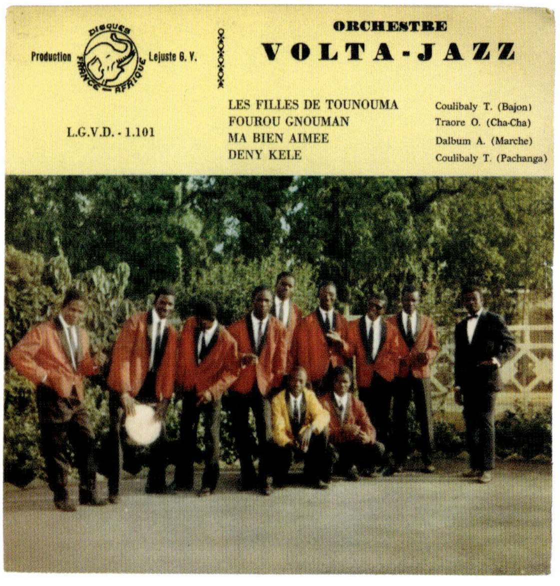
Production
DISQUES FRANCE-AFRIQUE
Lejuste G. V.
L.G.V.D. - 1.101
ORCHESTRE
VOLTA-JAZZ
LES FILLES DE TOUNOUMA Coulibaly T. (Bajon)
FOUROU GNOUMAN Traore O. (Cha-Cha)
MA BIEN AIMEE Dalbum A. (Marche)
DENY KELE Coulibaly T. (Pachanga)

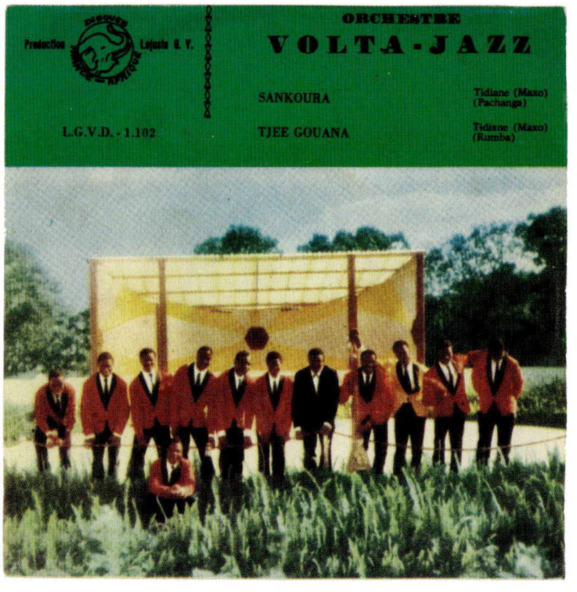
Production
DISQUES FRANCE-AFRIQUE
Lejuste G. V.
L.G.V.D. - 1.102
ORCHESTRE
VOLTA-JAZZ
SANKOURA Tidiane (Maxo) (Pachanga)
TJEE GOUANA Tidiane (Maxo) (Rumba)

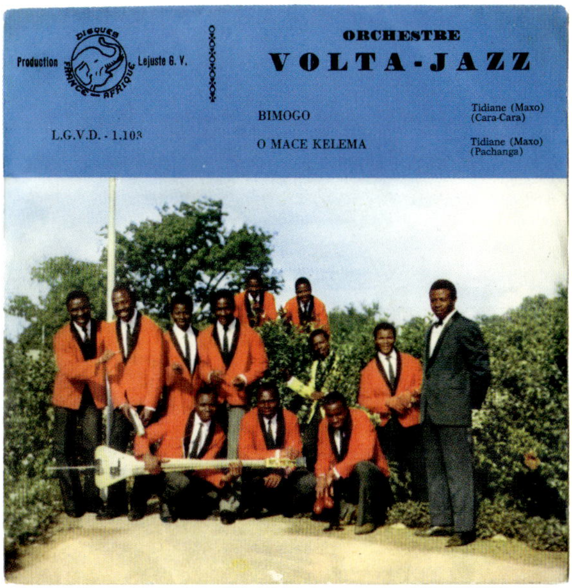

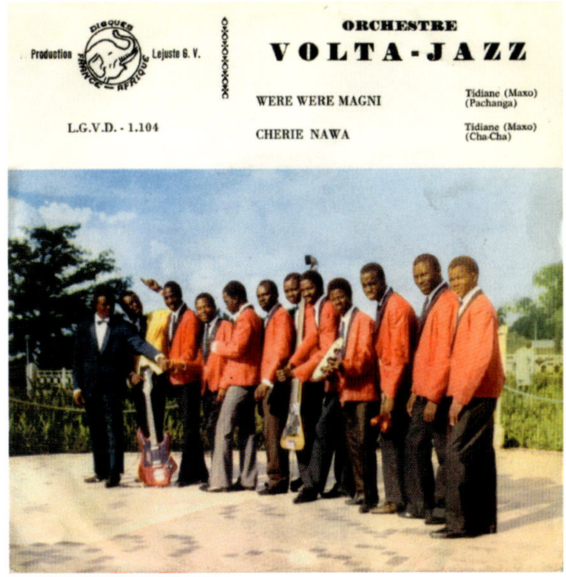

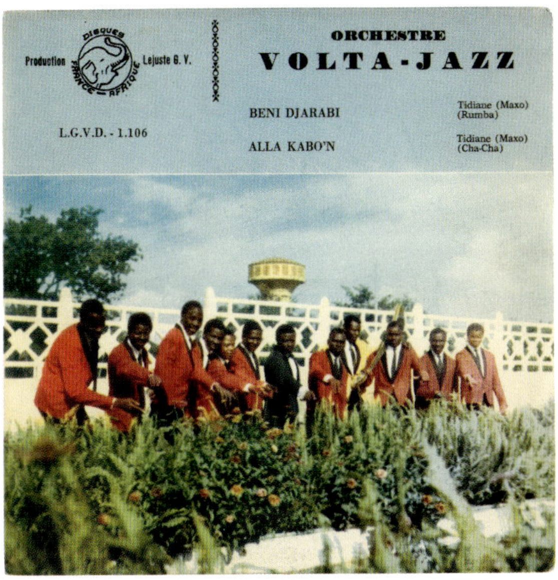

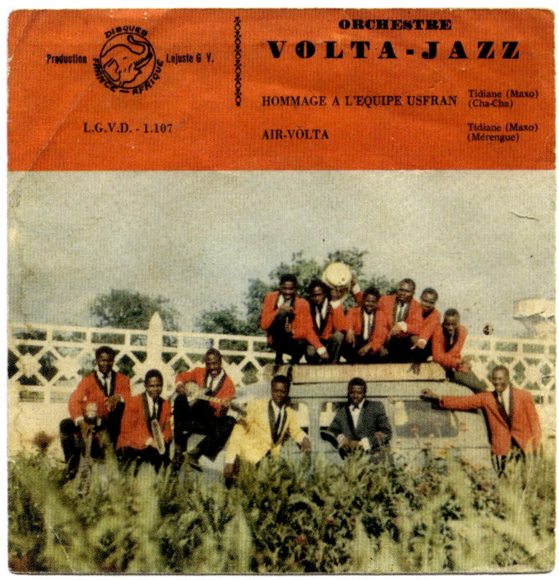

78b–i Disques France-Afrique / L.G.V.D. Productions

Volta Jazz 45-rpm record sleeves
Photographs by Ibrahima Sanlé Sory, c. 1968

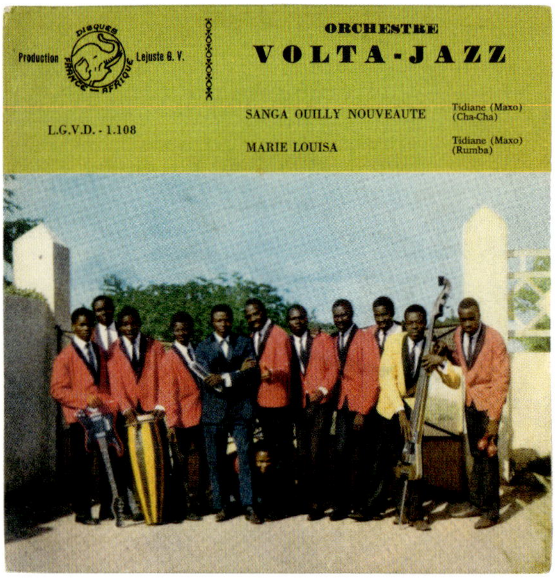

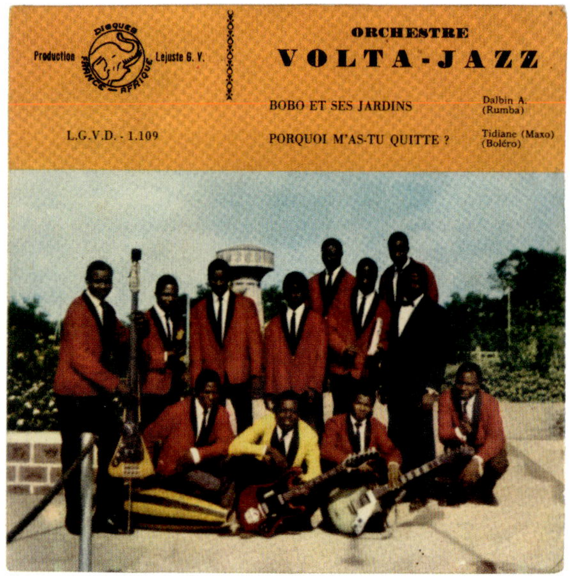

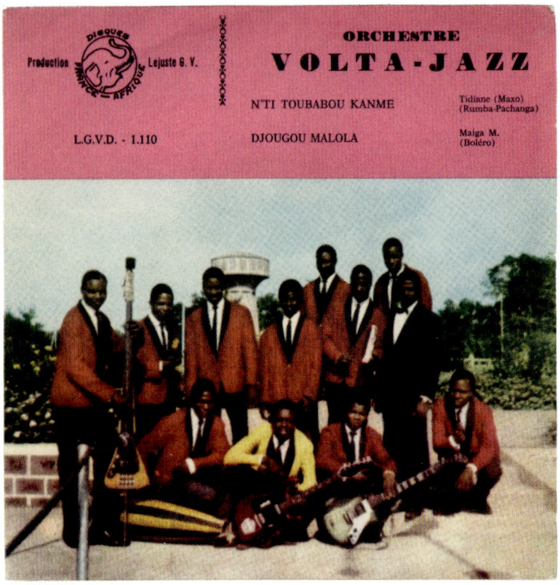

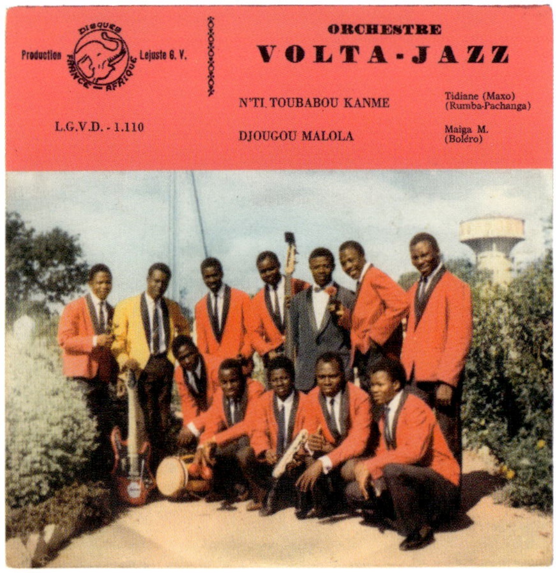

78j–n Disques France-Afrique / L.G.V.D. Productions

Volta Jazz 45-rpm record sleeves
Photographs by Ibrahima Sanlé Sory, c. 1968

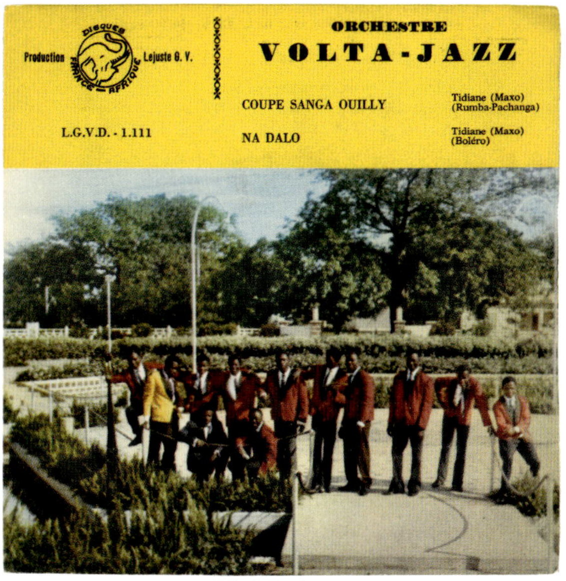

Baba Moussa

written by Tidiane Coulibaly

I arrived in Bobo-Dioulasso
Coming from Abidjan
The suitcase I had
A thief stole it from me
I went to the police station
Baba Moussa settled the case
With Lieutenant Moussa in Bobo
All the dirty business is over
Moussa Traoré
He has achieved good things
Baba Moussa
He has achieved good things
Lieutenant Moussa
He has achieved good things
Moussa the Sambla
He has achieved good things
Moussa Traoré
He has achieved good things
Lieutenant Moussa
He has achieved good things

Air Volta

Air Volta is arriving
Air Volta
The country's plane has landed
Air Volta
Air Volta is arriving
Air Volta
The country's plane is there
Air Volta
We go to Ouagadougou
Air Volta
I'm going to Ouahigouya
Air Volta
I'm going to Bobo-Dioulasso
Air Volta
I'm going to Banfora
Air Volta
I'm going to Koudougou
Air Volta
I'm going to Nouna
Air Volta
I'm going to Tougan
Air Volta
I'm going to Dédougou
Air Volta
I'm going to Diébougou
Air Volta
The plane of Upper Volta has landed
Air Volta is arriving
Air Volta
Air Volta is taking off
Air Volta
The plane of Upper Volta has landed
Air Volta
The country's plane has landed
Air Volta
The country's plane has landed
Air Volta
The country's plane has landed
Air Volta

Lyrics translated by Dragoss Ouédraogo

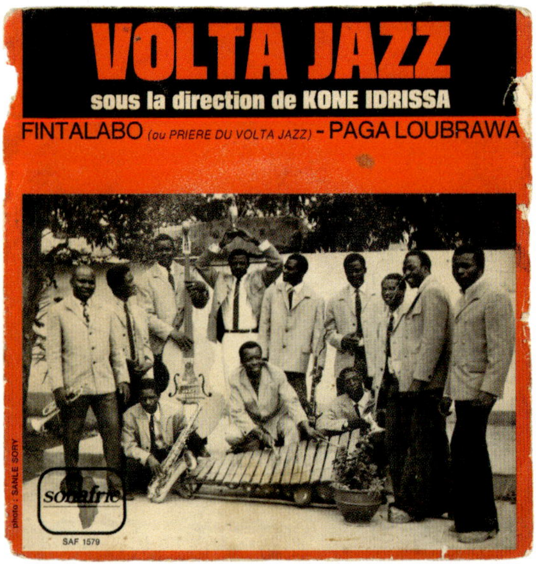

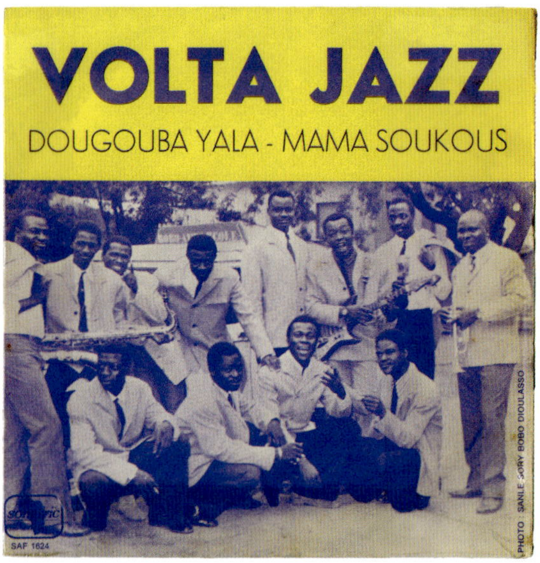

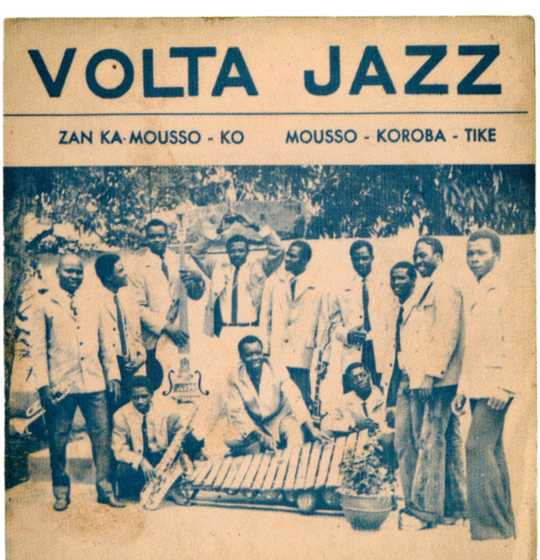

BB Peyrissac

If you want a pretty moped
If you want a good deal
If you're looking for good products
See you at Peyrissac
If you want a moped that softens hearts
If you want an affordable bike
Mopeds for young people and adults
They're found at Peyrissac
No more walking
See you at Peyrissac
A new moped and an affordable bike
They're sold at Peyrissac
If you don't have money
We can give you credit
and you'll pay bit by bit
BB Peyrissac
If you want a pretty moped
Go to Peyrissac
If you want a cheap bike
See you at Peyrissac
If you want a beautiful lady's bike
Go to Peyrissac
If you want a BB Jhonny
Go to Peyrissac
If you want a new Solex
See you at Peyrissac
If you want a 3 speed BB
See you at Peyrissac
If you want a new CT
See you at Peyrissac
If you want bike parts
See you at Peyrissac
If you want moped parts
See you at Peyrissac

Lyrics translated by Dragoss Ouédraogo

79a–b Sonafric (French)

80 Idrissa Koné Productions (Burkinabé)

Volta Jazz 45-rpm record sleeves
Photographs by Ibrahima Sanlé Sory, 1975–77

THE KEY TO SUCCESS: PHOTOGRAPHY AND FITNESS

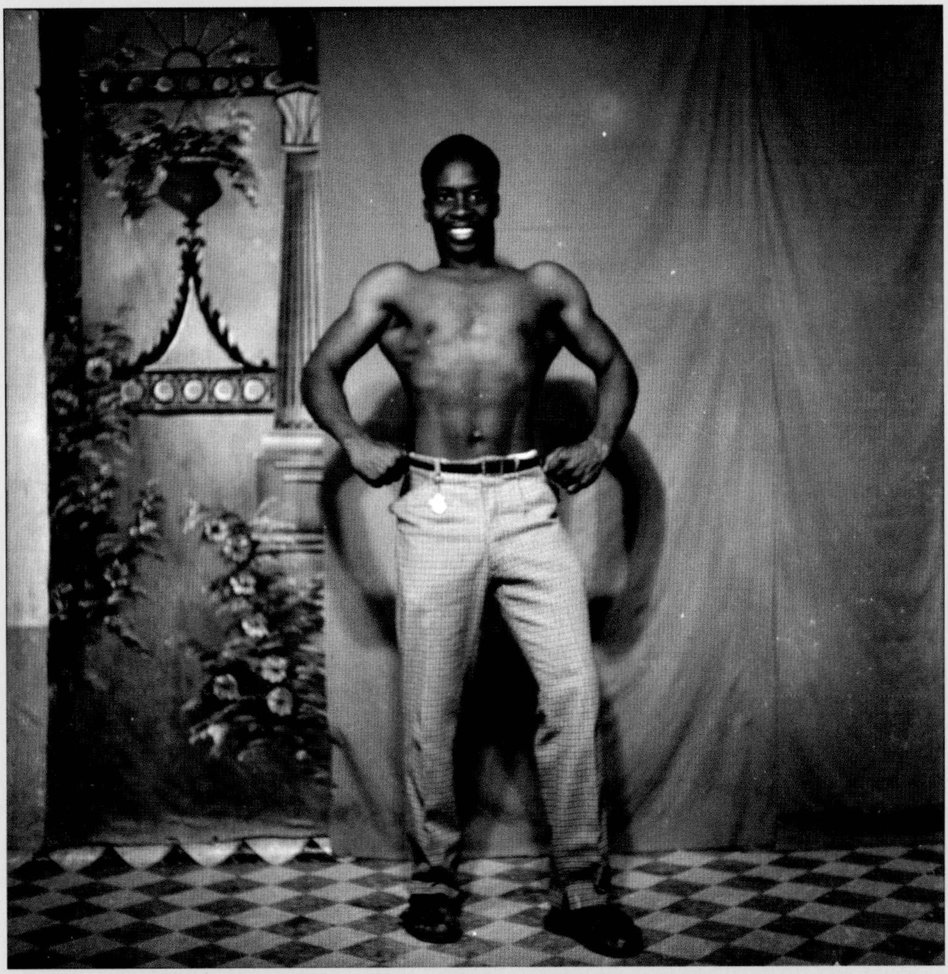

fig. 1 Untitled, 1965/75, printed 2017. 36 × 36 cm (image); 50 × 40 cm (sheet). The Art Institute of Chicago, gift of the artist and Florent Mazzoleni, 242564

MW: What are these two young fellows doing, here in front of the beach backdrop (p. 144)?

SS: The top one is showing he knows karate.

MW: A Bruce Lee effect?

FM: I think this picture is earlier.

MW: So karate was popular?

SS: Certainly. The "karate man" is Karamogo Koné. He's dead. He wasn't actually a karate follower.

FM: But you were.

SS: Not really. I was, but I resigned (laughs). I didn't have time. Training every evening, buying a lot of meat. Even if life was cheaper back then, with Coke at 25 francs a bottle.

MW: Where did you make the self-portrait in the mirror?

SS: In Diaradougou.

MW: You made a lot of self-portraits. Don't they cost money?

SS: Not once you're working in that field. How can you photograph others and not yourself, not modernize as you go along? Maybe someone will see such a picture and want something similar.

MW: Did your teacher Adomako pin up self-portraits in his studio?

SS: Certainly. He had pinned up his self-portrait separate from the others at his house, a picture taken in front of a backdrop painted with a fence, and a flowerpot as prop.

MW: You've said you made this self-portrait for your pleasure (plate 35). You liked looking at yourself at the time? This one is inscribed on the back: *Sory, Director of Photography.*

SS: Look at my face then and now, it's not the same any more (laughs)!

MW: Did you take self-portraits often? Monthly, daily?

SS: There were times when I was happy and wanted memories of myself. Photo means joy. If you're happy and proud, you want some kind of memory to look at one fine day, you never know … and then when you change clothing. You have to record your clothing, too.

That's at my boss's studio [Kojo Adomako]. Takes you way back (p. 12)! I did go to see my boss and the apprentices from time to time. And the boss did the same.

MW: So you saw him regularly.

SS: Of course, and Idrissa too—I sought their blessing. You must never abandon your boss. I'll never forget them until the day I die.

MW: Does that mean your apprentices came back to see you?

SS: Oh! They got discouraged, I told you, and decided they can't keep up with this business. I told you one of them left for the army, he doesn't write me.

FM: That disappointed you, hmm, Sory?

SS: Doesn't mean a thing to me. You know, I'm a simple guy. If you like me, I'm glad. If you don't like me, it's alright. I don't press anybody. That's how I am. So my

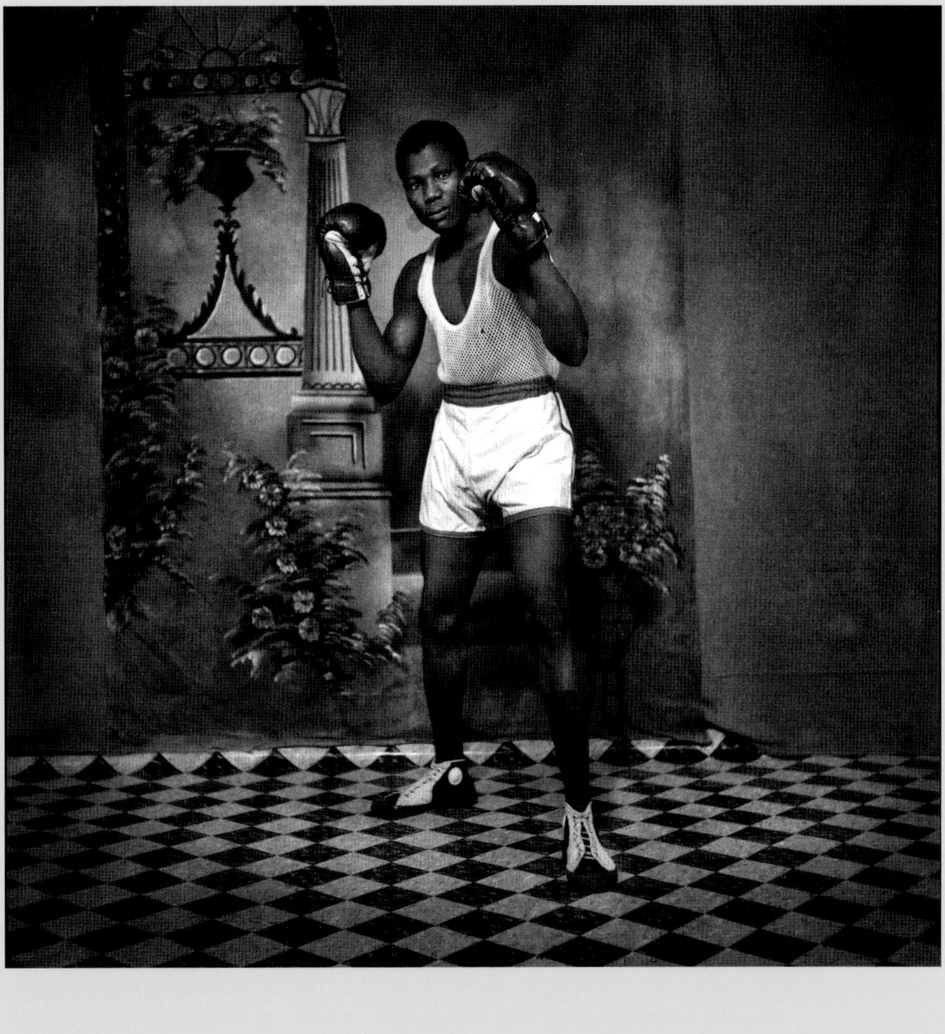

fig. 2 Abou, a Dafing boxer, 1965/75. 36 × 36 cm (image); 50 × 40 cm (sheet). Courtesy Florent Mazzoleni.

situation is uncomplicated. You can see it in my pictures. It's the same: people should be uncomplicated.

That's my sports trainer (plate 11).

FM: Standing with you. Two things here are interesting. First, whereas in those pictures you're documenting your new clothes—shoes, pants—here you're documenting your body itself. You've told me that you made a picture every week at the time to track the evolution of your body.

SS: That's right. And that's my trainer. He died at least three years ago. Ousmane, a Dafing.[21] I invited him to pose with me. I wanted a souvenir, as he was my sports trainer. [Long silence] The studio—I think it's Kojo's but an unusual backdrop.

MW: When and why did you start lifting weights?

SS: A man needs to exercise to keep healthy. When you don't do sports, you get old quickly, you fall apart. But when you do sports, your muscles tighten and you're ready for any kind of fight. Athletes in general are ready to solve problems. And lifting weights was something I could do.

FM: Was it your trainer who inspired you?

SS: When my trainer took his clothes off and you saw his muscles, you couldn't believe it. I admired him a lot. So I tried to define myself too, to be like him. Since I'm short, he was tall next to me (laughs).

AB: Did you put these photos up in the studio as well?

SS: No, these are personal photos, the sports ones—I didn't show them in the studio.

MW: Yet you were proud of them!

SS: If I'm proud it's for myself, not to show to the public. You can't advertise with those. You don't need to pin those up for people to come and say, "Sory looks like this or that." It was my personal collection to see my development through sports.

MW: I should say, Sory, that we really like your self-portraits and intend to feature them in the upcoming exhibition. Will that anger you?

SS: In the exhibition? Those who come to look won't know me. No problem then. If it were a local village or in Bobo, people would criticize and speak differently. Plus, if I show these photos today, no one will recognize me. If they see my picture now, they'll say it isn't true. For example, when you see my Afro here you say, it can't be (plate 92).

MW: Why did you take this picture?

SS: It was a moment of blossoming. When you're at full strength, you're proud and happy…

MW: What role are you playing in the image, with the turtleneck sweater and the Afro?

SS: My hair was changing, so I straightened it. And I wanted to show myself in thought. To think is a way of looking on the past. That's bound to please me. I took a pencil, what do you call it—

FM: —a makeup pencil.

SS: That's it, to pencil in the three lines [on my forehead]. To make a show. I didn't see that anywhere; I just liked it. I thought it up.

MW: You wanted to think up a look at the past?

SS: That's right. I said, If I make this hairstyle, pose like this, and take a picture, one day I'll like that. And here I am looking at it and very happy (big laugh).

MW: It has a certain intellectual look, maybe? Or am I wrong?

SS: You're not wrong. I was thinking about a lot of things, you see. At this time, going along, I would get up and say, "Okay, what should I do now?" I have to attack my work. Never give in, never let my guard down, have to be doing something. And in doing, to improve. Have to advance.

MW: Improve in what sense. Yourself?

SS: Improve myself. Well, I'm not so well schooled in French (laughs)—I get by. As time goes on, I can feel happy even wearing a turtleneck, so I call one of my assistants over to make this picture. Also, it was cold then. Sometimes it can get cold in Bobo.[22] In the morning you might want a sweater.

FM: Did you ever think your work—documenting the people of Bobo and its cultural scene—could be called intellectual?

SS: Not really. I did it to keep in shape and earn money.

21 The Dafing or Marka are a subgroup of the Mandé-speaking people who form communities on either side of the Burkina-Mali border.

22 Temperatures in Bobo-Dioulasso, a tropical region, range between around 20 and 40 degrees Celsius; monthly rainfall in summer can reach 250 mm or more.

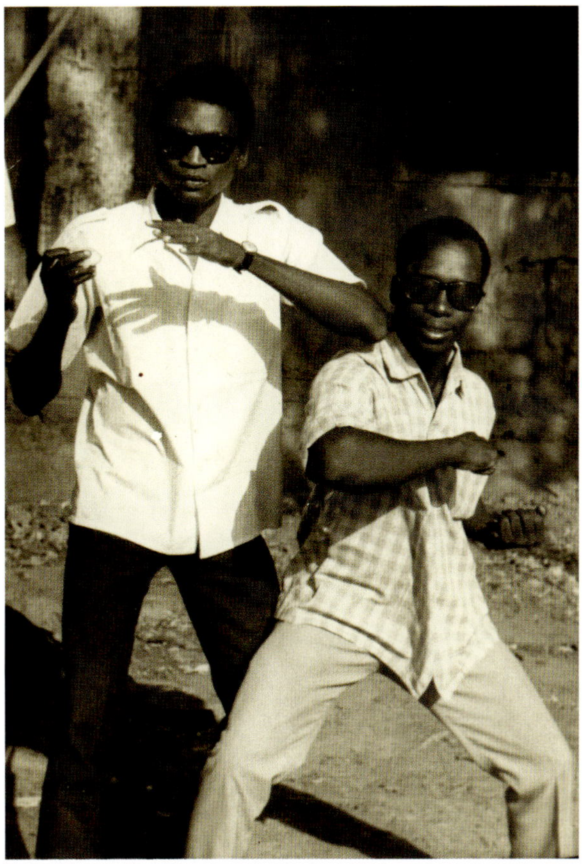

81 Self-portrait (right) with Karamogo, a managerial training specialist, 1965/75

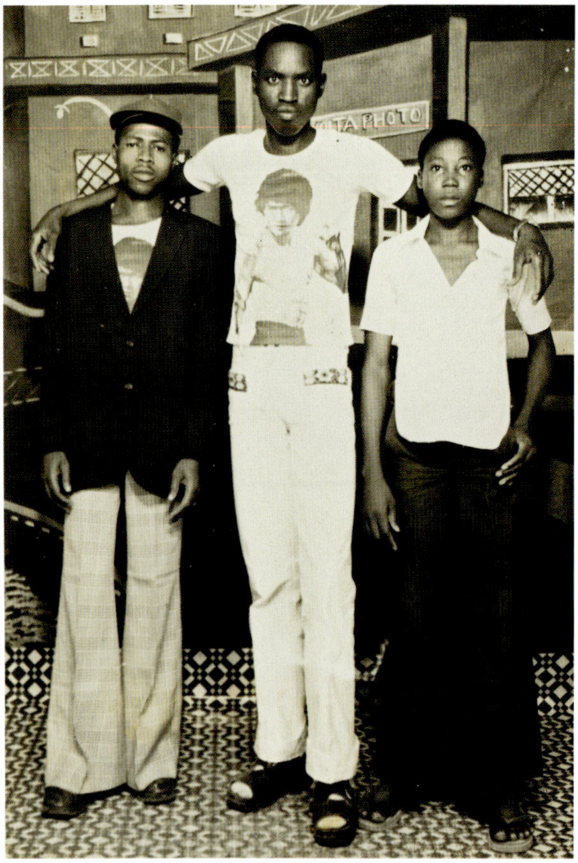

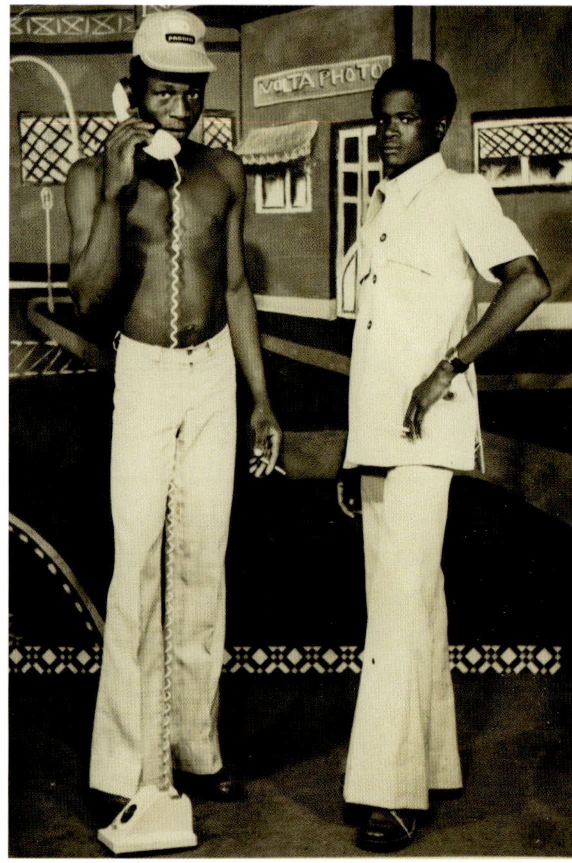

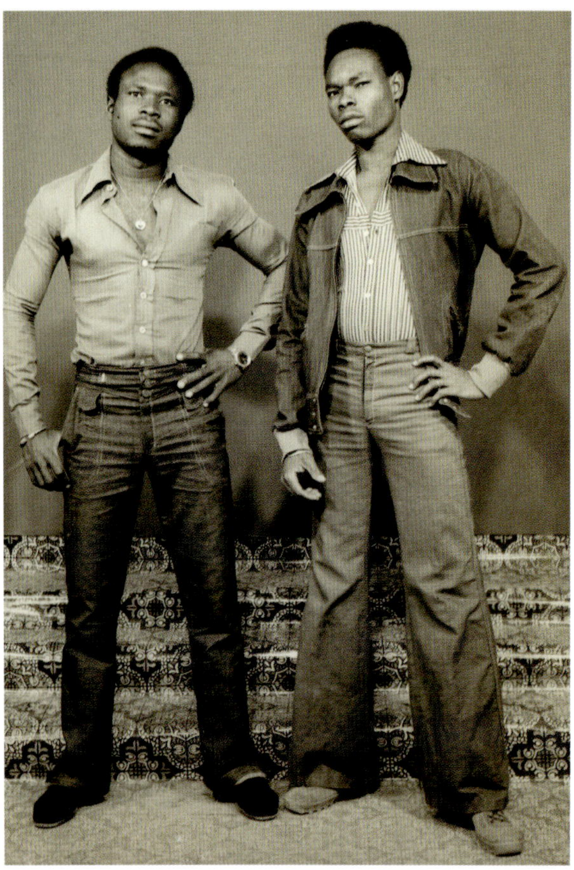

82–84 Untitled, 1965/75

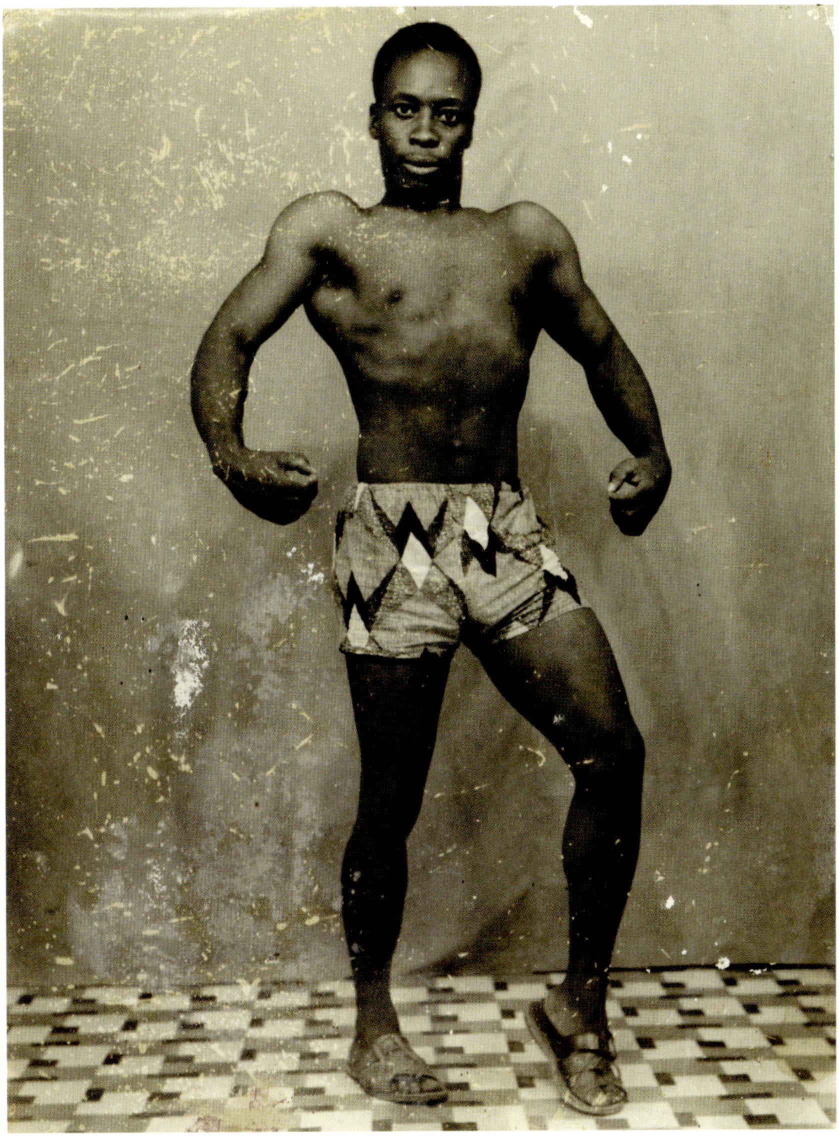

85 Self-portrait, 1960/65

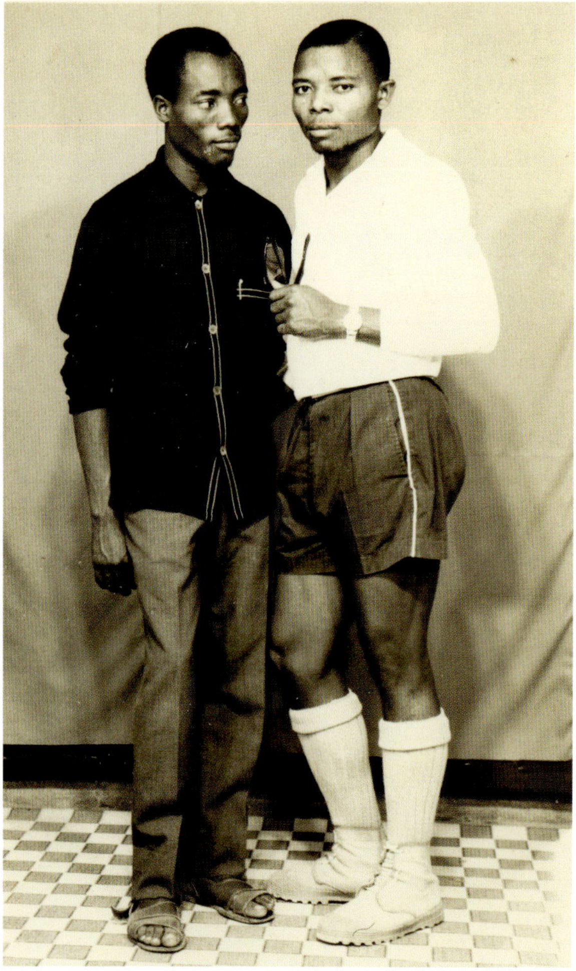

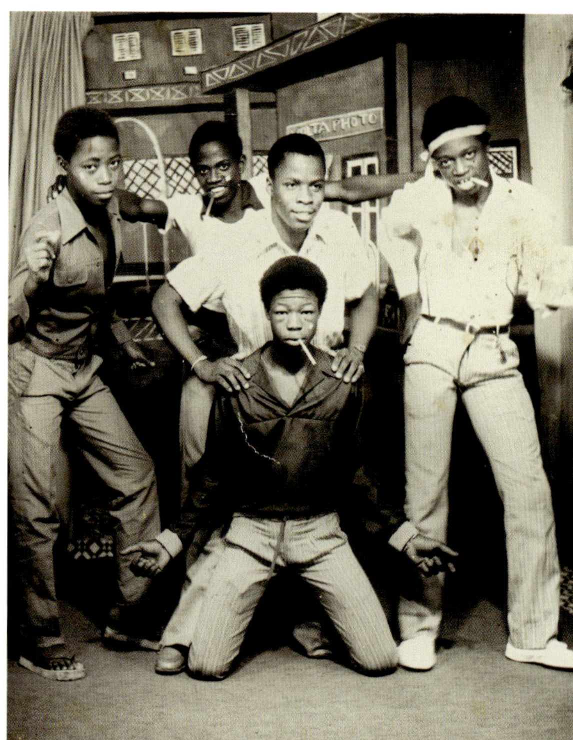

86 Untitled, 1970/80

87 Untitled, 1965/75

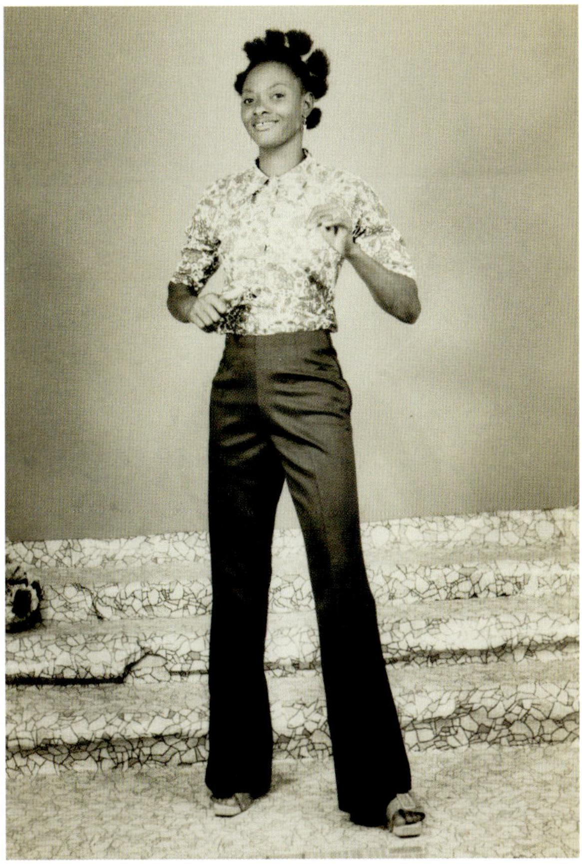

88 Untitled, 1965/75

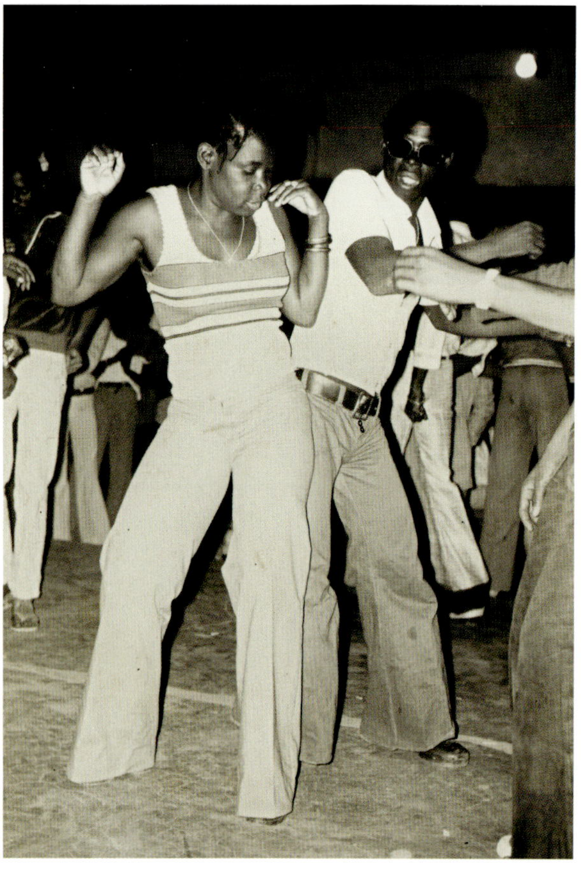

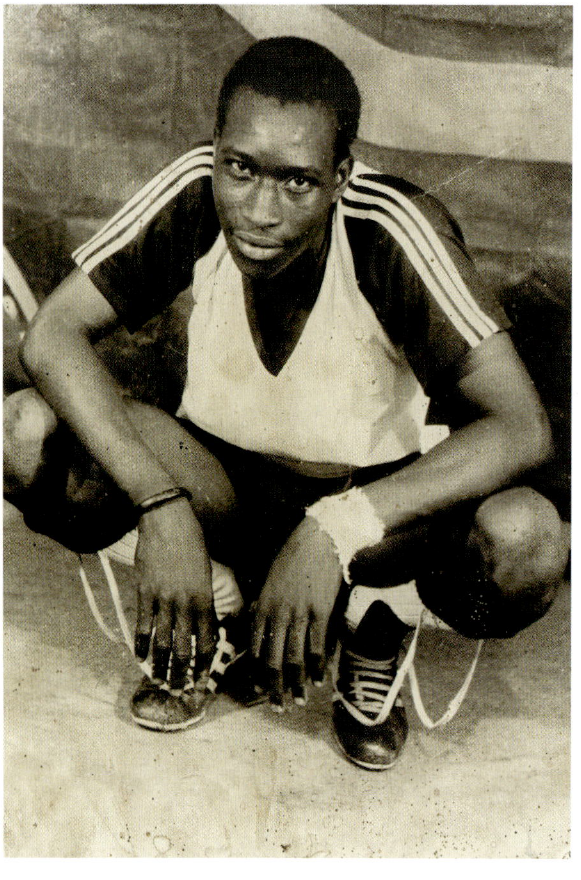

89 Untitled, 1970/80

90 Untitled, 1965/75

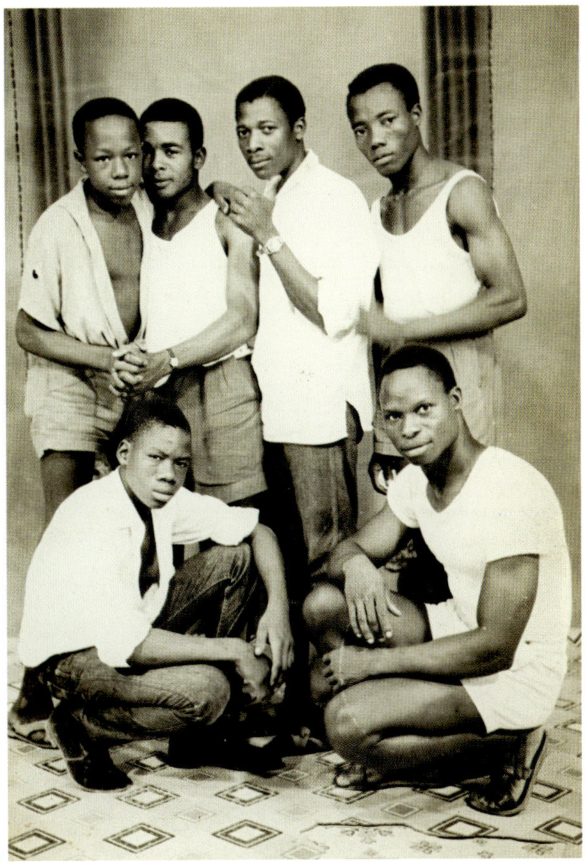

91 Untitled, 1965/75

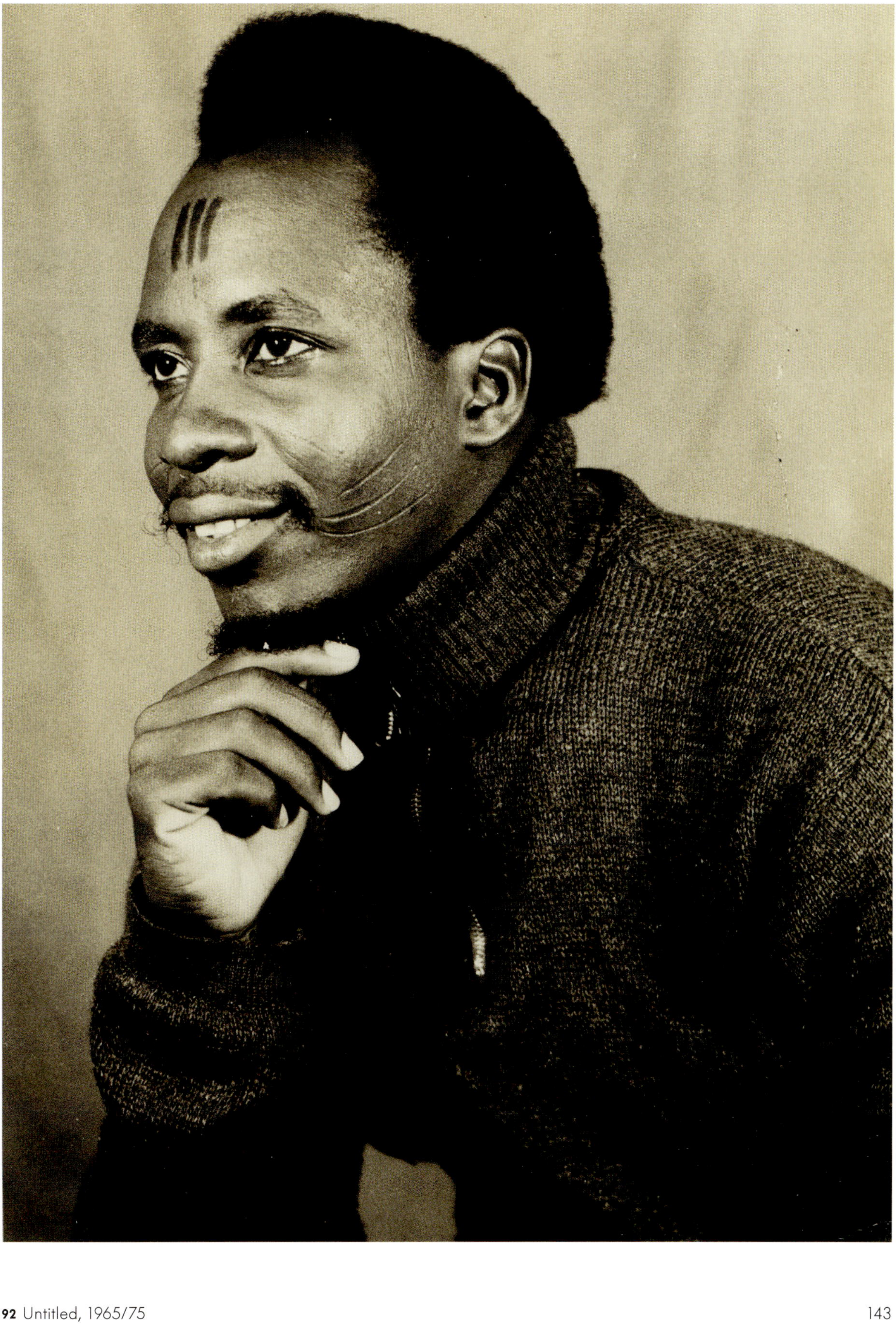

92 Untitled, 1965/75

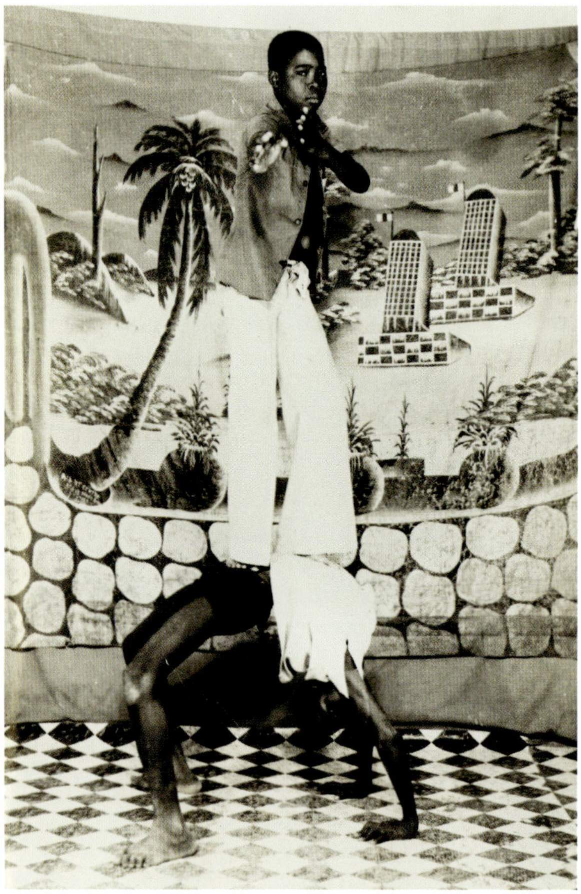

fig. 1 Untitled, 1965/75. 11.3 × 7.7 cm (image); 12.5 × 8.6 cm (paper). Private collection.

AMPLIFICATIONS: SANLÉ SORY'S GREAT MOVEMENTS BETWEEN PHOTOGRAPHY AND MUSIC

Antawan I. Byrd

A photograph by Sanlé Sory (fig. 2) shows a gushing young Fula man who has climbed on top of a Honda motorbike, removed his sunglasses, and steadied himself into a grand pose before the photographer and his medium-format camera. An audience of giddy kids enters this urban dirt-road scene on the left, while an elder stands captivated at the right of the frame. They bear witness to the man's performance and to the making of the photograph. If the attention of these onlookers, combined with the man's central and heightened placement within the image, were not enough to secure his status as its chief subject, his index finger points upward against a cloudless expanse of sky, dispelling any ambiguity. Through this most minor of gestures, he communicates that universal symbol of triumph and singularity known as "number one."

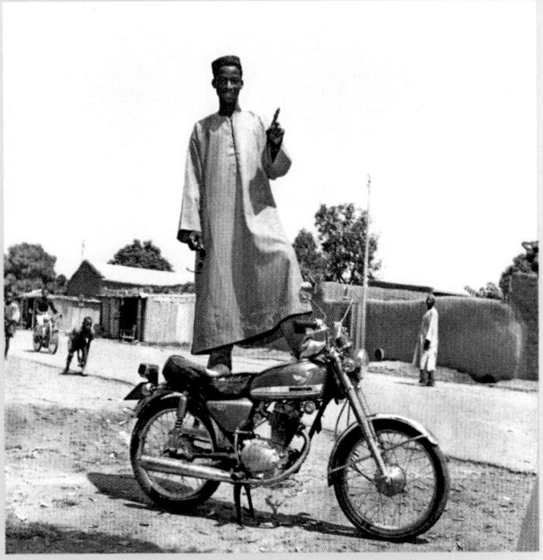

fig. 2 Untitled, 1965/75. Illustration from 6×6 cm negative. Courtesy Florent Mazzoleni

The upraised finger, a signifier of the subject's heightened stature, can serve as a metonymic indicator of Sory's practice and achievements as well; it symbolizes his knack for emboldening his portrait clients and the prominence he acquired as Bobo-Dioulasso's premier commercial photographer. Sory fulfilled his patrons' modest or outsized desires to see themselves from individuated perspectives, in ways that both registered and exceeded the ordinary. This assertion resonates in a picture (fig. 1), taken several years before the one of the man atop the motorcycle, which shows two Bobo kids, one standing on the other and enacting a karate move. The image derives its charm from the fantastic way the topmost boy's ascent eclipses the palm trees and buildings portrayed on the backdrop behind him.

The suggestions of scale and magnitude in these two works coalesce in a word: *amplification*. In a fundamental sense, the term describes abundance and the effort to make something more marked through enlargement, increase in volume, or the addition of details. Over the four principal decades of Sory's practice, from the 1960s through the 1990s (he continues to work

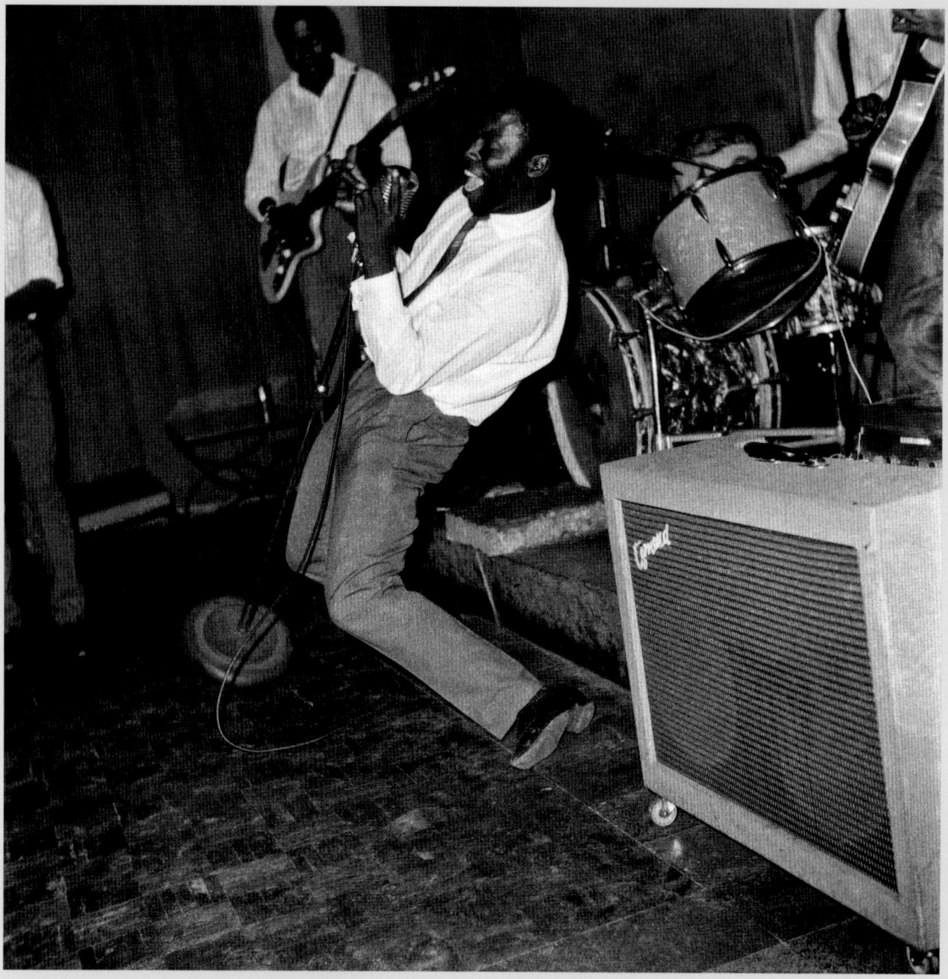

fig. 3 Jean Depara (Congolese, born Angola, 1928–1997). Untitled *(Kinshasa, between 1955–1965).* Courtesy Revue Noire Paris

somewhat today), ideas of amplification came to signify the varying scales at which the artist elaborated conventional definitions of studio practice. In addition to shuttling consistently between the studio and other urban spaces such as the street and the dance hall, he also practiced heavily in rural contexts. As part of its value in charting the experiences and social realities of postcolonial life in Upper Volta, Sory's archive—apparently more than eighty thousand surviving negatives and prints—magnifies other histories that developed in tandem with his image-making.[1] In particular, he combined his enthusiasm for photography with an intense love of music, and in so doing amplified the social value and aesthetic operations of both these popular technologies. The photographer chronicled Bobo youth and their insatiate appetite for the rhythms of Afro-Cuban, Afrobeat, soul, and rock music. He also fed it by supplying music at the dance parties

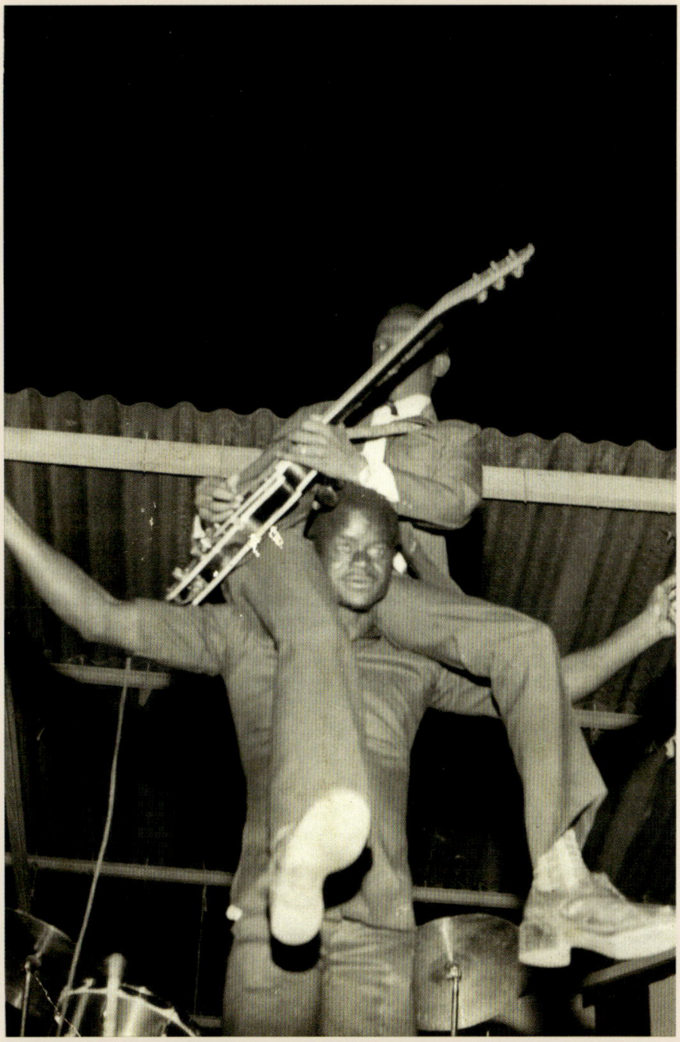

fig. 4 Tiamodjan, the lead guitarist for Echo del Africa Nacional, 1965/75
11.4 × 7.4 cm (image); 12.5 × 8.5 cm (paper).
The Art Institute of Chicago, promised gift of Ralph and Nancy Segall, 240656

he organized and emceed—parties that became a pretext for portrait commissions—and by collaborating on album-cover photography that, in turn, intensified the scale of reproduction, circulation, and exchangeability of his photographs in ways that continue through the present day.

Broad Movements

During the 1960s, the mass attainment of independence by nations across the African continent produced a manifest optimism: nation building, economic growth and upward mobility, rapid rural-urban migration, and increased investment in modern media infrastructures. Such optimism was tempered in Upper Volta by the dictatorial governance of the country's inaugural president, Maurice Yaméogo (1960–66), whose administration introduced inequitable economic policies, bureaucratic mismanagement, and assaults on traditional leadership.[2] Yet like many leaders, Yaméogo recognized the potential of radio broadcasting in communicating national political developments. In 1960, the year Sory opened his first studio, transmitters at Radio Haute Volta began broadcasting governmental policy, educational programs, and entertainment in multiple languages.[3] Two years later, a second station was launched in Bobo, followed by subsequent improvements to radio infrastructure in rural regions. The arrival of national radio brought ready and up-to-date access to the nation's political affairs; it also delivered a stream of foreign musical styles that, when combined with the increased availability of music on vinyl records and live performances, led to the birth of a modern listening public.[4]

If tuning into broadcasts or consuming vinyl records could shape Bobo listeners' worldview, then photography redoubled this experience, as subjects commissioned photographs that highlighted their participation in the growing commodity culture of popular music. A photograph by Sory from the early seventies (plate 61) shows a young man sporting sunglasses and wearing a mass-produced T-shirt emblazoned with dancing figures beneath text that reads, "SHAKARA," a reference to "Shakara Oloje," the 1972 hit by the Nigerian musician Fela Kuti. The sarcastic song, which lambastes braggarts and pretentiousness, became a nearly instant hit with listeners across West Africa. Sory had already established a reputation as a skilled and trustworthy portraitist, and perhaps from the later 1960s he had moved beyond the studio, accepting invitations to photograph at private "surprise parties" or chasing Bobo youth at area dance halls. He began to fulfill these commissions while he was in his early twenties and thus the same age as his customers. In her writing on the early work of famed Malian photographer Malick Sidibé (1936–2016), Candace Keller notes, "At parties, dances, and nightclubs, young people patronize photographers of their own generation, correctly presuming that their peers would be more sympathetic to their interests."[5]

Although Sidibé was a near contemporary of Sory's, the Malian photographer was a decade older and accordingly dispatched his younger assistants to photograph the Bamakois nightlife in addition to documenting it himself.[6] By contrast, Sory's assistants—Sibiri Ouattara and Mamoudou Bitenga, among others—did not attend parties on behalf of Volta Photo. Sory left them to run his studio while he set it in motion, traveling with camera and flash to fulfill commissions around town. It appears that Sory had become such a constant presence at music venues and nightly social events that, even as he aged, his relationship to them remained constant. A photograph from around the late 1970s (plate 72) captures a couple dancing amid other animated bodies at a surprise party. Their ebullient attention appears to be as much a response to the camera as it is to the man behind the lens. Becoming a party staple allowed Sory to reinforce his self-image as a man of the people rather than an impersonal photographer-for-hire. It also constituted an important form of cultural research and discovery, as he was able to stay au courant with Bobo's expansive and ever-changing music scene while also surveying the latest trends in fashion and dance—knowledge that came in handy during his own organization of parties outside the city.

One photographer with whom Sory shares a great deal is the Angolan-born, Congolese Jean Depara (1928–1997). In 1954 Depara opened his studio, Jean Whiskey Depara, on Kato Street in Kinshasa (then Leopoldville); this was a moment when the city held as many as three hundred nightclubs.[7] Depara likewise reveled in nightlife and was a pervasive presence on the city's social scene, snapping photographs of stylish subjects at popular nightspots such as Afro Negro and the Showboat. His images captured the attention of famed musician François Luambo Makiadi (known simply as Franco), the talented guitarist and vocalist of the pioneering band OK Jazz. "One evening," writes art historian Carole Naggar," passing 54 Kato Street, Franco saw Depara's photographs in his studio windows and invited the photographer to come hear him play. This encounter launched Depara's career: he became the popular musician's personal photographer; his images were featured on Franco's album covers and posters for his concerts."[8] This collaboration began at or soon after OK Jazz's 1956 public debut, and Depara's photographs (see fig. 3) conveyed the physicality and dynamic energy of their early live performances as well as the frenetic rhythms of their music. Nearly a decade later, Sory began his intense collaboration with bands in Bobo, frequenting the city's clubs to capture crowds dancing to performances by Volta Jazz, Echo Del Africa Nacional, and Dafra Star, among other bands. Although the music scene in Bobo was not saturated like that of Kinshasa, Sory's images suggest a similar vitality. His off-kilter photograph of members of Echo Del Africa Nacional (fig. 4), for instance, refracts the irrepressible energy and high-octane acrobatics that local bands delivered to their enthusiastic audiences.

Depara's collaboration with OK Jazz began, according to Naggar, with an invitation from Franco. This suggests that the handsome musician recognized that employing a photographer would help his commercial success. The collaborations between Volta Photo and Volta Jazz seem to have been motivated less by thoughts of personal publicity than a shared investment in national pride. Although Sory's familial connection to the band—it was founded in 1964 by his cousin and patron Idrissa Koné—certainly motivated his enduring relationship, the shared use of the country's name points to patriotism as the point of intersection between photography and

music. Patriotism and its amplification: throughout the 1960s and 1970s, photographs, as they are today, were often directly responsible for boosting the international visibility of a local music scene. In 1977 a music enthusiast from Bobo, Zongo Adrien Philippe, wrote to the popular Paris-based magazine *AfroMusic* : "I am a young twenty-five year-old Voltaic and big fan of your magazine. However, I would like to know why, since the advent of your journal, you've remained uninterested in Voltaic music?"
The editors' response indicated that they had little information to go on, and by way of redress they encouraged Philippe to send an article along with "two good black-and-white photos" for future publication.[9] Words alone cannot suffice.

Larger Scale

Around 1965 the West Indian composer Hervé Victor Lejuste founded the small recording company Production Lejuste G.V. (L.G.V.D) in Bangui, Central African Republic.[10] Perhaps to escape the political upheavals of Bangui's 1966–67 military coup, he relocated the company in 1967 to Abidjan, the cultural and economic capital of Ivory Coast. Soon after relocating, Lejuste traveled to Bobo and began a series of recording sessions with Volta Jazz that drew on their early repertoire of Afro-Cuban rhythms and structures with variations on the Congolese rumba. These recordings were issued in the early '70s as 45-rpm singles under the company's imprint, Disques France-Afrique (DFA). The production of these singles played a seminal role in bolstering local and regional popularity for Volta Jazz, and provided a new outlet for Sory to elaborate his collaboration with the band by creating portraits for their covers.

DFA had already honed its understanding of modern advertising by establishing a recognizable aesthetic for its entire discography. Black-and-white photographs of the musicians were printed edge to edge, and textual metadata appeared on monochromatic bands of color along a cover's top or right side. The label's elephant logo was featured alongside the band's name, song titles, catalogue numbers, and often the names of musical genres and lead performers. The graphic consistency of DFA record covers appears to reflect the mid-century boom in the mass production of consumer goods. Design consistency also streamlined the manufacturing process, perhaps expediting record releases. And it certainly established a visual identity that helped DFA compete in record stores with the dizzying array of imports from around the continent or overseas.

The photographs themselves varied widely in formal execution. One sleeve for a Bangui ensemble, Orchestre Centrafrican-Jazz, shows only the band's founder and guitarist Prosper Mayélé, who embodies the hip persona of a

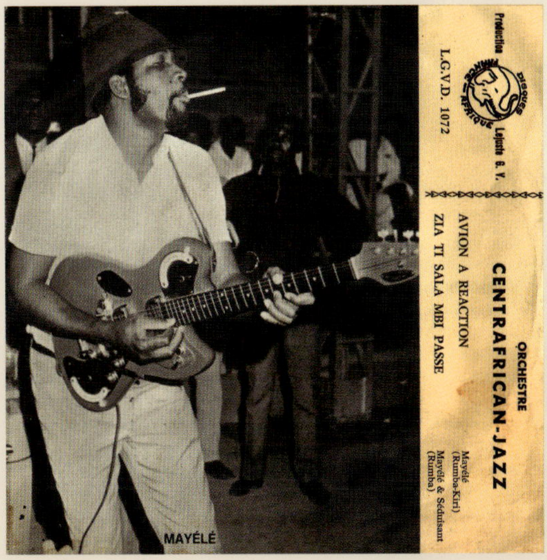

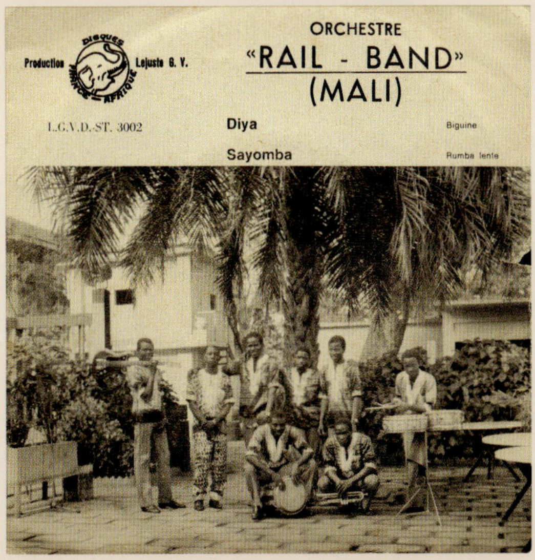

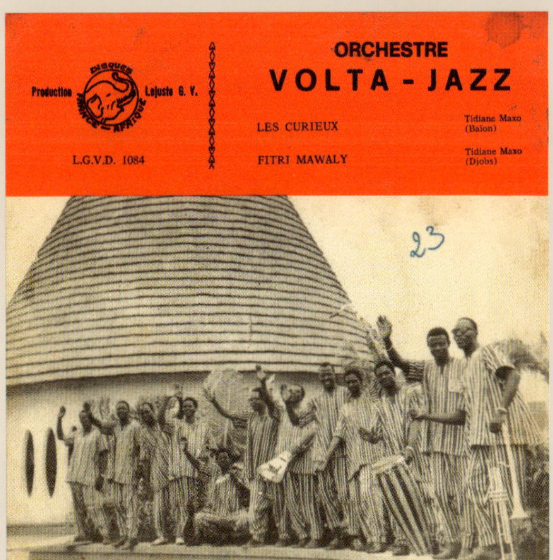

fig. 5 Disques France-Afrique / L.G.V.D. Productions. Orchestre Centrafrican-Jazz 45-rpm record sleeve. Photographer unknown, 1968/75. 18 × 18 cm. Courtesy Celine Bourdon-Ngo

fig. 6 Disques France-Afrique / L.G.V.D. Productions. Orchestre Rail-Band Mali 45-rpm record sleeve. Photographer unknown, 1968/75. 18 × 18 cm. Courtesy Florent Mazzoleni

fig. 7 Disques France-Afrique / L.G.V.D. Productions. Volta Jazz 45-rpm record sleeve. Photographer unknown, 1968/75. 18 × 18 cm. Courtesy Florent Mazzoleni

rock star, strumming an electric guitar with a cigarette at his lip (fig. 5). By contrast, a cover picture of the Malian group Rail Band de Bamako (fig. 6) reflects nationalist preferences for an aesthetic rooted in heritage and collectivity; the ensemble appears in matching outfits inspired by traditional dress. This heterogeneous aesthetic demonstrates efforts to interpellate different musical genres visually in ways that were responsive to prevailing sociocultural values; these interpellations reflected as well negotiated tastes between musicians and the ostensibly local photographers with whom they collaborated. In reconciling these divergent interests with the album cover's fundamental role as a material support and advertising vehicle for music, DFA regimented the interplay between image, text, and graphic design.

According to Lejuste catalogue numbers, printed sequentially on all his albums, the first wave of 45s that DFA released with Volta Jazz came in the early 1970s.[11] These sleeves show the band in front of traditional Burkinabé architectural structures, among other sites (see fig. 7). The band appears wearing striped and hand-woven cotton garments known in Dioula as *faso dan fani*, or "woven cloth of the homeland."[12] Taken by an unknown photographer, these covers, like the one by Rail Band, situated an image of Volta Jazz within a postcolonial framework of national identity and cultural pride, according to the communications logic analyzed by historian Michael Jarrett: "Record covers mirror back our perceptions of particular types of music, perceptions that are to a great extent visually and not musically determined."[13] The next set of Volta Jazz records released by DFA, however, began with a milestone—the label's one-hundredth album—and marked a sea change: the introduction of color photography, of Sory as album-cover photographer, and of European-style outfits for the band. Sory was apparently supplied with a single twelve-exposure roll of color film and tasked with producing a dozen images of the band in one day. He photographed the orchestra with their manager, Koné, who selected popular cultural locations in Bobo, such as the lush gardens and municipal bandstand adjacent to the zoo, and the city's Théâtre de l'Amitié. The film was sent back to Abidjan for processing, after which each image appeared on a separate album (see plate 78). The transition to color photography, whether the decision of Koné or Lejuste, imbued the band with a modern sensibility that cast the city of Bobo in a vibrant and picturesque light. This shift in representation may correspond to internal negotiations between Koné and Volta Jazz, concerned to transpose traditional musical influences into a contemporary repertoire with appeal for a youthful audience whose ears were increasingly turning toward soul and rock music.

Sory is explicit that he only took the photographs for these covers. Yet we should not dismiss his contribution on that account. This new collaboration furthered Sory's practice of fulfilling portrait commissions through negotiation with his customers. But the covers amplified that exercise in collaboration inasmuch as Sory was now operating within a culture industry and thus on a larger scale of production. The photographer-client dynamic was local but also transnational, with a record company based in Abidjan, a pressing plant in Italy, and potential audiences across Africa and elsewhere. That it was not deemed necessary for Sory to oversee any aspect of printing or design is already indicative of this shift in scale, for it illustrates how his creative contribution was subordinated to the broader aesthetic-commercial function imputed to photography as a vehicle of advertising. As such, one can argue that the shift to color resulted not only in a more modern approach to Volta Jazz's visual aesthetic, but, too, a more modern or industrialized scale of production for Sory. Indeed, although the number of records DFA produced is unknown, that these albums continue to circulate today alongside a recently manufactured box set of Voltaic music bearing Sory's photographs reaffirms this shift in scale while simultaneously underscoring the value of his contributions to Voltaic music.

Amped Up

For more than twenty years beginning in the early 1970s, Sory photographed his poor and working-class compatriots while emceeing parties for them on weekend nights in the floodplains of the Kou Valley, a regional hub of fisheries, rice paddies, and cotton farms about fifteen miles northwest of Bobo. He transported cameras, lighting equipment, loudspeakers, cassettes, and reproduction technologies in a French Citroën utility vehicle (see fig. 8 and plate 93). This van, which Citroën launched in Belgium in 1955, was aptly dubbed "La Week-End" and was marketed to consumers as a vehicle with "various possibilities of use" because of its "large side windows, [which] provide total visibility to travelers from the rear and front seats."[14] Sory exploited the conjunction of versatility and visibility by outfitting the vehicle with two hand-painted rectangular signs that read "VOLTA PHOTO" and by installing, in the Citroën's side windows, display boards on which he mounted an array of gelatin silver prints.

The patchwork of photographs served to demonstrate his formal and commercial achievements while also providing a menu of poses for potential patrons. Through this branding and mobility, Sory sought to increase his volume of clientele, especially in light of growing competition among photographers in Bobo. Writing on the history of portrait photography in Africa, art historian John Peffer reminds us that "even though the term 'studio' seems to imply a singular idea of place, it could also be understood to stand for a tension between mobility and emplacement, in a dual sense: photographers often moved from place to place and identities were actively created via images."[15] Indeed, through his commercial ambitions, Sory amplified the conception of the photography studio in the Hauts-Bassins region of Burkina Faso during the years of his practice.[16] For the artist and his patrons, the evolving Volta Photo came to represent an elastic enterprise whose domains of operation stretched from a home base in Farakan to nightclubs, parties, villages, and the city of Bobo with its streets, marketplaces, and other landmarks. Producing photographs in each of these contexts (and at times simultaneously across them with the aid of his assistants), Sory made the social continuity between these spaces not simply visible, but more markedly so. The "bush parties," as he calls them, helped not a little in this effort.

Sory describes these parties as follows: "I would drive down to some remote village in the bush, and I would set up a player, a few records, some loudspeakers, and a few lights and get the party going. We started

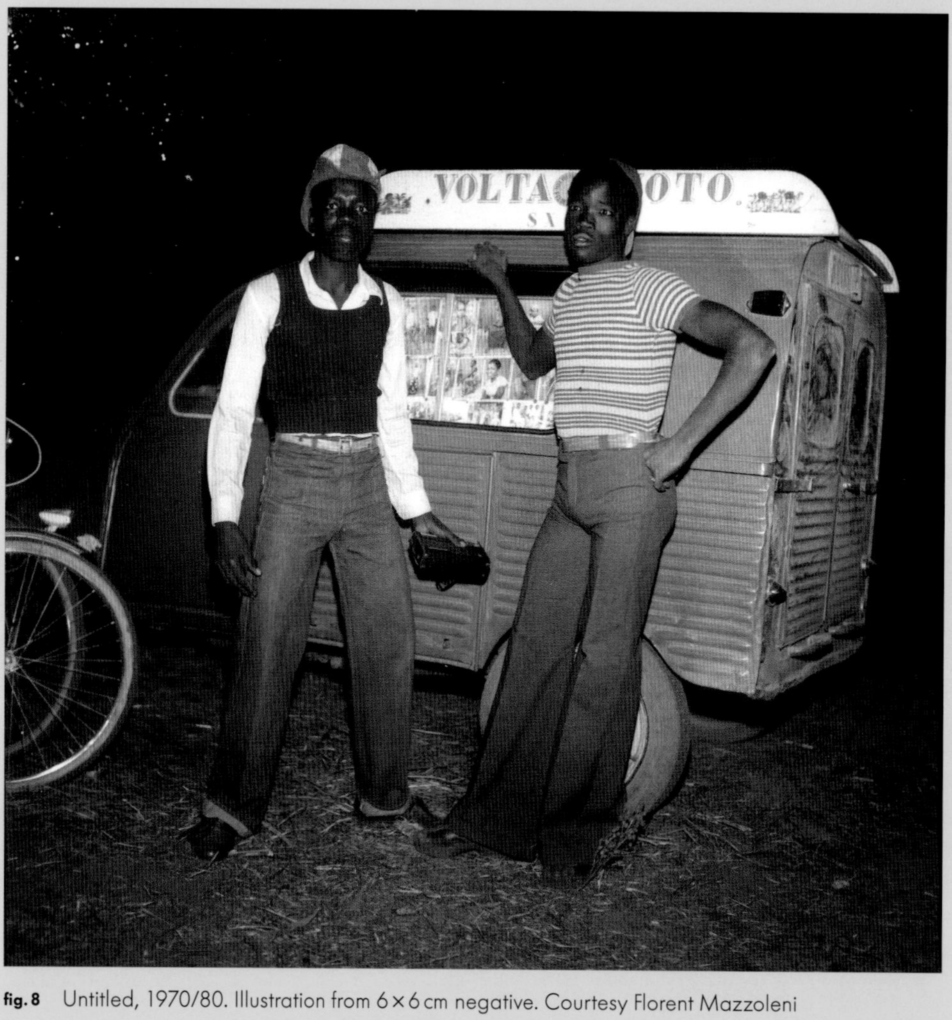

fig. 8 Untitled, 1970/80. Illustration from 6×6 cm negative. Courtesy Florent Mazzoleni

around 8:00 p.m. and people would tell me, 'Sory, you need to set the place on fire! It would go until 5:00 a.m.'"[17] Sory would often travel with friends—record shop owners and technicians from Bobo—who assisted the artist in amplifying music from cassettes that held jazz, rumba, highlife, and Afrobeat songs. The music enlivened those in attendance, while the loudspeakers carried sounds throughout the villages in ways that called attention to the soirées and summoned additional patrons. In expanding the audience of listeners to those beyond the parties, Sory was, in a sense, participating in broader sonic initiatives at the state level premised on bolstering continuity between the urban and the rural. In 1969, for example, the Voltaic government established Radio Rurale, a broadcasting station that included a network of radio clubs, mobile studio teams, and schemes for distributing portable radio sets to villages.[18] The station ran programs in multiple languages on health, popular music, cultural heritage, and agriculture, as well as other programs that strengthened links between city inhabitants and their rural counterparts by discussing sociocultural, political, and infrastructural changes underway across these spaces. Sory's travels to the village can thus be seen as continuous with dynamics spurred by the movement of people and things between rural and urban contexts, which is to say that these spaces were neither homogenous nor cut off from each other.

Sory's Multiblitz camera flash also bolstered his efforts to set the nights ablaze. "It's the flash," he remarks elsewhere in these pages, "that tells you the party's started." The photographer used the flash to throw bursts of artificial light on patrons not only as they entered the parties, but also throughout the night. With camera in hand, Sory often simulated the act of taking photographs by triggering the Multiblitz in order to keep his patrons animated. He knew that the attendees would get amped by the mere possibility of having their nights of dancing captured and returned to them in the form of illumined silver gelatin prints. Sory uses the expression "peep, peep, peep" to describe his near-stroboscopic delivery of light. If the word *peep* conjures the intimate, Sory's expression might equally indicate how the intense light of the flash rendered quasi-private moments hypervisible. The flash in one Kou photograph p. 102) spotlights a couple dancing in an embrace among other revelers inside a shanty. The couple acknowledges Sory but appears unfazed by his presence—being photographed was perhaps not an exception but an expectation.

Sory's clients at these parties often paid him in advance, by the roll, to capture them in candid fashion. This meant eschewing just-so compositions in favor of spur-of-the-moment shots that underscored the immediacy of dancing, social interactions, and the overall joie de vivre of the night. In this sense, the brightness of the flash spotlighted the very experience of consumption and made commissioning photographs all the more conspicuous. In her writing on the aesthetics of light in postcolonial Bahamian society, art historian Krista Thompson has noted that the concept of "bling," associated with performances and consumption practices in hip-hop culture, "characterizes both the threshold of absolute visibility and utter blindness." While the aesthetics of bling "seem on their surface to be about the production of glaring visibility, they simultaneously call attention, implicitly, to that which is rendered invisible at the moment it is seen."[19] One could extend Thompson's observations to say that, beyond its role as catalyst within the village milieu, the flash highlights the relative invisibility of rural lifeworlds in midcentury African studio photography, which was overwhelmingly concentrated on urban gatherings. As such, Sory's consistent engagements in the Kou Valley, his movement between the rural and the urban, marks one of his work's more distinguishing contributions to photography's postcolonial history in Africa.[20]

Another image taken in Kou (fig. 8) shows two young people illuminated by Sory's flash, one holding a radio in his hand; they pose before the window display board of the Volta Photo van as if to assign the vehicle the status of a backdrop. This and other such images in Sory's archives represent a recursive form of display. The viewer witnesses both the present moment of those being photographed and the framing of this moment against the photographer's past achievements, all taken from his Bobo studio. No set of Sory's pictures is more suggestive of the ways in which ideas of amplification characterized his practice, for they convolve past and present, singularity and multiplicity, rural and urban, mobility and emplacement, sound and image, all informed by the scale and intensity with which Sory shaped postcolonial social and cultural changes in and beyond Bobo. Standing before the display board of photographs with a radio between them, the subjects in this photograph are framed as consumers of a modern popular culture saturated by the reproduction of sound and photographic images alike, and as coproducers within this culture, assuming that they commissioned the picture. This reminds us that Sory's practices of amplification were driven not only by his entrepreneurial spirit and love of sound and image, but also by his customers' investment in seeing themselves from amplified perspectives.

I'm incredibly grateful to Matthew Witkovsky and Florent Mazzoleni for their insightful feedback on earlier drafts of this essay. For permission to reproduce particular images with this text, I thank Jean-Loup Pivin and Pascal Martin Saint Léon of Revue Noire Paris, Celine Bourdon-Ngo, and Florent Mazzoleni.

1 This figure was supplied by Florent Mazzoleni. The precise number of negatives Sory produced over his principal career is difficult to determine. The photographer destroyed a portion of his archive in the early 1990s as his studio work declined, because he felt these negatives were no longer of interest to his customers. The destruction of archives by West African studio photographers active during the second half of the 20th century is not uncommon and can be partly linked to the arrival of color photography in the 1980s and the concomitant rise of industrial-scale laboratories, which prompted the closure of many black-and-white studios in the region.

2 Ernest Harsch, *Burkina Faso: A History of Power, Protest, and Revolution* (London: Zed Books, 2017), 22-26.

3 Radio Haute-Volta was established by decree on October 25, 1959, and was on air with the implementation of independence on August 5, 1960. See Richard Fardon and Graham Furniss, *African Broadcast Cultures: Radio in Transition* (Oxford: James Currey, 2000), 84–85.

4 Auguste F. Kaboret and Oger Kabore, *Histoire de la musique moderne du Burkina Faso: Genèse, évolution et perspectives* (Ouagadougou: EDIPAP International, 2004), 37.

5 Candace M. Keller, "Framed and Hidden Histories: West African Photography from Local to Global Contexts" *African Arts* 47, 4 (2014): 39.

6 Ibid., 39-44; see also Malick Sidibé, "Studio Malick" in André Magnin and Brigitte Ollier, *Malick Sidibé: Mali Twist* (Paris: Xavier Barral Publisher, 2017), 115–6.

7 Gary Stewart, *Rumba on the River: A History of the Popular Music of the Two Congos* (London: Verso, 2003), 74.

8 Carole Naggar, "Jean Depara: Night and Day in Kinshasa," *Aperture* No. 207 (Summer 2012): 28-31; see also Pascal Martin Saint Leon and Jean Loup Pivin, *Jean Depara: Kinshasa, Night and Day, 1951–1975* (Paris: Revue noire, 2011).

9 Zongo Adrien Philippe, "Et la musique voltaique," *AfroMusic* 19 (1977): 4. *AfroMusic* magazine was founded in Paris by the pioneering Cameroonian musician Manu Dibango (b. 1933) in 1976 and ceased publication in 1978. The publication's coverage focused on musical developments in Africa and throughout the diaspora, and targeted Francophone audiences in Africa.

10 Although not much on Lejuste or the history of his record company has been committed to print, some discussion appears in Florent Mazzoleni, *Burkina Faso: Musiques Modernes Voltaïques* (Bordeaux: Castor Astral, 2011), 25–27.

11 Here I draw from the Lejuste discography found on the website *Radio Africa*, which was compiled by Geoff Bale, Graeme Counsel, and other contributors; see: radioafrica.com.au/ Discographies/ LGVD.html.

12 Lawrence Rupley, Lamissa Bangali, and Boureima Diamitani, *Historical Dictionary of Burkina Faso* (Lanham, MD: Scarecrow Press, 2013), 76.

13 Michael Jarrett, *Drifting on a Read: Jazz As a Model for Writing*, (Albany, NY: State University of New York Press, 1999), 199. The use of music and visual imagery to bolster national cultural policies was especially pronounced in Guinea, where beginning in the 1960s president Sékou Touré offered robust support of national bands through the state-run label Editions Syliphone Conakry. Between 1967 and 1983 this label released more than 150 recordings with bands such as Bembeya Jazz, Orchestre de la Paillotte, and Orchestre du Jardin de Guinée. On this, see Maja Kominko, *From Dust to Digital: Ten Years of the Endangered Archives Programme* (Cambridge: Open Book Publishers, 2015), 555–7.

14 See citroenet.org.uk/ foreign/ belgium/ belgium2.html.

15 John Peffer, "Introduction," in John Peffer and Elisabeth L. Cameron, *Portraiture and Photography in Africa* (Bloomington, Indiana: Indiana University Press, 2013), 8.

16 According to Sory, he was the only photographer in the Hauts-Bassins region who developed an expansive model of studio practice by working between the urban and rural contexts.

17 Sory Sanlé, *Sory Sanlé: Volta Photo 1965-85* (London: Reel Art Press / Morton-Hill, 2017), 79.

18 Philippe Essomba, "Radio rurale voltaïque: 1,300 villages," *Bingo* 314 (March 1979): 29–30.

19 Krista Thompson, *Shine: The Visual Economy of Light in African Diasporic Aesthetic Practice* (Durham, NC: Duke University Press, 2015), 198–9.

20 On this point, Sory's Kou photographs establish parallels with the Togolese photographer Cornélius Augustt Azaglo (1924–2001) who, like Sory, apprenticed in Bobo-Dioulasso with an itinerant Ghanaian photographer in the 1950s. Azaglo went on to establish Studio du Nord in the small Ivorian town of Korhogo and traveled throughout the region producing ID portraits of village farmers. In 1963 the Senegalese photographer Oumar Ly (1943–2016) opened Studio Thioffy in the northern town of Podor on the Senegal River. In addition to making studio portraits of subjects posing with record sleeves and modern commodity objects, Ly also traveled to nearby villages to fulfill portrait commissions. See Jean-Christophe Deberre et. al., *Cornélius Yao Augustt Azaglo: Photographies, Côte D'Ivoire, 1950–1975* (Paris: Revue Noire, 1996); and Frédérique Chapuis and Florence Pacaud, *Oumar Ly: Portraits de Brousse Podor 1963/1978* (Trézélan: Filigranes, 2009).

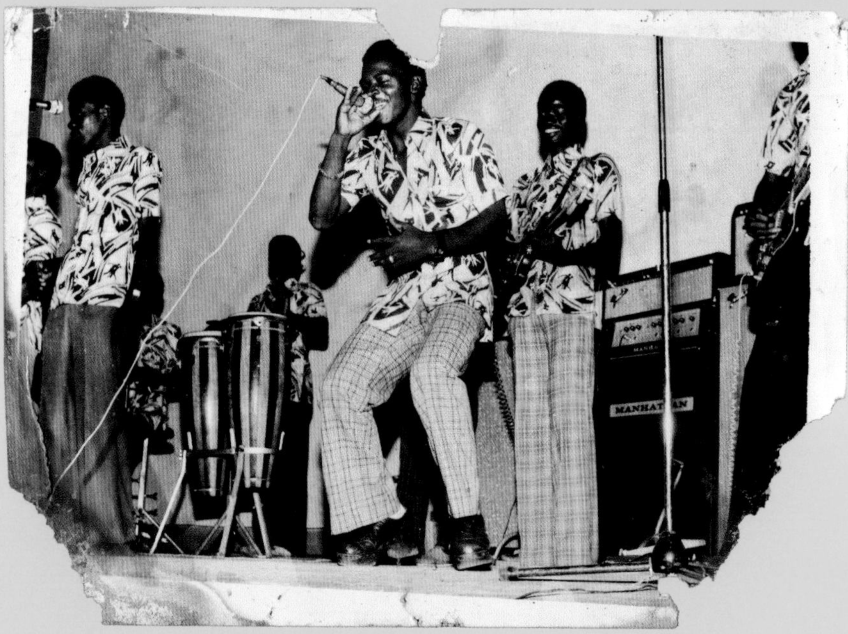

fig. 1 Untitled, 1965/75. 11.4 × 16.3 cm (image); 12.5 × 17.6 cm (paper). Private collection

MODERN TIMES IN UPPER VOLTA: VOLTA JAZZ AND THE BOBO MUSIC SCENE

Florent A. Mazzoleni

Upper Volta, an independent country since August 1960, had its name Africanized in 1984 under the rule of socialist revolutionary Thomas Sankara, becoming Burkina Faso, an expression in Moré and Dioula (the country's main languages) meaning "land of upstanding people."[1] The ideals embodied in Sankara's chosen name had arguably come to fruition two decades earlier in Voltaic music, which emerged in the 1960s as a force for genuine cultural revolution. Musical innovation at that time was centered in the southwestern city of Bobo-Dioulasso, a pluralistic, relatively prosperous hub of international exchange in an otherwise poor and isolated fledgling nation-state.

Predominantly Islamic, Bobo is nevertheless home to people of various religions as well as a number of entrepreneurial cultures, including Dioula traders, seminomadic Fula farmers, and Senufo and Bobo craftspeople. Cotton was developed into an industry in the 1920s, and a train line connecting Bobo to Abidjan, the capital of neighboring Ivory Coast, opened in 1934. Bamako and Kumasi, principal cities in Mali and Ghana, respectively, are not so distant. (The Voltaic capital, Ouagadougou, located 360 kilometers further north, lies at a greater remove from vibrant cities in countries that border Burkina Faso and never benefited from a railroad connection.) Colonists and other businesspeople from across French West Africa were drawn to Bobo by these possibilities.

Unsurprisingly, the city became the first in Upper Volta to host modern popular musicians. The first music group may have arisen in the 1930s within the Société Amicale de la Jeunesse Dorée (The Golden Youth Friendship Association), one of a very few local youth clubs. Bobo musicians played the French accordion to the rhythms of *goumbé* (a regional form of modern folk music) and to orchestrations involving a further mix of local and Western instruments, for example the Senufo balafon and the guitar. The French authorities moved to suppress *goumbé* and all music sung in local languages.[2] Partly to rival such attractions from below, by the mid-1940s a colonial orchestra, led by a French businessman, started to play in and around Bobo. One can imagine that the local youth, rather than simply resenting official music, may have looked on enviously at colonial ballroom dances.

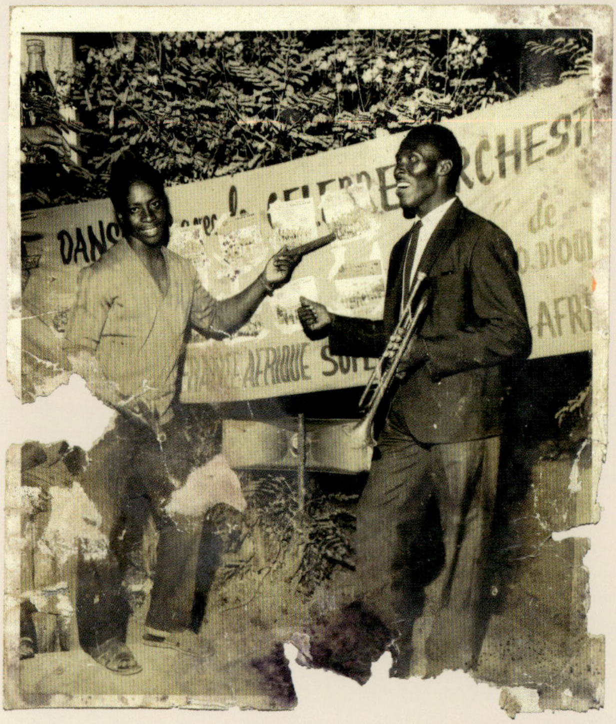

fig. 2 Sanlé Sory and Volta Jazz member Abou Traoré at a promotional event for the band, 1965/75. 13.2 × 11.7 cm (image); 14 × 12.5 cm (paper). Private collection

An Ivorian musician, Moussa Diomandé, was one of the first Africans to lead a professional band in Bobo, starting the Ivoiri Jazz Orchestra in 1945 with several young civil servants. Renamed Le Rossignol (Nightingale) two years later, the group was impressive for its size and composition, which included about one dozen musicians, among them a violin player. After colonial Upper Volta was restructured in 1947, the authorities, in a show of tolerance, supplied the band with some instruments and equipment. All the same, subtle anticolonial messages entered into the lyrics, as with the Kaira (enlightenment) movement that accompanied the proindependence political party RDA (Rassemblement Démocratique Africain, or African Democratic Assembly), founded in nearby French Sudan (Mali) in 1946.

Le Rossignol disbanded in 1956, having set a precedent for musical formations that enjoyed colonial support while resisting colonial power through their words. Newer bands, among them the Sahara Orchestra and Harmonie Voltaïque, continued in this vein; the governor of Upper Volta, Salvador Jean Etcheber, managed the first band, and musicians in both were drawn from the entire region as well as the ranks of French expatriates.

The reference points claimed by these groups laid an important basis for popular music in the coming independence years. Horns, guitars, drums,

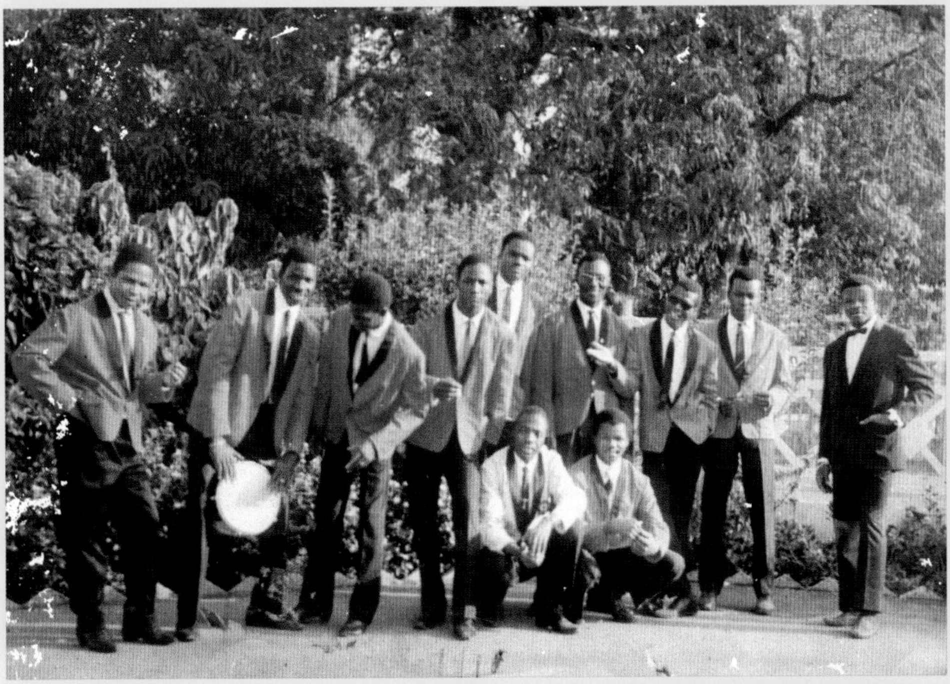

fig. 3 Volta Jazz, c. 1967. 11.5 × 16.5 cm (image); 12.4 × 17.4 cm (paper). Private collection

and accordions were the key instruments—all Western—but the sounds they played mixed military marches, French chansons, and the modern ballroom staples of waltz and foxtrot with Afro-Latin dances such as the cha-cha, bolero, and merengue. The bands also played in the open air, at events known as *bals poussière* (dust balls), indicating a growing popular interest in the music they brought to this desert region throughout the 1950s.

Popular music nevertheless shifted noticeably in the wake of independence, a development that galvanized French West Africa.[3] In Guinea, which declared independence on October 2, 1958, two days before the declaration of the French Fifth Republic, President Sékou Touré instated a politics of cultural authenticity that included music. Epic songs in the Mandingo tradition, declamatory griot singing, and balafon performances all received government funding and joined with Franco-European and Afro-Latin sounds or their domesticated versions, such as the Congolese rumba. This expanded mixture of sources inspired a new wave of orchestras in Bobo after Upper Volta gained independence in 1960 (fig. 1).

Throughout the 1960s and '70s, Upper Volta lacked a proper recording studio or record-pressing plant. Nevertheless, a great deal of popular music circulated in the country, on the radio (a national station was declared in late 1959 in Ouagadougou and began broadcasting in Bobo in 1962) and through sales (or later, pirated cassette copies) of imported 7-inch records and the occasional LP album. Studio facilities in Kumasi, Abidjan (Ivory Coast), Bamako, and Cotonou (Benin) became especially widely used. The very experience of traveling abroad exposed Voltaic artists further to other musical styles. In the early 1960s as well, renowned African orchestras—the Congolese outfits OK Jazz and Les Bantous de la Capitale, Ghanaian highlife bands such as E. T. Mensah's Tempos and the Kumasi Stargazers, and the Ivorian Eléphants Noirs de Bouaké—played to receptive audiences in Upper Volta.

By the mid-1970s, Bobo held around one dozen record stores, including Black Soul Music, Etablissements Antoine D'Albin, Carrefour du Disque, Music Hall, and Voix de l'Afrique. Musicians traveled to the city to spend time in these stores and at concerts, coming from Mali, the Ivory Coast, Senegal or Guinea. They made the journey in part to connect with a strong Mandingo heritage that had its beginnings in Bobo-Dioulasso.[4] The city had also shown strong if sporadic resistance to the French when they conquered territories of the former Malian empire in the 1890s. Malian orchestras in particular often visited the city, among them the star groups Rail Band de Bamako and Zani Diabaté's Super Djata Band.

Bobo bands played modern arrangements of established local melodies and rhythms, and they began to amplify their Western instruments—rented, for the most part, as the musicians could not afford to purchase them.[5] Two of the earliest Bobo orchestras were Dynamic Jazz (later called Echo del Africa Nacional) and Tropic Jazz.[6] Jean-Pierre Bordas, a real-estate entrepreneur and amateur guitar player, founded the latter group and paid for its instruments, earning the right to join the band members onstage. Tropic Jazz became a school for musicians, including Tidiane Coulibaly, the outstanding lead singer for Volta Jazz.

Bordas may have inspired Idrissa Koné, another Bobo entrepreneur, to found Volta Jazz—and he definitely gave Koné his musical instruments. Ambitious and well connected, Koné had served in the French colonial army and had used his pay, as well as his training, to open the first driving school in Bobo. A guitar enthusiast like Bordas and a small-time performer, Koné started Volta Jazz in 1964. It is possible that he took the name of his orchestra from Volta Photo, the portrait studio he had helped to start for his cousin Sanlé Sory four years earlier. Sory, as recounted elsewhere in this book, would become the group's chronicler and sometime publicity photographer (fig. 2).

Volta Jazz made an impression in concerts across the country and inspired the formation of further bands in several larger cities. They brought an emphasis on Mandingo songs and Afro-Cuban structures, mixed with Bobolais rhythms and languages. Koné and his musicians aimed explicitly to valorize local culture, both as heritage and in its contemporary manifestations. Early Volta Jazz songs were named for Bobo's zoo and gardens and even Peyrissac, a hardware store that also sold mopeds and scooters. (See p. 128 for lyrics to this song.) As Koné recalled, he pursued musical excellence as part of the "cultural promotion of Voltaic youth."[7]

The Volta Jazz orchestra grew to one dozen musicians and even spun off a "B formation," but at its core stood four members: the multitalented Ibrahima Traoré, singer Tidiane Coulibaly, guitarist Dieudonné Koudougou, and bassist Abdoulaye Yago. Traoré had played with Koné in a previous band and thus claimed seniority as the dean of Volta Jazz. Coulibaly, a railroad worker whom Koné spotted in the lineup of Tropic Jazz, became the group's principal bandleader and songwriter. Koné similarly offered Koudougou and Abdoulaye, two fans of Congolese pop music who had performed together since 1961, prominent positions in his new formation.

The group's early songs drew heavily on Afro-Cuban music, particularly *pachanga*, *charanga*, and cha-cha. For African musicians, adapting such source material felt at once like domesticating something exotic and bringing exported ancestral sounds back home. Koudougou and Yago, who tended to emphasize melodic line, exercised their fascination for Congolese rumbas (originally sung in Lingala) by adapting them for rendition in Dioula. All the band members listened closely to Radio Bobo and followed developments through records arriving in local stores.

Volta Jazz played at dinners and events across the Bobo region, especially those for the Red Cross and the Rotary Club, of which Koné was an influential member. They also featured regularly at music halls, first the Normandie Bar and then the Calebasse d'Or (Golden Calabash), subsequently renamed Volta Dancing and later owned by Koné. Entry cost 100 francs on weeknights and an additional 50 francs on Saturday evenings. Koné acted as a true patron, purchasing instruments for the musicians and subsidizing their rehearsal and performance expenses. He also held the members to a demanding schedule, asking that they rehearse daily and having them perform every Thursday and Saturday, excluding tour dates. Their Sundays and Mondays were usually free.

Bands in Upper Volta lacked state support; this was in contrast to the situation in Guinea, where orchestras acted as quasi-official ambassadors of national culture, or Mali, where the Bamako railway station volunteered its name and a part of its space to the hit formation Rail Band.[8] West Indian composer Hervé Victor Lejuste had begun a record company in 1965 in Bangui, capital of the Central African Republic. In 1967 he relocated his operation to Abidjan, and soon after Volta Jazz came to play there at the Hôtel Ivoire. The band would eventually release 7-inch singles with Lejuste under his L.G.V.D. label and then under the name Disques France-Afrique.

Lejuste traveled to Bobo to record the band live at Volta Dancing and at a bandshell in the city park, among other locations. With only two microphones—one for the musicians and another for vocals—Lejuste caught the vivid sound of Volta Jazz in the late 1960s. He captured four to eight songs in each of a series of sessions that ultimately yielded more than twenty singles. Nearly pristine, the outdoor recordings were interrupted on occasion by noises coming from the nearby zoo! One of the last surviving witnesses to these sessions is Lolita, a fifty-year-old female chimp, who for some years now has been the only animal remaining in that decrepit institution.

The sleeves to these records form a series that is illustrated with color photographs of the group, dressed in matching, elegant tuxedo suits and posing in various Bobo locations (fig. 3). These pictures are all the work of Sanlé Sory, indebted as ever to Koné for financing his initial investment in the Volta Photo studio. Sweet and candid, the imagery constitutes some of the few known images of Bobo in that time. One sleeve shows the orchestra standing alongside the sign for the city limits; on others they appear near the park bandshell, in the zoo, or in the nearby municipal gardens. Koné's driving school even features in some of the pictures. In a further indication of this frugal yet ambitious operation, all the photographs were taken on a single day, although the records appear to have been released over a two-year period.

The tuxedos—one of at least three uniforms that Koné commissioned for the group's members—carry a particular set of associations. They project an air of cosmopolitan chic that could be associated with a suave orchestra for a grand hotel somewhere in Europe or with the bespoke suits worn by Ivorian president Félix Houphouët-Boigny. Koné devised a scheme that—for a time at least—overlaid this Eurocentric élite attire with a sense of repertorial democracy: red jackets would be for every band member; the yellow jacket would be worn by each member in turn, for one month only, while he accepted the rotating responsibility of bandleader. (Koné reserved the blue tuxedo jacket for himself as "president" of the orchestra.)

Prior to Volta Jazz, Koné had played in a *goumbé* music ensemble that entertained at dust balls held by the RDA political party, which had expanded from Mali to a number of former French West African colonies.

He undertook other music ventures in the 1960s and '70s in a spirit of idealism similar to that embodied in the shared yellow tuxedo jacket. In December 1966, for example, Koné organized a large balafon competition he called the Olympiade, at a local soccer stadium. He subsequently launched a modern orchestra competition modeled on a Guinean annual contest called National Weeks, which lasted a few years.

Koné also started a Volta Jazz B lineup, with bass player Sanou Kotalama as leader. In the early 1970s he supervised Les Anges Noirs (The Black Angels, not to be confused with a Congolese band of the same name) headed by singers Otis and Siaka Ouattara; the latter was called Elvis for his pompadour hairstyle. One can see here the increasing influence of American pop culture, which added a further layer of international references to Bobo music beginning in the later 1960s.

After a year of repertory structure, meanwhile, Koné proposed in 1967 that Coulibaly assume permanent leadership of the A lineup for Volta Jazz, a position that the singer held until 1974. In that time Coulibaly composed over eighty songs, many of them key tunes, and gave the orchestra much of its repertoire. As an example, "Baba Moussa," written during a rehearsal session, is an ode to the Congolese rumba named for a Bobo police detective. The song, which showcases Coulibaly's enthusiastic singing and pays homage to a local hero, became a staple in the band's repertoire, according to recollections by Yago and Ibrahima Traoré. Another Coulibaly hit, "Air Volta," celebrates the national airline in imitation of "Air Guinée" by the Guinean group Bembeya Jazz (see p. 127 for lyrics).

Ibrahima Traoré brought Senufo influences and played guitar, organ, percussion, and balafon, the last as a nod to the popularity in Bobo of the Senufo grand balafon with twenty-three strips. Although sometimes uncredited, he wrote songs for both Koné and Coulibaly and, like others, helped to fuse Mandingo and Afro-Cuban influences. As Koné recalled in 2011:

At that time, Congolese music and Cuban music were truly part of our influences. We even ordered a Cuban upright bass in order to obtain the sound we were looking for while everyone else used a regular bass guitar. We had seven horns, Abou Traoré on the trumpet and trombone, Christophe Adjahi on the trombone. Moustapha Maïga led the three saxophone players. They worked in series. During musical competitions, our horns allowed us to engage in battle, thanks to our Cuban style arrangements. I kept saying "Launch the horns" whenever we could take over the opposing orchestra. That's how we defeated Maurice Semporé's mighty Harmonie Voltaïque in Ouagadougou in 1967 and 1972.[9]

Volta Jazz used the Congolese *mi-solo* guitar routine, with a third guitarist playing between lead and rhythm guitars in a way that emphasized rhythmic patterns. Yago played the Cuban upright bass mentioned by Koné, and later bass guitar, while Ardjouma Soré and Sibiri "Le Grand" Koné played the drums and tumbas. Maïga, Abou Traoré, and Adjahi also sang backing vocals. Dieudonné Koudougou excelled at slide guitar in the manner of Congolese master Docteur Nico. Brothers Paul and Souleymane Sanon, or occasionally Traoré, took turns on rhythm guitar.

While Coulibaly was the main singer for Volta Jazz, others included "Elvis" Ouattara, Ousmane "Mano Le Prince" Traoré, Michel Traoré, and Saïdou Sanou, each specializing in a particular repertoire. Other performers, such as Dominique Valléa or future African music star Georges Ouédraogo, had their start with Volta Jazz. The founding patron, Koné, played guitar only occasionally and barely sang (fig. 4). He did execute lead vocals on the rare song "Fintalabo" (Nothing Can Outdo God), subtitled "the Volta Jazz prayer." This tune was first performed live at the Maison du Peuple in Ouagadougou during a festival organized by the Lion's Club in February 1972.

With numerous instrumentalists and a rich vocal team, Volta Jazz soared in the later 1960s. As mentioned before, they took the train to Abidjan to play at Hôtel Ivoire, a luxury venue. In July 1969, under the aegis of Koné and fired by Coulibaly's enthusiasm, the group played at the Festival Panafricain in Algiers. One hymn from that era, composed and performed by Maïga on vocals and saxophone, is "Djougou Malola" (Shame on Evil People): "Ah, young people of Bobo, evilness is a lie!" he sings in part. Praising Bobo and its inhabitants, this bolero embodies the thinness, remoteness, and grace of modern Voltaic music. The voice is so frail and breathless that one can imagine Maïga bursting into tears as his saxophone overflows with emotion. Yet he keeps this possibility ever so slightly in check, delivering a breathtaking song akin to OK Jazz boleros or Guinean ballads of the time.

The eerie "Na Dalo" (Young Lady), sung in the Bobo language by Coulibaly, sounds similarly timeless. Crystalline in its fragility, this bolero features heady vocals, airy guitar, and whispered saxophone. "B. B. Peyrissac," the song about a local hardware store, remarkably makes problems with mopeds and scooters into a moving tune. "Bi kaméléou" (Young People of Today), an upbeat number, stands as a testament to Voltaic garage rock, which flourished in Bobo as well, with the raw recordings and performances typical of that genre. "Young people of today know how to flatter women / But I warn you beware of him, go away from him, he's gonna destroy you," sings Coulibaly as a message to the young ladies.

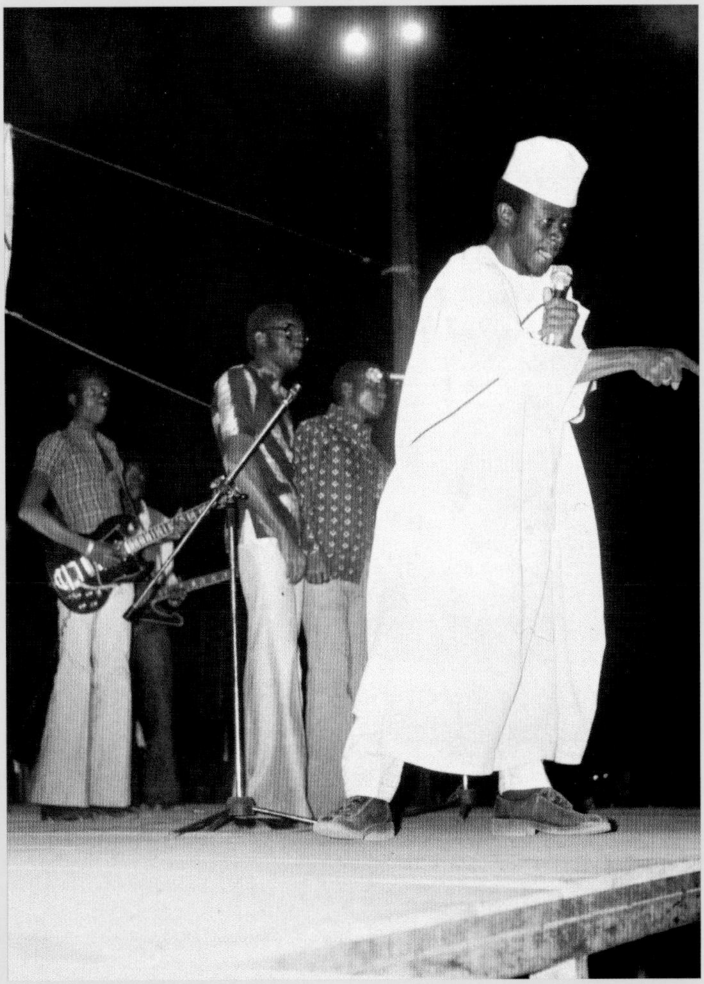

fig. 4 Idrissa Koné emceeing at a Volta Jazz event; Dieudonné Koudougou on guitar at left, 1974/75. 10.7 × 7.7 cm (image); 12.5 × 8.5 cm (paper). Private collection

Around 1970, following the success of the Disques France-Afrique releases, which were recorded between Bobo and Abidjan, Idrissa Koné started his own imprint, Disques Paysans Noirs (Black Farmer Records). He issued at least one single by troubadour Pierre Sandouidi and some feverish singles by the Volta Jazz B formation, such as "Mama Soukous." Raw, fierce, and syncopated, in a rock vein, these songs—particularly "Mousso Koroba Tike" (Mature Lady, Don't Do It)—are among the greatest the band ever recorded. (Most of the songs hold a message, in this case warning against adultery, as if Volta Jazz were the buoyant keeper of Bobo morality.)

The very vibrancy of the music scene in Bobo began to make it an increasingly competitive city in which to perform. Weeknights were still manageable: on Tuesdays, the Imbattables Léopards (Unbeatable Leopards) played the Lion d'Or or Chez Samy, while Echo del Africa Nacional took the stage at Normandie Bar on Wednesdays, and Volta Jazz performed on Thursdays at its eponymous Volta Dancing. Dafra Star, a direct rival to Volta Jazz begun in 1975 by Coulibaly, played on Fridays at its own namesake venue: Dafra Bar. There were still other bands to hear on these nights, however, and on Saturdays many of them might be playing simultaneously. There was further competition to secure traveling engagements, and all of the groups just named released singles for sale as well.

Volta Jazz resisted updating its repertoire as the years went on, preferring to keep to a mixture of Afro-Cuban, Mandingo, and Congolese influences. At the same time, they reemphasized their regional African identity in new ways. Moved by resurgent nativism across Africa, for example, Koné ordered black-and-white striped outfits for the musicians that distinctly recall the *faso dan fani*, a cotton garment popular in southern Burkina. Later singles by the group show black-and-white cover photographs—no longer in color, and not taken by Sory—in which the members pose in these costumes at culturally resonant sites in Abidjan or Ouagadougou.

Coulibaly launched Dafra Star after a Volta Jazz meeting at which Koné voiced disappointment in the band while displaying, according to Ibrahima Traoré, a lack of vision for either of its stage formations. Several members followed Coulibaly, while others clung to Koné. Proud of his Mandingo culture and origins, Coulibaly named his new group after the tiny Dafra river, which crosses Bobo at a point where the goddess Sya supposedly lies waiting to protect the city. Koné persevered, meanwhile, and even recorded a full-length LP album with his B formation, released in 1977 through the Sonafric label in Paris. Unfortunately, the album lacks outstanding songs. Koné subsequently disbanded the group, recalling that he gave the instruments and equipment to a Youth Club in the nearby town of Banfora. "Tidiane was the best Voltaic singer," Koné remembered with pride. "If he became so, it is because I had decided so. A lot of musicians came to find a position within the Volta Jazz. I had the luck and opportunity to gather and undertake many musical ventures and eventually to find talents as great as Tidiane Coulibaly."

Thanks to Sanlé Sory, Idrissa Koné, Ibrahima Traoré, Yago Abdoulaye, Moustapha Maïga, Drabo, Abdoulaye Cissé, and Dragoss Ouédraogo.

1 While the country name Burkina Faso is a phrase in Moré and Dioula, the inhabitants are called *Burkinabé*, a locution in Fula.

2 British and Belgian authorities in Africa, by contrast, allowed the use of local languages for music and dances. Modern African music began in the British colonies of Ghana and Nigeria (highlife in the 1930s and '40s) and in the Belgian Congo (rumba in the 1940s).

3 In 1957 Ghana was the first African colony to declare independence under the leadership of Kwame Nkrumah. It was followed in October 1958 by the French colony of Guinea, whose president, Sékou Touré, declared, "We prefer freedom in poverty than slavery in riches." By 1960 more than fifteen French African colonies had gained independence, including Mali (former French Sudan), Ivory Coast, Niger, Togo, and Benin, all countries that bordered Upper Volta.

4 Most of present-day Burkina Faso once belonged to the Malian Empire, which was established in the 13th century. Under Emperor Sundiata Keita, Mali stretched for several decades from Niger in the east to Senegal in the west, from Mauritania in the north to Ivory Coast in the south—the territory of approximately ten modern African countries. Within this empire, the Mandé region formed a triangle between the countries of Mali and Guinea. Among the cultural productions from this region was the griot tradition, which involved songs of praise (for example, of Sundiata Keita himself). The griots played balafon, *kora* (twenty-one-string harp) and *ngoni* (four-string lute/ guitar) as they created an oral history of the region. The term *Mandingo* refers to the Mandé culture.

5 Personal communication from many musicians of that generation, including Ibrahima Traoré and Moustapha Maïga.

6 Beginning in the late 1940s, several orchestras in French West Africa used the word *jazz* in their name: Ségou Jazz in Mali (1949) and, in Congo, African Jazz (1953) and OK Jazz (1956). The international popularity of these groups, especially African Jazz and the first Panafrican hit, "Indépendance Cha-Cha" (African Jazz, 1960), contributed to this vogue for band names across the continent.

7 Conversation with the author, Bobo-Dioulasso, 2011; all quotations from Koné are taken from this conversation.

8 For information on postwar popular music in Francophone West Africa, and on Rail Band in particular, see Eric Charry, *Mandé Music: Traditional and Modern Music of the Maninka and Mandinka of Western Africa* (Chicago: University of Chicago Press, 2000); Graeme Counsel, *Mandé Popular Music and Cultural Policies in West Africa: Griots and Government Policy Since Independence* (Germany: VDM Verlag, 2009); Jacob B.Y. Daboué, *Musique moderne et langues nationales au Burkina Faso* (Paris: L'Harmattan, 2012); Florent Mazzoleni, *L'Epopée de la musique africaine* (Paris: Hors Collection, 2008); and Mazzoleni, *Afro Pop: L'Âge d'or des grands orchestres africains* (Bordeaux: Le Castor Astral, 2011).

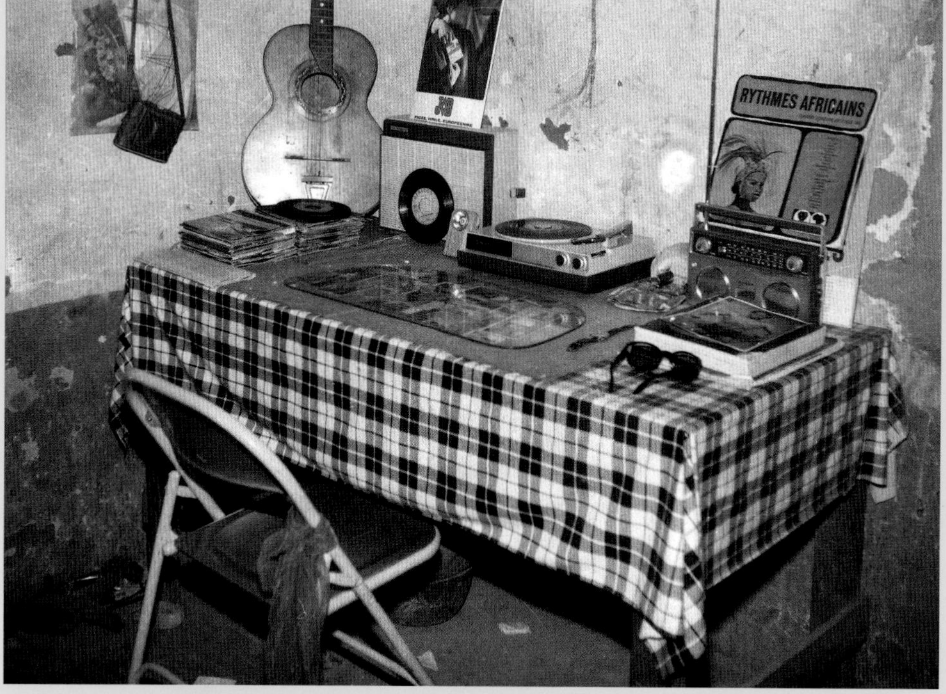

fig. 1 Untitled, 1965/75. Illustration from 6×6 cm negative. Courtesy Florent Mazzoleni

Sanlé Sory's work corner is crowded with a turntable and transistor radio, a guitar that he occasionally played, and an array of his photographs on the wall, including the self-portrait taken at Black Farmer Square (plate 1).

AB: Did you commonly see Volta Photo prints in people's houses in Bobo?

SS: Some folks have my pictures in their albums to this day!

FM: Not on the walls, though.

SS: To put a picture on the wall you need a good size print. If not it's not even worth framing. We start [with that] at 18 × 24 size. 13 × 18 [cm] is too small. 18 × 24 you can frame. But a print at that size costs money, so people don't buy one every day. People who want such a print are doing well. Ha!

MW: Did any such people come to see you?

SS: There are certainly people who asked for big prints: bought and framed, and they're off. You can't ask to visit such people afterward.

MW: These were not your friends, then.

SS: They parked their car and came in with the family, the kids; I put them in order like that in the studio and went click, then they asked me to make a great big framed print. Fine. But when it's your little brother running around town—

MW: —then it's a little print.

SS: Yep.

AB: Was it common for people to write messages on the photos?

SS: Sometimes people wrote what they liked on the picture and sent it to their friends.

AB: Even abroad?

SS: You put the photo with a letter in the envelope. Whoever receives it reads and rips up the letter but keeps the photo because it makes him happy. It's easy.

FM: What did people think of photographs in their homes at the time? Was it special?

SS: When people come to your house, they don't even look at the photos. They've come for business. They could care less about the photo. It's meaningless. You made the photo so you know its significance. The person looking at it, it means nothing to him at that time.

MW: Does that also mean people did not know how to pose for a camera?

SS: Photos aren't something people need. If you've opened a studio, it is already advertised for all to see, for anyone at all. Someone who comes in ready to pay has already learned where he or she can go to have a picture taken well. That's how it worked. People said "Sory will give you pretty pictures, or someone else will give you pretty pictures." I run a shop like any other.

MW: What are the important moments to photograph?

SS: The Ramadan holy days. Weddings, although some folks get married without a photographer. It depends what sort of person. Some people marry, and it doesn't even cost 100,000 francs. Others pay double or triple that—they kill a lot of chickens and sheep. Same for the drinks.

AB: Did people use your pictures for wedding invitations?

SS: Yes, some paid me properly, even ahead of time, for the film and so forth.

MW: Were you called regularly for any other ceremonies?

SS: Saturday and Sunday things were going on at least in town. But getting together didn't necessarily involve asking for a photographer. And I didn't go looking for that kind of work. Folks came to see me as needed. If they didn't call you, it wasn't worth going. Dance parties are another matter.

MW: This is a photo you took (plate 51).

SS: Yes. It's a lady from Bobo. It's from the same group as the one with the ceremonial headdress, the one with the three women. But it's not the same woman here.

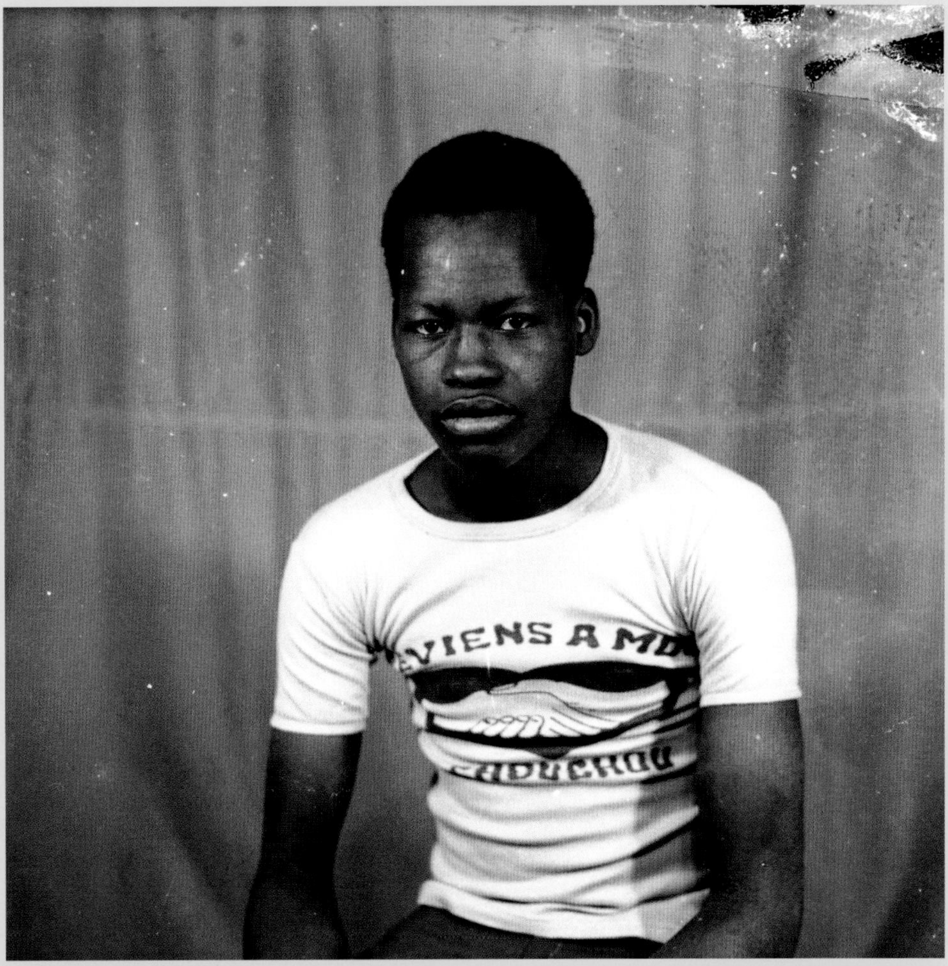

fig. 1 Untitled, 1965/75, printed 2017. 36 × 36 cm (image); 50 × 40 cm (sheet). The Art Institute of Chicago, gift of the artist and Florent Mazzoleni, 242562

MW: So perhaps not the same year but the same time of year?

SS: That's right, the time of this festival, *kurubi*, when the Bobolaises have their hair done like that.[23] They dance until dawn. You tell all the stupid things you've done, and then it's over—you have to wait until the next year.

FM: A confession day.

SS: The others come and insult you, tell you you're not good. You can't say anything on this day, that's the rule. People can tell you that you're bad or mean. They dance and you can't talk back. It doesn't last more than three or four days. It's not like someone comes and parks at your door. No. They gather in a crowd. (Looks for his camera.)

MW: You have a recent photo of this?

SS: Yes (looking through the pictures on his camera screen). You see this getup? It's that kind of thing. Women only. Any men there are taking care of kids. All the women are there, ancient or babies. If you can travel, you follow them.

AB: A final question: what do you think of the fact that your photographs are now in museums? What do you make of the undeniable success that Volta Photo is having internationally?

SS: It moves me a great deal. Florent told me I'll be out in public and I didn't know what to say. I'm very proud and happy. I pray to god for a successful business.

MW: What more would you like to see for your photographs?

SS: I want them to bring us all happiness, prosperity, and health, and for us to have a long life so we may enjoy to the fullest. I regret having burned so many photos—I've said so. You buy gasoline, pour it on, and they burn.

AB: And the people of Bobo-Dioulasso, do you have thoughts on what they might think it means to be shown across the world?

SS: Many have gone up to paradise. Those who have stayed behind, if they see a photograph, in their current state, they won't even recognize themselves. There are people who can't even recognize their own picture. If they are in a group [photo] they say they aren't there.

23 *Kurubi* is a festival held during Ramadan and attended by both men and women, although Dioula girls and young women are the principal performers since the 1960s. In earlier times, Muslim clerics would assemble to read Koranic passages, and men engaged in competitive dancing while women competed in displays of dress, jewelry, and beauty. In the decades covered by Sory's photographs, and through to the present, women typically wear headdresses and waist beads, carry horsehair fly-swatters, and may appear in bras or fully uncovered above the waist (see p. 57, and plates 51 and 59). A festival with similar dress and performance, connected to Ashura, the Muslim New Year, is called *Jomɛnɛ*, an annual confirmation of progress in society and the spiritual realm. See Katja Werthmann, "Transformations d'une élite musulmane en Afrique de l'Ouest: Le cas des Dioula de Darsalamy (Burkina Faso)," *Cahiers d'Etudes Africaines* 52 (4): 845-876. Thanks to Constantijn Petridis for this and other references.

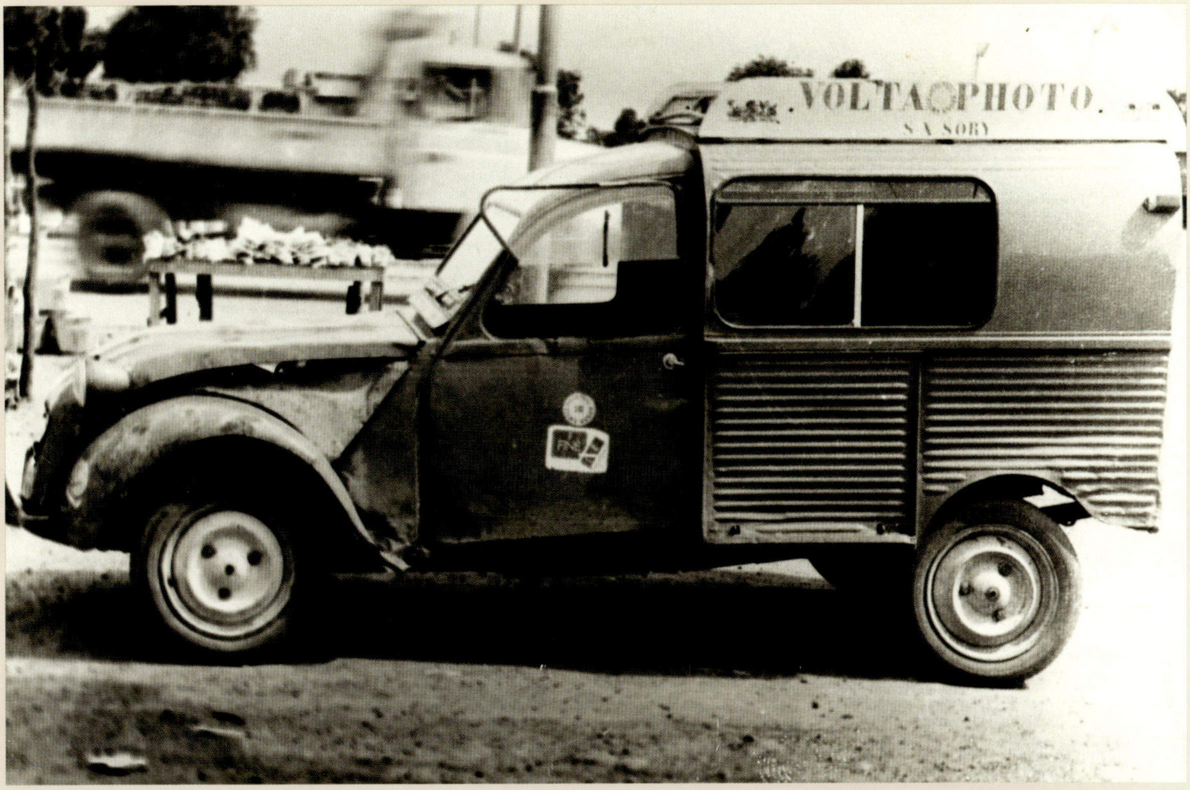

93 Sory's work van, 1970/80

LIST OF ILLUSTRATIONS AND EXHIBITION CHECKLIST

Double-exposure self-portrait in Place du Paysan Noir (Black Farmer Square), c. 1970
22.5 × 16.4 cm (image); 23.7 × 17.7 cm (paper)
The Art Institute of Chicago, gift of the artist, 2017.384
Illustrated p. 2 [1]

Fula men seated outside the Farakan studio, 1970/80
12.5 × 17.5 cm (image/paper)
Private collection
Illustrated p. 4 [2]

Self-portrait at the studio of Kojo Adomako, 1960/70
22.5 × 16.6 cm (image); 23.7 × 17.8 cm (paper)
Private collection
Illustrated p. 12 [fig. 1]

Self-portrait, 1965/75
17 × 11.4 cm (image); 18 × 12.6 cm (paper)
Private collection
Illustrated p. 180 [94]

Self-portrait, 1965/75
22.6 × 16.8 cm (image); 23.8 × 17.8 cm (paper)
The Art Institute of Chicago, promised gift of Ralph and Nancy Segall, 240646
Illustrated p. 180 [95]

ID photo, 1965/75
11.2 × 7.5 cm (image); 12.5 × 8.8 cm (paper)
Private collection
Illustrated p. 15 [fig. 2]

Teenage girl in the village of Dandé, photographed at home on market day, 1970/80
11.5 × 7.8 cm (image); 12.8 × 8.7 cm (paper)
The Art Institute of Chicago, restricted gift of Peter J. Cohen, 2017.371
Illustrated p. 17 [fig. 3]

A customer at Calebasse d'Or (Golden Calabash, later named Volta Dancing), 1965/75
11.4 × 7.9 cm (image); 12.5 × 8.7 cm (paper)
The Art Institute of Chicago, promised gift of Ralph and Nancy Segall, 240598
Illustrated p. 19 [fig. 4]

Untitled, 1965/75, printed 2017
36 × 36 cm (image); 50 × 40 cm (sheet)
The Art Institute of Chicago, gift of the artist and Florent Mazzoleni, 242556
Illustrated p. 24 [fig. 1]

Kouloubi, younger sister of Yakaridjan and girlfriend of Sory at the time, 1960/65
13 × 8 cm (image); 13.7 × 8.7 cm (paper)
The Art Institute of Chicago, promised gift of Ralph and Nancy Segall, 240645
Illustrated p. 33 [3]

Untitled, 1965/75
11.4 × 7.9 cm (image); 12.4 × 8.8 cm (paper)
Private collection
Illustrated p. 34 [4]

Untitled (taken by an apprentice), 1965/75
11.3 × 7.8 cm (image); 12.8 × 8.6 cm (paper)
Private collection
Illustrated p. 34 [5]

Untitled, 1965/75
Gelatin silver print
11.3 × 7.8 cm (image); 12.4 × 8.6 cm (paper)
Private collection
Illustrated p. 180 [96]

Untitled, 1965/75
11.6 × 7.8 cm (image); 12.5 × 8.7 cm (paper)
Private collection
Illustrated p. 180 [101]

Untitled, 1965/75
11.5 × 7.5 cm (image); 12.5 × 8.3 cm (paper)
Private collection
Illustrated p. 181 [103]

Untitled, 1965/75
11.6 × 7.5 cm (image); 12.5 × 8.3 cm (paper)
Private collection
Illustrated p. 181 [104]

Untitled, 1965/75
22.5 × 16.7 cm (image); 23.8 × 17.8 cm (paper)
Private collection
Illustrated p. 181 [111]

Untitled
1965/75
11.7 × 7.7 cm (image); 12.7 × 8.7 cm (paper)
Private collection
Illustrated p. 35 [6]

Untitled, 1965/75
7.7 × 11 cm (image); 8.7 × 12.5 cm (paper)
Private collection
Illustrated p. 35 [7]

Untitled (taken by an apprentice), 1965/75
7.6 × 11.8 cm (image); 8.7 × 12.5 cm (paper)
The Art Institute of Chicago, restricted gift of Peter J. Cohen, 2017.369
Illustrated p. 36 [8]

Yao Pelé, 1965/75
16.3 × 11.6 cm (image); 17.7 × 12.5 cm (paper)
Private collection
Illustrated p. 37 [9]

Untitled (taken by an apprentice), 1965/75
16.9 × 11.4 cm (image); 17.9 × 12.5 cm (paper)
The Art Institute of Chicago, promised gift of Ralph and Nancy Segall, 240654
Illustrated p. 37 [10]

Sanlé Sory in gymnastic attire next to his sports trainer, Ousmane, 1957/65
12.9 × 7.7 cm (image); 13.7 × 8.9 cm (paper)
Private collection
Illustrated p. 38 [11]

Self-portrait (left) with Yakini, a Yoruba youth, and Adama, a Bobo youth, 1960/65
7.7 × 11.7 cm (image); 8.2 × 12.2 cm (paper)
Private collection
Illustrated p. 39 [12]

Self-portrait (center) with two apprentices, 1960/65
11.8 × 16.1 cm (image); 12.8 × 18 cm (paper)
Private collection
Illustrated p. 39 [13]

Untitled, 1965/75
11.4 × 7.7 cm (image); 12.5 × 9 cm (paper)
The Art Institute of Chicago, promised gift of Ralph and Nancy Segall, 240687
Illustrated p. 40 [14]

Untitled, 1965/75, printed 2017
36 × 36 cm (image); 50 × 40 cm (sheet)
The Art Institute of Chicago, gift of the artist and Florent Mazzoleni, 242559
Illustrated p. 42 [fig. 1]

Untitled, 1965/75
11.6 × 16.1 cm (image); 12.4 × 17.7 cm (paper)
Private collection
Illustrated p. 45 [15]

Untitled, 1965/75
16.5 × 11.2 cm (image); 17.5 × 12.4 cm (paper)
Private collection
Illustrated p. 46 [16]

Untitled, 1965/75
16.5 × 11.5 cm (image); 17.7 × 12.5 cm (paper)
Private collection
Illustrated p. 46 [17]

Fula man, 1970/80
17 × 11.2 cm (image/paper)
The Art Institute of Chicago, promised gift of Ralph and Nancy Segall, 240567
Illustrated p. 47 [18]

Woman in a ceremonial headdress, 1965/75
12.8 × 7.8 cm (image); 13.7 × 18.7 cm (paper)
The Art Institute of Chicago, promised gift of Ralph and Nancy Segall, 240585
Illustrated p. 48 [19]

Four women in ceremonial headdresses, 1965/75
7.8 × 11.7 cm (image); 8.7 × 13.7 cm (paper)
Private collection
Illustrated p. 48 [20]

Untitled, 1965/75
11.2 × 7.8 cm (image); 12.4 × 8.5 cm (paper)
Private collection
Illustrated p. 49 [21]

Untitled, 1965/75
11.5 × 7.8 cm (image); 13.7 × 8.6 cm (paper)
Private collection
Illustrated p. 49 [22]

Untitled, 1965/75
11.5 × 7.5 cm (image); 12.5 × 8.4 cm (paper)
Private collection
Illustrated p. 50 [23]

Untitled, 1965/75
11.4 × 7.8 cm (image); 12.4 × 8.6 cm (paper)
The Art Institute of Chicago, promised gift of Ralph and Nancy Segall, 240576
Illustrated p. 51 [24]

Two Fula women, 1965/75
11.5 × 7.4 cm (image); 12.4 × 18.7 cm (paper)
Private collection
Illustrated p. 51 [25]

Untitled, 1965/75
16.7 × 11.8 cm (image); 17.5 × 12.5 cm (paper)
The Art Institute of Chicago, promised gift of Ralph and Nancy Segall, 240679
Illustrated p. 52 [26]

Untitled, 1965/75, printed 2017
36 × 36 cm (image); 50 × 40 cm (sheet)
The Art Institute of Chicago, gift of the artist and Florent Mazzoleni, 242554
Illustrated p. 54 [fig. 1]

Untitled, 1965/75, printed 2017
36 × 36 cm (image); 50 × 40 cm (sheet)
The Art Institute of Chicago, gift of the artist and Florent Mazzoleni, 242561
Illustrated p. 57 [fig. 2]

Untitled, 1965/75, printed 2017
36 × 36 cm (image); 50 × 40 cm (sheet)
The Art Institute of Chicago, gift of the artist and Florent Mazzoleni, 242557
Illustrated p. 60 [fig. 3]

Untitled, 1965/75
11.2 × 7.8 cm (image); 12.5 × 8.5 cm (paper)
The Art Institute of Chicago, promised gift of Ralph and Nancy Segall, 240583
Illustrated p. 63 [27]

Yao Pelé, an apprentice who later joined the army and became a lieutenant, 1965/75
16.5 × 11.7 cm (image); 17.6 × 12.5 cm (paper)
Private collection
Illustrated p. 64 [28]

Untitled, 1965/75
10.6 × 16.1 cm (image); 11.8 × 17.6 cm (paper)
Private collection
Illustrated p. 64 [29]

Untitled, 1965/75
16.3 × 11.8 cm (image); 17.6 × 12.5 cm (paper)
Private collection
Illustrated p. 65 [30]

Untitled, 1965/75
16.6 × 11.8 cm (image); 17.7 × 12.5 cm (paper)
The Art Institute of Chicago, promised gift of Ralph and Nancy Segall, 240639
Illustrated p. 65 [31]

Untitled, 1965/75
Gelatin silver print
16.8 × 11.9 cm (image); 17.5 × 12.5 cm (paper)
Private collection
Illustrated p. 180 [98]

Untitled, 1965/75
11.4 × 7.7 cm (image); 12.4 × 8.6 cm (paper)
Private collection
Illustrated p. 180 [100]

Untitled, 1965/75
11 × 17.6 cm (image); 13 × 8.9 cm (paper)
Private collection
Illustrated p. 180 [102]

Tidiane Coulibaly and another man, 1965/75
Gelatin silver print
11.7 × 16.3 cm (image); 12.4 × 17.5 cm (paper)
Private collection
Illustrated p. 181 [105]

Untitled, 1965/75
11.6 × 7.8 cm (image); 12.5 × 8.5 cm (paper)
Private collection
Illustrated p. 181 [106]

Untitled, 1965/75
11.6 × 7.8 cm (image); 12.4 × 8.5 cm (paper)
Private collection
Illustrated p. 181 [108]

Untitled, 1965/75
7.5 × 9.4 cm (image); 8.7 × 12.1 cm (paper)
Private collection
Illustrated p. 181 [109]

Untitled, 1965/75
14.5 × 10.1 cm (image/paper)
The Art Institute of Chicago, promised gift of Ralph and Nancy Segall, 240688
Illustrated p. 64 [32]

Untitled, 1965/75
11.8 × 7.7 cm (image); 12.5 × 8.8 cm (paper)
The Art Institute of Chicago, promised gift of Ralph and Nancy Segall, 240575
Illustrated p. 65 [33]

Untitled, 1965/75
7.6 × 11.3 cm (image); 8.5 × 12.5 cm (paper)
Private collection
Illustrated p. 65 [34]

Self-portrait on postcard stock, addressed on reverse: "SORY X. Director of Photography. Bobo B.P. 139," 1960/65
12.4 × 7.7 cm (image); 13 × 8.3 cm (paper)
The Art Institute of Chicago, promised gift of Ralph and Nancy Segall, 240571
Illustrated p. 68 [35]

Untitled, 1965/75
11.6 × 7.8 cm (image); 12.5 × 9 cm (paper)
The Art Institute of Chicago, promised gift of Ralph and Nancy Segall, 240624
Illustrated p. 69 [36]

Untitled, 1965/75
10.9 × 7.7 cm (image); 12.4 × 8.8 cm (paper)
Private collection
Illustrated p. 69 [37]

Untitled, 1965/75
16.9 × 11.3 cm (image); 18 × 12.9 cm (paper)
The Art Institute of Chicago, promised gift of Ralph and Nancy Segall, 240642
Illustrated p. 69 [38]

Untitled, 1965/75
16.5 × 11.3 cm (image); 17.5 × 12.5 cm (paper)
Private collection
Illustrated p. 69 [39]

Untitled, 1965/75
11.5 × 7.6 cm (image); 12.6 × 8.7 cm (paper)
The Art Institute of Chicago, promised gift of Ralph and Nancy Segall, 240621
Illustrated p. 70 [40]

Untitled, 1965/75
12.6 × 7.8 cm (image); 12.5 × 8.6 cm (paper)
Private collection
Illustrated p. 70 [41]

Untitled, 1965/75
16.5 × 11.5 cm (image); 17.2 × 12.2 cm (paper)
The Art Institute of Chicago, restricted gift of Peter J. Cohen, 2017.372
Illustrated p. 71 [42]

Untitled, 1965/75
16.6 × 11.5 cm (image); 17.7 × 12.6 cm (paper)
The Art Institute of Chicago, promised gift of Ralph and Nancy Segall, 240661
Illustrated p. 71 [43]

Untitled, 1965/75
9.7 × 7.8 cm (image); 12.4 × 8.8 cm (paper)
Private collection
Illustrated p. 72 [44]

Untitled, 1965/75
11.8 × 7.7 cm (image); 12.4 × 8.9 com (image)
Private collection
Illustrated p. 72 [45]

Untitled, 1965/75
16.5 × 11.4 cm (image); 17.5 × 12.5 cm (paper)
Private collection
Illustrated p. 73 [46]

Untitled, c. 1983
10.4 × 7.8 cm (image); 12.5 × 8.7 cm (paper)
Private collection
Illustrated p. 74 [47]

ID photo, 1965/75
11.3 × 7.5 cm (image); 12.2 × 8 cm (paper)
The Art Institute of Chicago, promised gift of Ralph and Nancy Segall, 240636
Illustrated p. 75 [48]

Untitled (taken by an apprentice of his girlfriend), 1965/75
11.5 × 8 cm (image); 12.4 × 8.7 cm (paper)
Private collection
Illustrated p. 75 [49]

Untitled, 1965/75
11.2 × 7.6 cm (image); 12.8 × 8.7 cm (paper)
Private collection
Illustrated p. 76 [50]

Untitled, 1965/75, printed 2017
36 × 36 cm (image); 50 × 40 cm (sheet)
The Art Institute of Chicago, gift of the artist and Florent Mazzoleni, 242555
Illustrated p. 80 [fig. 2]

Bobo woman in a ceremonial headdress, 1965/75
16.5 × 11.5 cm (image); 17.6 × 12. cm (paper)
The Art Institute of Chicago, promised gift of Ralph and Nancy Segall, 240635
Illustrated p. 83 [51]

Photographer unknown
Hunter, perhaps from the Wassoulou region
Reprinted by Ibrahima Sanlé Sory, 1970/80
16.6 × 11.4 cm (image); 17.7 × 12.7 cm (paper)
Private collection
Illustrated p. 85 [52]

Untitled, 1965/75
16.7 × 11.5 cm (image); 17.6 × 12.5 cm (paper)
Private collection
Illustrated p. 86 [53]

Untitled, 1965/75
11.4 × 7.5 cm (image); 12.4 × 8.7 cm (paper)
Private collection
Illustrated p. 87 [54]

Untitled, c. 1980
11.7 × 7.7 cm (image); 12.5 × 8.7 cm (paper)
Private collection
Illustrated p. 87 [55]

Untitled, 1965/75
10.9 × 7.6 cm (image); 12.2 × 8.7 cm (paper)
The Art Institute of Chicago, promised gift of Ralph and Nancy Segall, 240623
Illustrated p. 88 [56]

Untitled, 1965/75
22.2 × 16.5 cm (image); 23.6 × 17.5 cm (paper)
The Art Institute of Chicago, promised gift of Ralph and Nancy Segall, 240691
Illustrated p. 89 [57]

Untitled, 1965/75
11.5 × 7.4 cm (image/paper)
The Art Institute of Chicago, promised gift of Ralph and Nancy Segall, 240684
Illustrated p. 89 [58]

Untitled, 1965/75
16.7 × 11.5 cm (image); 17.7 × 12.5 cm (paper)
The Art Institute of Chicago, promised gift of Ralph and Nancy Segall, 240613
Illustrated p. 90 [59]

Untitled, 1965/75, printed 2017
36 × 36 cm (image); 50 × 40 cm (sheet)
The Art Institute of Chicago, gift of the artist and Florent Mazzoleni, 242560
Illustrated p. 93 [fig. 1]

Les Afro-Pop, 1965/75, printed 2017
36 × 36 cm (image); 50 × 40 cm (sheet)
The Art Institute of Chicago, gift of the artist and Florent Mazzoleni, 242565
Illustrated p. 94 [fig. 2]

Yacouba Zéro, 1965/75, printed 2017
36 × 36 cm (image); 50 × 40 cm (sheet)
The Art Institute of Chicago, gift of the artist and Florent Mazzoleni, 242558
Illustrated p. 97 [fig. 3]

Untitled (taken by apprentice Sibiri Ouattara), 1979/84
16.5 × 22.4 cm (image); 17.5 × 23.5 cm (paper)
Private collection
Illustrated p. 105 [60]

Yao Pelé, 1965/75
11.3 × 7.8 cm (image); 12.5 × 8.6 cm (paper)
The Art Institute of Chicago, promised gift of Ralph and Nancy Segall, 240620
Illustrated p. 106 [61]

Village party in the Kou Valley, 1970/80
10.9 × 8.2 cm (image); 12.6 × 8.5 cm (paper)
Private collection
Illustrated p. 106 [62]

Village party in the Kou Valley, 1965/75
10.6 × 7.9 cm (image); 12.4 × 8.8 cm (paper)
The Art Institute of Chicago, promised gift of Ralph and Nancy Segall, 240600
Illustrated p. 107 [63]

Echo del Africa Nacional in concert, 1975/1980
9 × 7.7 cm (image); 12.4 × 8.9 cm (paper)
Private collection
Illustrated p. 108 [64]

Amadou Diallo (center), record seller and party organizer, 1970/80
11.3 × 7.9 cm (image); 12.5 × 8.6 cm (paper)
Private collection
Illustrated p. 109 [65]

Fans of Cuban music holding a record by Belisario López, May 16, 1967
7.9 × 11.7 cm (image); 8.6 × 12.4 cm (paper)
Private collection
Illustrated p. 109 [66]

Untitled, 1965/75
12 × 7.8 cm (image); 13.2 × 8.7 cm (paper)
Private collection
Illustrated p. 109 [67]

Party at the Messe des garnisons (Officers' Mess), 1965/75
11.6 × 7.7 cm (image); 12.4 × 8.6 cm (paper)
The Art Institute of Chicago, promised gift of Ralph and Nancy Segall, 240599
Illustrated p. 110 [68]

Pierre Sandouidi, 1965/75
11.4 × 14.8 cm (image); 12.4 × 17.5 cm (paper)
Private collection
Illustrated p. 111 [69]

The Five Jamaicans of Bobo-Dioulasso, a reggae fan club, 1965/75
30 × 23.5 cm
Private collection
Illustrated p. 113 [70]

Dancing the blues, perhaps at Volta Dancing, 1965/75
11.3 × 7.7 cm (image); 12.4 × 8.6 cm (paper)
Private collection
Illustrated p. 114 [71]

"Surprise party," 1978/1980
11.5 × 7.8 cm (image); 12.5 × 8.6 cm (paper)
Private collection
Illustrated p. 114 [72]

Tidiane Coulibaly performing at Volta Dancing, c. 1976
7.6 × 11 cm (image); 8.1 × 12 cm (paper)
Private collection
Illustrated p. 115 [73]

Untitled, 1965/75
11.6 × 7.8 cm (image); 12.5 × 8.5 cm (paper)
Private collection
Illustrated p. 116 [74]

On a garden terrace in Bobo, 1965/75
11.6 × 7.6 cm (image); 12.5 × 8.8 cm (paper)
Private collection
Illustrated p. 117 [75]

Untitled, 1970/80
11.6 × 7.7 cm (image); 12.5 × 8.4 cm (paper)
Private collection
Illustrated p. 117 [76]

The Osmonds, a fan club in an outlying Bobo neighborhood, 1971/72
7.7 × 11.6 cm (image); 8.5 × 12.5 cm (paper)
Private collection
Illustrated p. 118 [77]

Untitled (taken by an apprentice), 1965/75, printed 2017
36 × 36 cm (image); 50 × 40 cm (sheet)
The Art Institute of Chicago, gift of the artist and Florent Mazzoleni, 242563
Illustrated p. 121 [fig. 1]

Untitled, 1965/75
11.2 × 7.6 cm (image/paper)
The Art Institute of Chicago, promised gift of Ralph and Nancy Segall, 240618
Illustrated p. 180 [98]

Untitled, 1965/75
11.8 × 7.5 cm (image/paper)
Private collection
Illustrated p. 180 [100]

Untitled, 1965/75
11.2 × 7.8 cm (image); 12.5 × 8.7 cm (paper)
Private collection
Illustrated p. 181 [107]

Disques France-Afrique / L.G.V.D. Productions
Volta Jazz 45-rpm record sleeves
Photographs by Ibrahima Sanlé Sory, 1968/75
18 × 18 cm (approx.)
LGVD numbers 1.100 (color), 1.101, 1.102, 1.103 (black/white), 1.106, 1.107*, 1.108–1.111
Courtesy Florent Mazzoleni
LGVD number 1.100* (black/white)
Courtesy Radio Africa (Graeme Counsel)
LGVD numbers 1.103* (color), 1.104*
Courtesy Numero Group
LGVD number 1.110* (alternate, plate 79m)
Courtesy Benjamin Pelletier
Illustrated pp. 123-127 [79a-n]
* Not in exhibition

Disques France-Afrique / L.G.V.D. Productions
Volta Jazz 45-rpm record sleeves
Photographer unknown, 1968/75
18 × 18 cm
LGVD number 1.080,1.082, 1.083,
1.085 not illustrated
LGVD number 1.084 illustrated p. 151 [fig. 7]
Courtesy Florent Mazzoleni

Sonafric (French)
Volta Jazz 45-rpm record sleeve
Photograph by Ibrahima Sanlé Sory, 1975/76
18 × 18 cm
Courtesy Florent Mazzoleni
Illustrated pp. 128 [80a-b]

Idrissa Koné Productions (Burkinabé)
Volta Jazz 45-rpm record sleeves
Photographs by Ibrahima Sanlé Sory, 1975/77
18 × 18 cm (approx.)
Courtesy Florent Mazzoleni
Illustrated p. 128 [81]

Untitled, 1965/75, printed 2017
36 × 36 cm (image); 50 × 40 cm (sheet)
The Art Institute of Chicago, gift of the artist and Florent Mazzoleni, 242564
Illustrated p. 129 [fig. 1]

Abou, a Dafing boxer, 1965/75, printed 2017
36 × 36 cm (image); 50 × 40 cm (sheet)
Courtesy Florent Mazzoleni
Illustrated p. 131 [fig. 2]
*Not in exhibition

Self-portrait (right) with Karamogo, a managerial training specialist, 1965/75
10.3 × 7.3 cm (image); 11.3 × 7.9 cm (paper)
Private collection
Illustrated p. 135 [81]

Untitled, 1965/75
11.7 × 7.8 cm (image); 12.6 × 8.6 cm (paper)
Private collection
Illustrated pp. 136 [82]

Untitled, 1965/75
16.7 × 11.7 cm (image); 17.6 × 12.5 cm (paper)
The Art Institute of Chicago, promised gift of Ralph and Nancy Segall, 240686
Illustrated p. 136 [83]

Untitled, 1965/75
11.7 × 7.9 cm (image); 12.5 × 8.8 cm (paper)
The Art Institute of Chicago, promised gift of Ralph and Nancy Segall, 240628
Illustrated p. 136 [84]

Self-portrait, 1960/65
22.6 × 16.8 cm (image); 23.7 × 17.7 cm (paper)
The Art Institute of Chicago, restricted gift of Peter J. Cohen, 2017.370
Illustrated p. 137 [85]

Untitled, 1965/75
12.8 × 8 cm (image); 13.9 × 8.9 cm (paper)
The Art Institute of Chicago, promised gift of Ralph and Nancy Segall, 240622
Illustrated p. 138 [86]

Untitled, 1965/75
15.3 × 11.6 cm (image); 17.6 × 12.5 cm (paper)
The Art Institute of Chicago, promised gift of Ralph and Nancy Segall, 240655
Illustrated p. 138 [87]

Untitled, 1965/75
17 × 11.7 cm (image); 17.9 × 12.5 cm (paper)
The Art Institute of Chicago, promised gift of Ralph and Nancy Segall, 240563
Illustrated p. 139 [88]

Idrissa Touré and apprentices in traditional medicine, 1965/75
7.8 × 11.1 cm (image); 8.7 × 12.5 cm (paper)
Private collection
Illustrated p. 181 [110]

Untitled, 1970/80
11.6 × 7.6 cm (image); 12.8 × 8.6 cm (paper)
Private collection
Illustrated p. 140 [89]

Untitled, 1965/75
22 × 16.4 cm (image); 23.7 × 17.6 cm (paper)
Private collection
Illustrated p. 140 [90]

Untitled, 1965/75
17 × 11.9 cm (image); 18 × 12.8 cm (paper)
The Art Institute of Chicago, promised gift of Ralph and Nancy Segall, 240682
Illustrated p. 141 [91]

Self-portrait, 1965/75
22.1 × 16.1 cm (image); 22.9 × 17.4 cm (paper)
The Art Institute of Chicago, promised gift of Ralph and Nancy Segall, 240660
Illustrated pp. 143 [92]

Untitled, 1965/75
11.3 × 7.7 cm (image); 12.5 × 8.6 cm (paper)
Private collection
Illustrated p. 144 [fig. 1]

Tiamodjan, the lead guitarist for Echo del Africa Nacional, 1965/75
11.4 × 7.4 cm (image); 12.5 × 8.5 cm (paper)
The Art Institute of Chicago, promised gift of Ralph and Nancy Segall, 240656
Illustrated p. 147 [fig. 4]

Untitled, 1965/75
11.4 × 16.3 cm (image); 12.5 × 17.6 cm (paper)
Private collection
Illustrated pp. 158 [fig. 1]

Sanlé Sory and Volta Jazz member Abou Traoré at a promotional event for the band, 1965/75
Photograph by apprentice Mamoudou Bitenga
13.2 × 11.7 cm (image); 14 × 12.5 cm (paper)
Private collection
Illustrated p. 160 [fig. 2]

Volta Jazz, c. 1967
11.5 × 16.5 cm (image); 12.4 × 17.4 cm (paper)
Private collection
Illustrated p. 161 [fig. 3]

Idrissa Koné emceeing at a Volta Jazz event; Dieudonné Koudougou on guitar at left, 1974/75
10.7 × 7.7 cm (image); 12.5 × 8.5 cm (paper)
Private collection
Illustrated p. 167 [fig. 4]

Untitled, 1965/75, printed 2017
36 × 36 cm (image); 50 × 40 cm (sheet)
The Art Institute of Chicago, gift of the artist and Florent Mazzoleni, 242562
Illustrated p. 173 [fig. 1]

Sory's work van, 1970/80
8 × 12.5 cm (image); 8.7 × 13 cm (paper)
Private collection
Illustrated p. 175 [93]

The following works are illustrated together on pp. 182-183

Volta Photo studio backdrop, c. 1965
Commissioned by Ibrahima Sanlé Sory from a Ghanaian sign painter
233.7 × 191.8 cm
Painted canvas
Courtesy of Sanlé Sory

Philips-France (founded 1930s or 1940s as a subsidiary of Philips, founded Netherlands, 1891)
L3F21T All Transistor radio, 1962
Plastic exterior
Courtesy of Florent Mazzoleni

Air Afrique (Various African countries and France, 1961-2002)
Carry-on travel bag, date unknown
Polyester fabric
Courtesy of Florent Mazzoleni

Studio lamps, c. 1965
Welded metal
Commissioned by Ibrahima Sanlé Sory from a Bobo artisan
Courtesy of Sanlé Sory

Ericsson-Colombes, France (subsidiary of Ericsson, founded Sweden, 1876)
Telephone, 1959
Bakelite plastic
Courtesy of Sanlé Sory

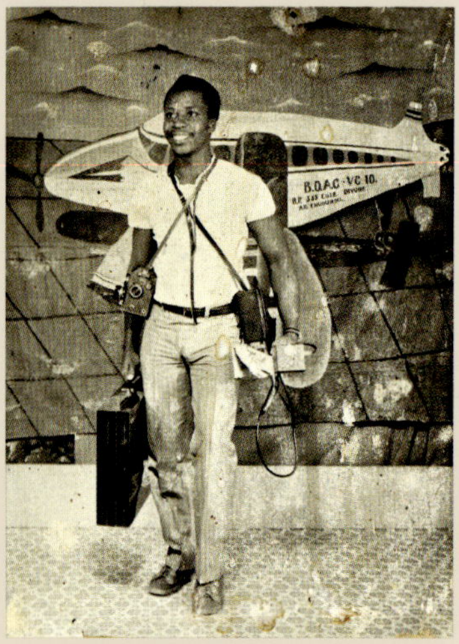

94

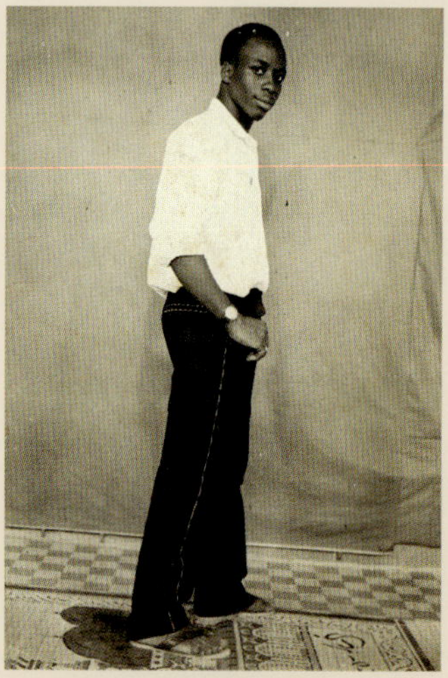

95

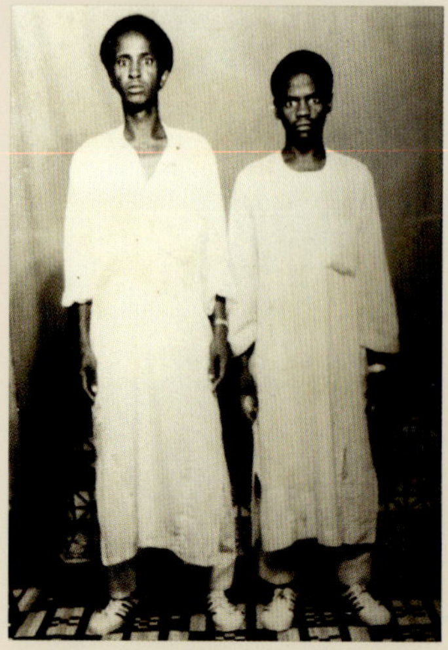

96

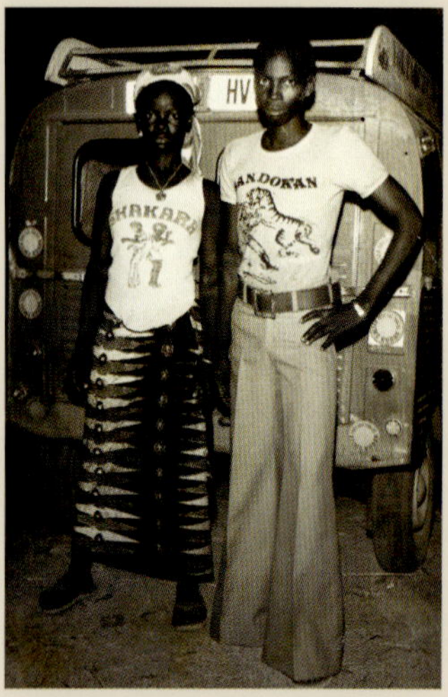

97

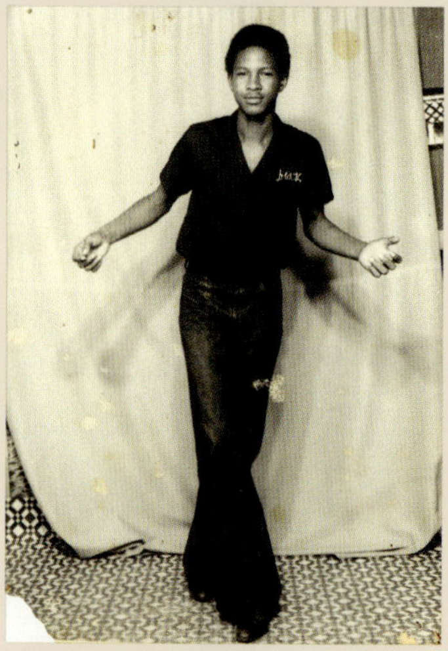

98

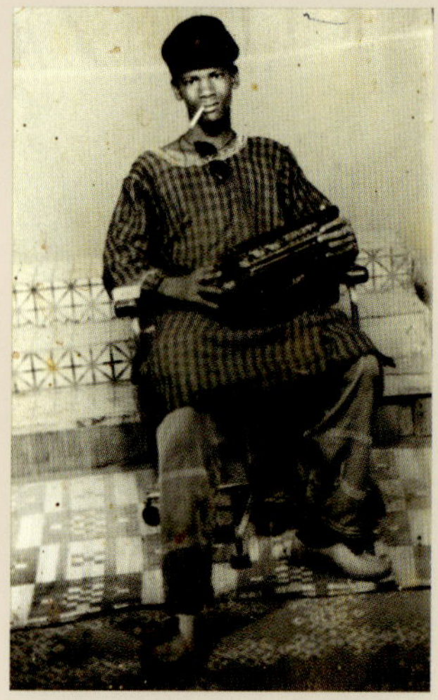

99

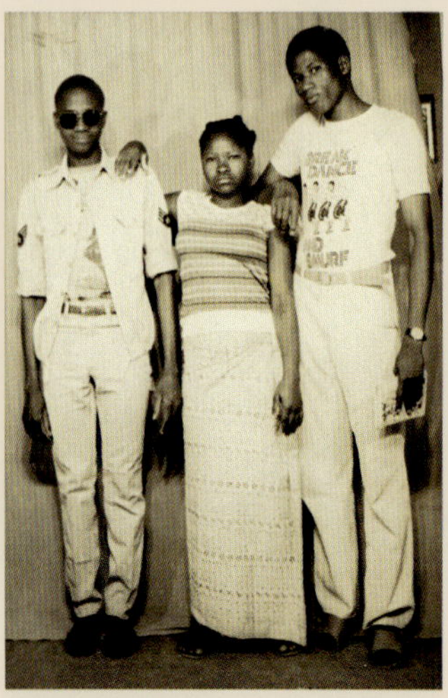

100

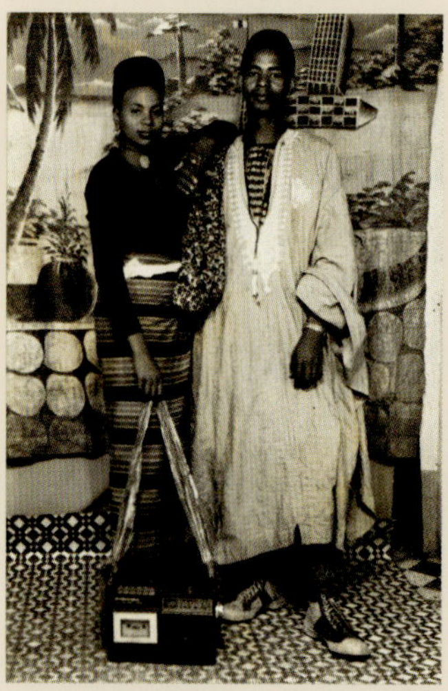

101

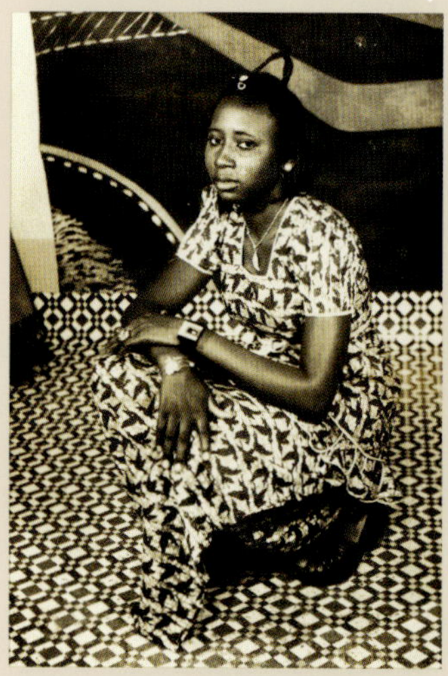

102

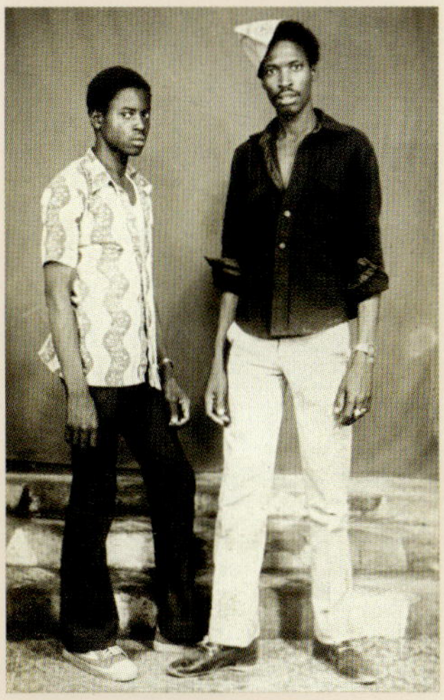

103

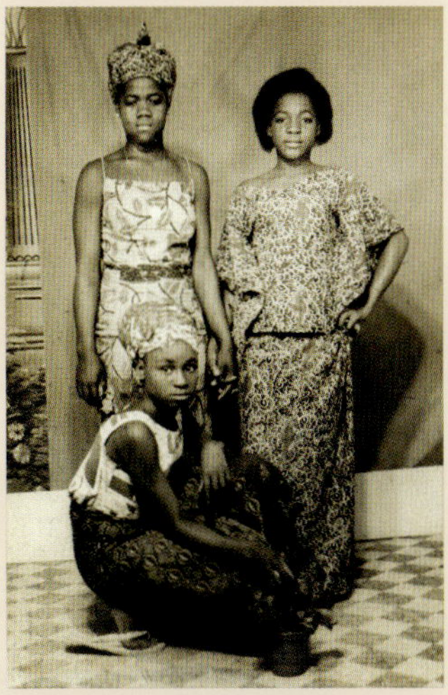

104

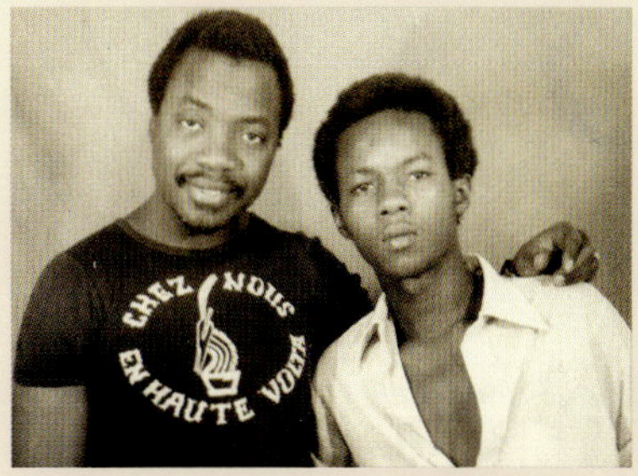

105

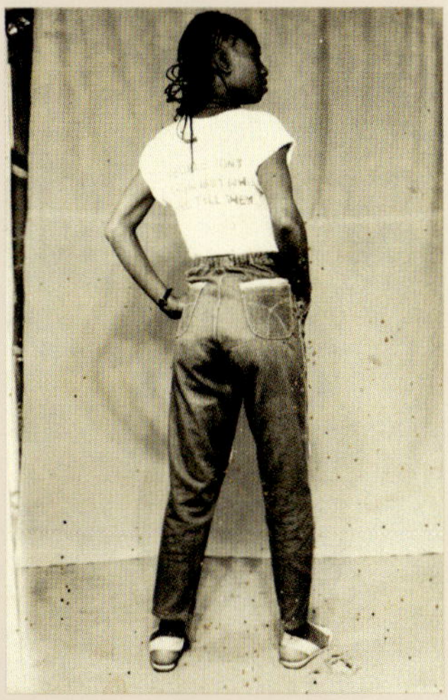

106

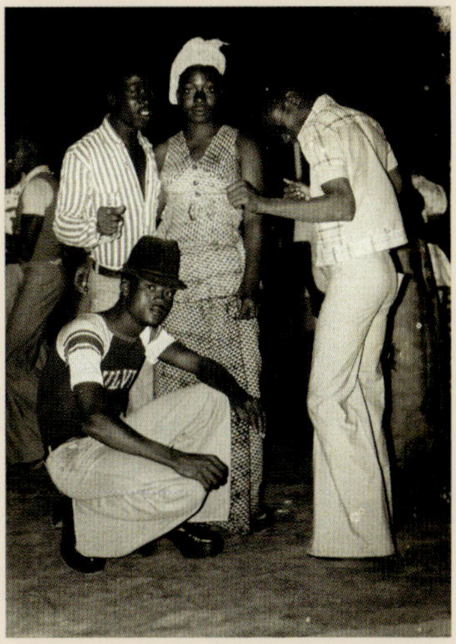

107

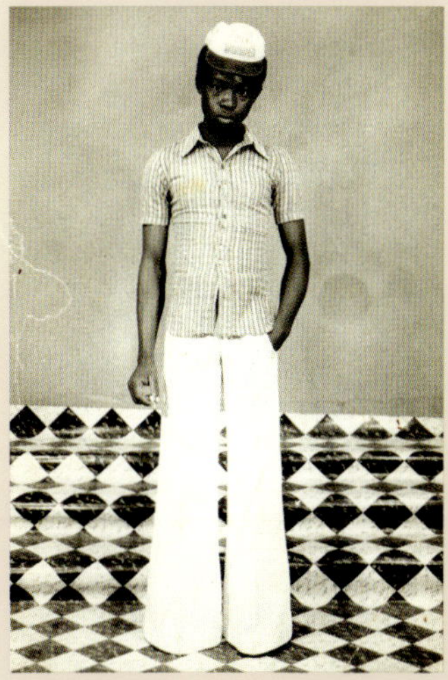

108

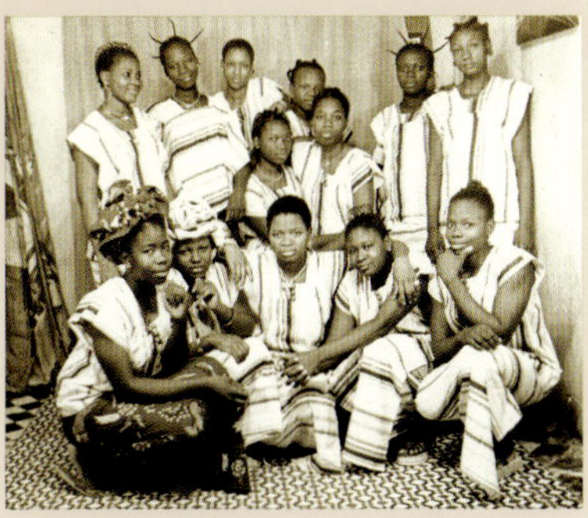

109

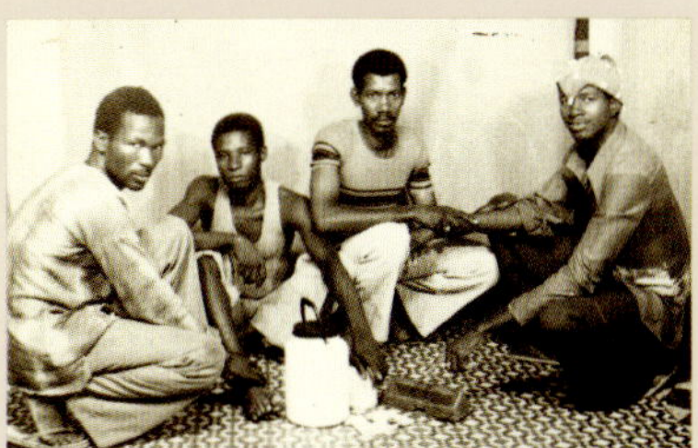

110

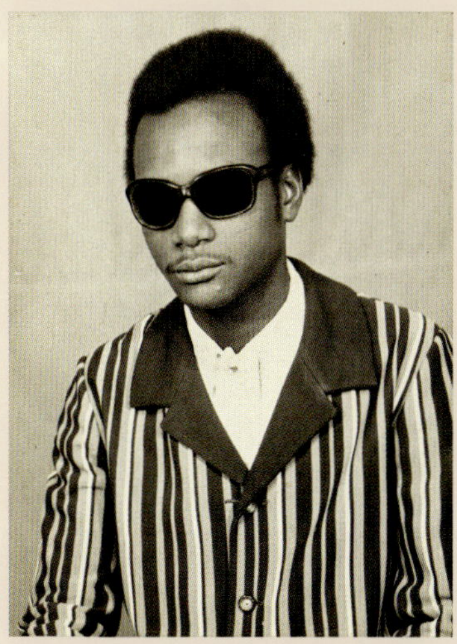

111

This final illustration shows a canvas backdrop, two studio lamps, and three props from Volta Photo, photographed in the imaging studio at the Art Institute of Chicago, 2018.
Backdrop (233.7 × 191.8 cm) painted around 1965 by an unknown Ghanaian sign painter according to instructions dictated by Ibrahima Sanlé Sory. Photograph by Chris Gallagher.

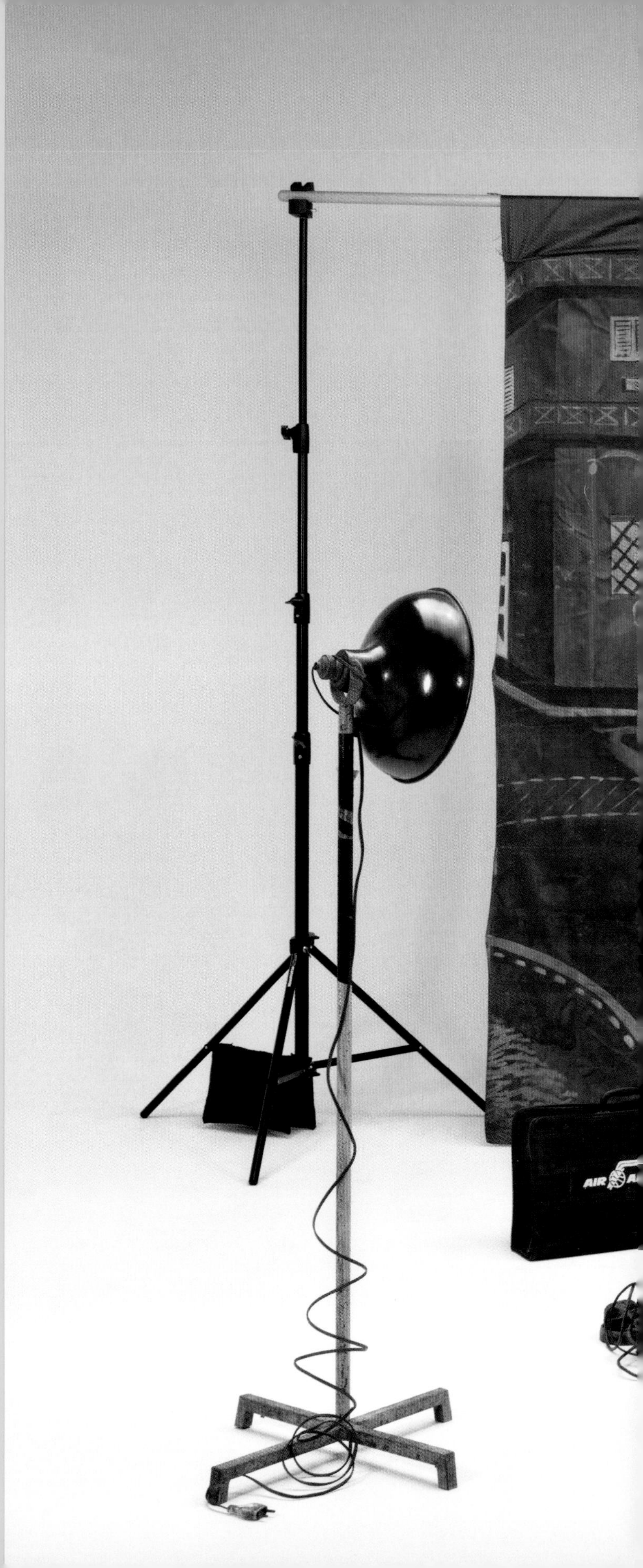

First edition published in 2018

Unless otherwise noted, all images of photographs by Sanlé Sory, his props, and record covers that include his photographs were made by the Department of Imaging at the Art Institute of Chicago.

Book design: Holger Feroudj

Separations by Steidl image department
Production and printing: Steidl, Göttingen

Steidl
Düstere Str. 4 / 37073 Göttingen, Germany
Phone +49 551 49 60 60
Fax +49 551 49 60 649
mail@steidl.de
steidl.de

ISBN 978-3-95829-400-4
Printed in Germany by Steidl

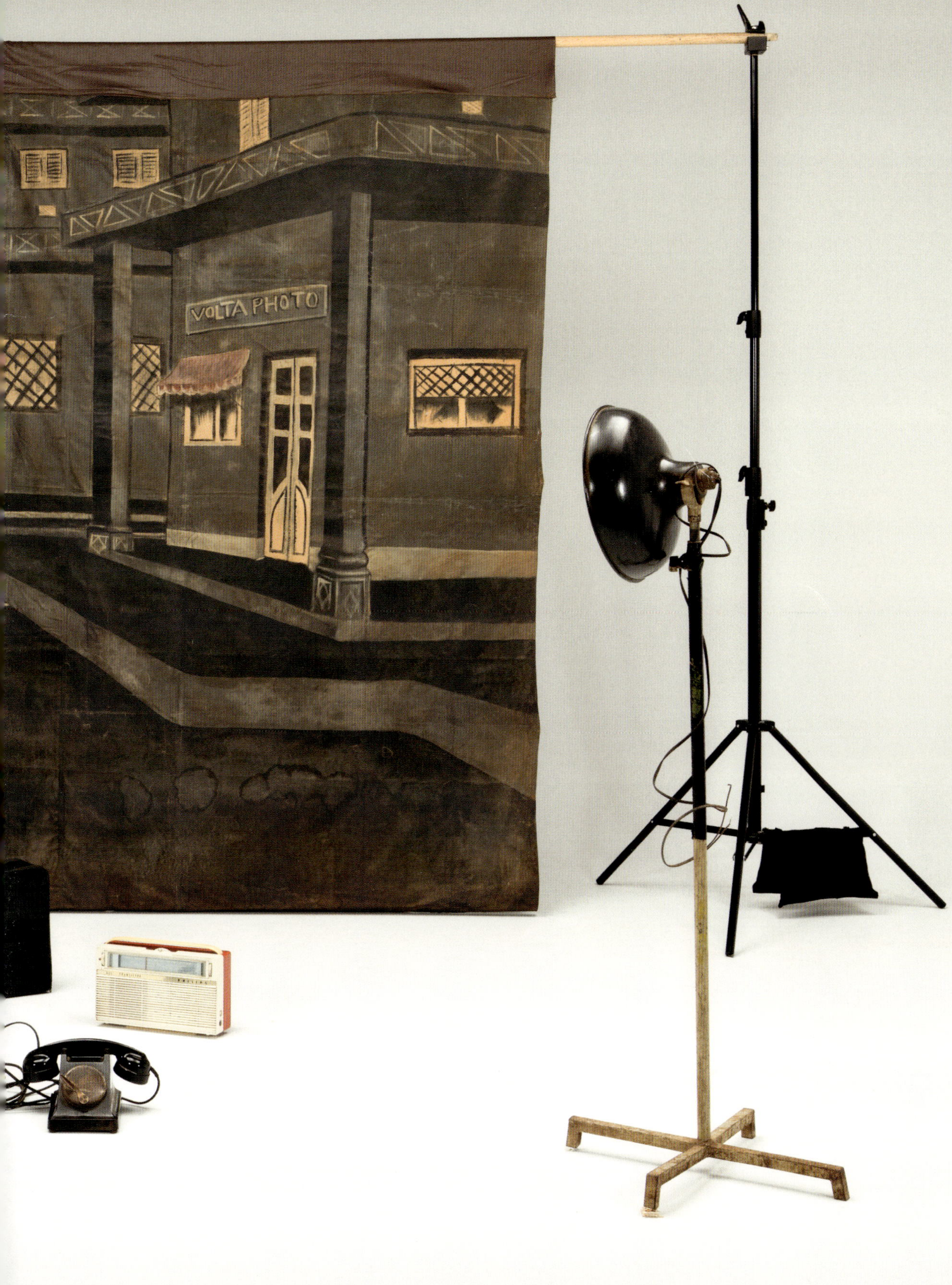
VOLTA PHOTO